LETTER TO THE PAST

LETTER TO THE PAST

AN AUTOBIOGRAPHY

GEORGE WOODCOCK

Fitzhenry & Whiteside
Toronto Montreal Winnipeg Vancouver

Typesetting by Jay Tee Graphics Ltd.

Fitzhenry & Whiteside Limited
150 Lesmill Road
Don Mills, Ontario, Canada M3B 2T5

Canadian Cataloguing in Publication Data
Woodcock, George, 1912-
   Letter to the past

Includes index.
ISBN 0-88902-715-3 (v.1)

1. Woodcock, George, 1912 - Biography.
2. Authors, Canadian (English - Biography.)*
3. Historians - Canada - Biography. I. Title.

PS8545.062Z53 1982   C818'.54'09
PR9199.3.W66Z468   C82-095132-3

Thanks to the Ontario Arts Council and the Canada Council for their kind assistance in the publication of this book.

CONTENTS

I

THE FAMILY BUSH

I WAS BORN IN WINNIPEG, where I struggled into life before dawn on the 8th May, 1912, in the old Grace Hospital. I spent my first months in the wooden apartment block where my parents lived on Portage Avenue, but I remember nothing of this, and my first recollections are of my parents' native Salopian countryside. My mother took me back to England on the *Aquitania* in the autumn of that year, and I was baptized in the Market Drayton church where my grandfather was the vicar's warden.

On both sides my forefathers were Shropshire people, inhabitants of the Welsh Marches around the Wrekin where, despite Offa's Dike, the Saxon and the Celtic races have mingled since the middle ages. The two strains meet in me.

I have never felt an urge to probe far back into my ancestry, perhaps because of a sense that there would be nothing of great interest to discover, that we were never any other than peasants and their descendants. The first ancestor of whom I know, my great-great-grandfather William Woodcock, was born about 1780 and farmed land at Norton-in-Hales, a village tucked into the north-eastern angle of Shropshire where it touches both Cheshire and Staffordshire. He and his wife were celebrated for their longevity. When I was a boy my father took me to Norton, going by way of Blore Heath, to look at the muddy little river which local lore claimed had run for three days with blood at the great battle there during the Wars of the Roses. In the church vestry at Norton I saw the fading sepia photograph of William and his wife, fragile and fustily clothed, in their nineties.

William Woodcock lived out his long years in relative prosperity; they were the times of the corn laws when English farmers were protected. He moved into the town of Market Drayton before he died, and I also saw as a boy his gravestone against the back wall of the old red sandstone church on the clifftop overlooking the valley of the Tern. It has since vanished, as any real memory of the man had done long before, for no one could tell me anything that illumined his character.

His son, my great-grandfather Thomas Woodcock, ran into trouble and tragedy. He too prospered in the beginning and raised by his first wife a family of four daughters. All of them were married when he became a widower, and as his second wife he took a girl no older than they. My grandfather, Samuel Woodcock, born in 1860 from this second marriage, was his only son. With some wonder, as a child, I would see grey-haired men as old as he — one of them a gaitered Archdeacon and the others well-to-do farmers — calling him Uncle; they were the sons of his half-sisters.

After his second marriage, my great-grandfather's fortunes declined. The late 1860s were a bad time for English farmers, for the corn laws had been repealed and cheap wheat was coming in from Canada and the United States and ruining the local market. Thomas Woodcock died, like Speke and many other Victorians, by dragging a cocked shotgun through a quickset hedge and blasting his side in; it was regarded as a gentlemanly way of committing suicide, and juries always returned a verdict of accidental death. The reason in my great-grandfather's case became evident when his farm was sold by his creditors and my great-grandmother was evicted. In those days there were no widows' pensions and to avoid the dreaded workhouse she moved to a village cottage and made a poor living by taking in washing.

My grandfather began his working life delivering laundry baskets to the houses of the vicar and the doctor and the few other people in the village well enough off to afford the services of a washerwoman. This he did in the evenings, after school; he left school entirely at the age of twelve to earn a few shillings working as a "crow-starver" for a local farmer, keeping the birds away from freshly-mown fields with a rattle and stones. Then, as a lesser evil than the drudgery of a life of farm labouring, my grandfather chose the only alternative then available to young villagers. He entered service, as it was then called, in one of the great country houses that dotted the north Shropshire countryside, becoming a pageboy to the Longvils of Shavington Hall, one of the several families of that area who were of real Norman descent.

In those days there was still a semi-feudal relationship between villagers and squires in border counties like Shropshire and Herefordshire, somewhat resembling that between a Scottish highlander and his laird. In the 1870s the landowning families were still at the height of their prosperity and political power, and gave employment as a social duty; service in their homes carried its own pride in valued skills and created its own hierarchy, with the butler and the housekeeper, the cook and the lady's maid forming a powerful patriciate. Working in the big houses of the countryside was too common a village occupation — and too evidently preferable to labouring in the fields — for any rural stigma to be attached to it. It was townspeople who regarded an ancestor in service as something to be hidden like a touch of the tar-brush (as Dickens did) or to be used *pour épater les bourgeois* (as Wells did once he began to consort with the newly rich). Certainly my parents' generation, who lived through the breakup of rural relationships after 1914, and had seen the old landowners replaced by men who had made their money in trade and had no sense of feudal obligation, were uneasy about the facts about *their* parents' servant pasts popping out of nicely-papered-over cupboards, but this was largely because they themselves had become somewhat urbanized, and in an urban context being in service connoted a skivvy, pale as celery in the basement kitchen and incessantly bullied by some shopkeeper's wife.

My grandfather's own attitude to that part of his past doubtless grew ambivalent when he became a merchant and in a small way a landowner himself, but he never denied it. He would sometimes talk in a very lively way about the days in the early 1880s when, having graduated from a footman, he became valet to Reggie Longvil, the eldest son of the family, who established himself in London rooms with the Wildean address of Half-Moon Street just about the time of Wilde's arrival in London. I have often speculated on the thought that Reggie Longvil may have been one of the young men Wilde met in the Mayfair houses of that time, and perhaps a partial model for Algernon Moncrieff in *The Importance of Being Earnest*, which starts off in Half-Moon Street, in which case Lane, Moncrieff's man-servant, might have been partially modelled on my pre-bearded grandfather. Not that my grandfather ever mentioned Oscar Wilde; when I knew him he was too much the evangelical Christian even to acknowledge such a name.

When the Half-Moon Street years came to an end, my grandfather decided it was time to get out of country house service. An alternative to valeting or labouring had finally appeared in the local countryside, for the railway had recently been built from Wellington to Crewe, passing through Market Drayton. My grandfather left behind his livery and took instead a ticket-collector's uniform on the Great Western Railway, which my other grandfather, Henry Lewis, had joined not long before as a signalman.

Samuel Woodcock celebrated his release from domestic service by performing another act of liberation when he enticed away and married the Longvil's lady's maid. Her name was Hannah Rodgers; she came from Oswestry, the nearest Shropshire town to Wales, and all her life she retained a strong Welsh accent, the manners of an old-fashioned Welsh woman of respectable status, and a dumpy resemblance to Queen Victoria. She was ten years older than Samuel, and she had spent her time profitably by accumulating a nestegg and the skills that enabled her to set up a dressmaking establishment where shopkeepers' wives could go to be fashionably costumed. In a few years she and my grandfather were able to parlay her earnings into a retail coal business which enabled Samuel to leave the railway. This was some time in the 1890s. By the time I became aware of such matters twenty years or so later, he was the leading coal merchant in Market Drayton, a light in the town council, and warden of the dissident evangelical congregation of Emmanuel Church.

He and Hannah had four children, all sons. The eldest, named Reggie after the Longvil heir, died in childhood and so did the youngest, Norman, a fair Victorian average. The two who survived were my father, Samuel Arthur, and his younger brother, Harold. Physically, they exemplified the scope of our ancestry: my father a little more than the average height, with clear grey eyes and a Nordic profile; his brother short, dark and Celtic.

I tell as I have heard it the modest history of the period before I knew any of these people. My own recollections date from the end of the Great War, when my grandfather was in his fifties, my father in his early thirties and my uncle in his twenties.

My mother, Margaret Gertrude Lewis (whom I and all her friends and relatives knew as Maggie), was the daughter of a strange, dour rebel named Harry Lewis whose blood I have always felt running strongly and bitterly in my veins. His mother, like my paternal grandmother, was Shropshire Welsh and he took her name, for he was the natural son of the rich gentleman farmer named Bourne whose dairymaid she had been. He grew up hating the well-to-do. In reaction against the prevalent Anglicanism of the region he became an ardent Baptist, and in reaction against the prevalent Toryism he became a radical Liberal of the Lloyd George chapel type, for he loathed the Asquith Whigs as much as he detested the Conservatives. He was an early member of the railway workers' union, though by the time I knew him he was denouncing the powers which the union leaders had amassed.

Indeed, Harry Lewis hated authority of any kind. Even as an old man he would tell, vividly and with relish, the histories of the great Shropshire poachers and their feuds and battles with the gamekeepers and the police. Or the tale of that well-remembered day in the 1860s when, over some forgotten grievance, the people had surged out of Ranter's Gullet and the Town Well, out of the Shutt and the Drumble and the other haunts of poverty, to riot and wreck the heart of Market Drayton. As a boy, he sat in a tree and watched the Irish labourers from the railway line marching in, four abreast with pick-staves on their shoulders, to join in the fighting merely for the fun of it. A day later he sat in the same tree and saw the yeomanry riding in, farmers' sons in red dragoon jackets with unsheathed sabres flashing in the sun, to rout the rioters and take their leaders off to Shrewsbury gaol.

Harry Lewis's father had endowed him, when he came of age, with a few hundred pounds. Accepting them without gratitude, Harry reverted immediately to the peasant past of all of us and bought himself a modest holding in the village of Little Drayton, west of Market Drayton on the road to Shrewsbury; there were four acres with a good orchard and a sandstone cottage. In the same way my other grandfather, Samuel Woodcock, as soon as he became a coal merchant, also bought four acres of orchard and meadow. Nominally it was to graze the horses for his coal wagons, but really it was because he wanted to own land as his father had done before he lost it; he could easily have kept his horses in a stable and fed them on hay and oats as the other coal merchants did. These two plots of land — the holdings of my grandfathers — became the vital terrains of my childhood.

Harry Lewis married Betsy France and when he was old and she was dead and I was a boy he would tell me how he had seen her dancing, nimblest of all the girls, in the midsummer night's moonlight on the lawn of Hawkestone Hall, and had decided at once that he must marry her. Hawkestone was the country house of Viscount Hill, whose father had fought under Wellington in the Peninsular War and filled the estate with Regency follies. Betsy's family, who lived in the tiny village of Marchamley near the Hall, claimed that their real name was Franck and that their Dutch ancestor had come to England in the train of William of Orange. Her father was Lord Hill's bailiff, and she was a maid in the Hall.

Betsy France's mother was a woman of singular spirit, and once, when a deserter came limping through Marchamley at the time of the Crimean War, she had put him in the great baking oven outside her house, piled logs and kindling in front of him, and talked his pursuers into parting. I never knew old May France but her story, which my grandfather Harry Lewis told me with zest, impressed me when I was a child, and perhaps some memory of it encouraged me to become an objector when the wars of my own time came to pass.

I remember my grandmother Betsy only as a little and very lively old woman, though perhaps she was not so old as she seemed, for she died early of cancer when I was young, no more than five, and at that time anyone over forty seemed old to me. She and Harry had six children, and all but one lived to adulthood.

The one who died was the boy I knew as "Uncle Jack." Long decades after the day he went bird-nesting at the age of twelve and fell from a high elm on to a spiked iron fence, my grandfather, not a man to show his emotions, had tears in his eyes when he would say, "Jack was the flower of the flock!" I never heard my mother or anyone else in the family disagree; there must have been some special quality of spirit in him, which I never understood and nobody could quite describe to me.

Annie, a dreamy and vaguely Burnes-Jonesish woman with a bird's nest of fine fair hair, was the eldest; she married a leather merchant from Bridgend in South Wales, named Daffyd Llewelyn Jenkins, a fiery Welsh Calvinist preacher with a remarkable physical resemblance to Gandhi.

Harry, the family black sheep, was a tall, lanky man, with a resemblance I realized when I looked at World War I cartoons, to Little Willie, the Crown Prince William of Germany. Growing into manhood, he drank, smoked, gambled and wenched; for a while he earned his living acting as the "dreadful example" of the confirmed drunkard at temperance meetings and as the penitent who threw himself on the mercy seat at revivalist gatherings to encourage the congregation. Eventually, to get out of some especially serious scrape, he joined the Coldstream Guards. But he accepted the King's Shilling in the wrong year; it was 1914. In a few months Harry became an unwilling member of the British Expeditionary Force sent out in the vain hope of saving Belgium from the advancing German Army; he quickly contrived to get himself taken prisoner and he does not enter my memory until he returned in 1918, emaciated and uncommunicative, from four years in the Ruhleben prison camp.

Next to Harry, and his complete opposite in character, came Alice, a dark and bitter woman in whom the worst side of our Celtic ancestry emerged. Her husband, Dick Newing, kept a bicycle shop in Colwyn Bay and looked and talked like a character from *Mr. Polly*.

My mother was a little younger than Alice, and then came my Aunt Jessie, slim and fair, with the sharp-witted pertness of a spoilt youngest child. With Aunt Jessie my memories swing into focus. I was three when she married a pharmacist from Ellesmere named Joseph Cooke. The year was 1915, and though Aunt Jessie is many years dead, Joe Cooke still lives, well into his nineties, as my good and loyal friend, a sardonic link with that far-off day of earliest recollections.

Their wedding is the first event to stand out in the mist of half memories of my earliest consciousness. It took place in the Baptist Church where my grandfather was an elder and his daughters sang in the choir. I remember the Biblical texts glittering in gold lettering as the sun shone through the windows on the green walls, and the loud and sonorous singing, for there was much Welsh blood among the Market Drayton Baptists and their renderings of Handel were greatly admired. Singing, flowers, the smell of polished pews and then, clear as a photograph, the scene as we left the chapel: the older men in frogged and braided frockcoats; the women corsetted into hour-glass dresses, topped by hats like great extravagant mushrooms, and enveloped in the ostrich feather boas that were still having a last flicker of fashion in that backwater of social change; and me, among them, a lumpy infant in a brown velvet suit and a large and detested lace collar. I remember the excitement of jumping and shouting among a crowd of adults who had lost their customary gravity, wildly hurling confetti at my aunt, and then the swaying clatter of the horse cab as we rode away, the mouth-drying smell of dust and straw in its upholstery, and the grinding sound of its iron-tired wheels clattering over the cobblestone streets to my grandfather's cottage.

There the wedding breakfast took place, in the great living-room-kitchen where hams and flitches of smoked bacon hung from the smoke-black beams. Here the territory to which my stature entitled me was the floor of worn bricks which I shared with Jack, my grandfather's mongrel dog, the dearest friend of my infancy. I was observant of what happened at the table, standing tiptoe with my chin on the edge, fascinated by the little silver balls on the wedding cake that was served to me in homeopathic mouthfuls. But the most exciting incident of all, which perhaps imprinted the wedding so sharply on my mind, was Jack's feat of catching a mouse that had incautiously emerged to share in the feast. He ate it in front of the assembled guests, and I remember the guts of the mouse spurting out around his teeth like grey spaghetti in tomato sauce as he bit the poor beast in two.

THE PERSONAL HISTORY which brought me to that wedding began when my father and mother, both of them born in 1883, were first drawn together by their love of music. My mother sang Handel, and her contralto voice was good enough for her to take part in the Three Choirs Festival when she lived for a while in Hereford. My father was a pianist, good enough for his part to be encouraged by Edward German who came from Whitchurch, a few miles away from Market Drayton. With his friend Kent Godwin, a dark saturnine giant who became one of the dominant figures of my childhood, my father organized a band that played at dances and other gatherings in the small towns around the Wrekin and sometimes at the balls in country houses to which the gentry rode in their four-in-hand coaches and their early motor cars.

My mother left the church school near her home in Little Drayton to become an apprentice milliner, first in Market Drayton and then in a large store in Hereford where the staff lived in; it must have been very like the drapers' shops in which H. G. Wells served and which he described so vividly in *Kipps*. My father went on to the old grammar school by the church in Market Drayton which Robert Clive had once attended, and then left to work in the Wedgwood laboratories at Etruria in the heart of Arnold Bennett's Five Towns, which we called the Potteries. Later he became a clerk on the Great Western Railway, but it was music that he wanted most to follow as a career. He was a good tympanist as well as a pianist, and his opportunity seemed to have come when Edward German recommended him for a place in the orchestra of the Stafford theatre.

But while my grandparents were all in favour of music as a genteel amateur pastime, they were imbued with the fear of the artistic life that haunted almost every respectable Victorian or Edwardian, particularly after the trial of Oscar Wilde. My father's musical friends had already led him into whatever modest Bohemianism could flourish in small Shropshire towns; many years later when she found out I had been drinking in the Bell Inn at Market Drayton, my mother reinforced her disapproval by telling me that there had been trouble, long ago, over my father's entanglement with the barmaid in the same tavern. To my grandmother, the theatre seemed the very heart of corruption, which nobody could touch without being irremediably ruined, an attitude then shared by most rural people, so that even when I was a boy in the 1920s it was taken for granted that the actresses in the companies that toured the small towns with their shallow farces were "loose women" and probably prostitutes.

My grandfather cannot have been without some understanding of my father's desire to break free, for Market Drayton gossip credited him with being something more than a philanderer in the days before he became a churchwarden. But he was, as I long afterwards discovered, a hypocrite on a grand scale, supporting the hysterical protests of my grandmother, of whom he was afraid, by offering my father a partnership in his coal business as a bribe to keep away from the world of the arts.

I recognize much that has gone into my own character when I think of my father, too gentle to rebel, too obstinate to comply, taking neither course, and retreating from confrontation in a physical as well as a mental way. It was 1907. Canadian immigration agents were combing Britain for emigrants to dilute the great flow of East Europeans brought into the prairies by Clifford Sifton's immigration policies. To my grandmother's chagrin, my father decided to escape the constrictions of his life at home and try to make a new one in what the English still called "the colonies"; to the end of her days she would refer to Canada as "that terrible country" and refuse to discuss it any further.

My father was twenty-four when he sailed from Liverpool to New York. Before he left, he and my mother became engaged and she promised to join him as soon as he had made a position for himself. He spent a little time in New York and rather more in Chicago, where he was fascinated by the new ragtime music which he encountered there and immediately adopted. All through my childhood, whenever he could get to a piano, he would play excellent ragtime, though he never moved on to jazz and never even liked it.

From Chicago he went to Winnipeg, and then to the Manitoba prairie, up towards Riding Mountain, where he worked on the ranch of a Shropshire gentleman farmer; he acted as a groom, tending the hunters and carriage horses that were the appendages of a transported gentility. Soon he tired of life in the stables and in the spring went to work as hired hand for a young Englishman who had settled on a remote homestead.

Though he never complained of it, I am sure my father did not enjoy the long days of pioneer toil, the hard work of breaking the prairie, but he did remember, with amusement and often with nostalgia, the circumstances that accompanied it. He would talk often of the wide prairie skies and the aurora borealis building its crackling cathedrals of light; of the great flocks of migratory birds; of the pink-breasted hawks and the coyotes howling through the night; and of the snakes infesting the stables which the hands would kill, seizing them by their tails and cracking them like whips. He would describe the weekly buggy trips over the rough prairie trails from the homestead into Minnedosa, their nearest settlement, where they would eat enormously, take a bath at the Chinese laundry where they left the weekly washing, and return with provender to keep them going until the next Saturday, including always a great rice pudding made in an enamel wash basin. Half a century later in a small prairie town somewhere about 1965, I was delighted when the waiter in the Chinese restaurant served us helpings of rice pudding cooked in the same way.

A season of pioneering was enough for my father. When fall came and the first snows dusted the land he had helped to plough, he drifted back into Winnipeg and got a job as clerk on the Canadian National Railway. He joined the mildly Bohemian circle that gathered in Rudi's café to talk into the small hours over Milwaukee beer. He encountered Charlie Chaplin there, still an unknown comic in Fred Karno's travelling show, and he struck up a friendship with a down-and-out prize fighter named Victor McLaglen, who later became a Hollywood star and even a good actor in films like *The Informer*.

McLaglen and my father heard there was money to be picked from the ground up north in Cobalt, and they went to try their fortunes in the silver mines, but they found they were years too late; all the claims were taken and they had to work as labourers to pay their way back to

Winnipeg. Pleasure and curiosity led my father to other places in the Shield, and I remember a photograph from that period, showing him and a friend in wasp-striped bathing suits reaching almost to the knees, standing in the shallow water of a lake sombrely framed by spruce woods.

Whether there were any successors in Winnipeg to the barmaid from the Bell Inn I never learnt, but my father's Bohemian connections led him at times into odd company. He told me that he had once played as accompanist to a man acquitted of murder by a prairie jury, though as everyone knew and he did not attempt to deny he had shot his man dead in a quarrel at a free lunch counter in a saloon. The killer had a good baritone voice, my father remembered, and altogether seemed an amiable, relaxed kind of person. A last image of my father's Winnipeg life was a photograph that fascinated me throughout my childhood; firemen's hoses had turned a burned building into a glittering palace of ice. Not until I read Wyndham Lewis's *Self Condemned* decades later did I find literary justice done to that splendid visual metaphor.

A little while after he returned from Cobalt, my father got a job with the Imperial Oil Company as a bookkeeper. He was soon promoted to accountant and decided the time had come for him to write to my mother.

For her they had been trying and restless years. After an attack of rheumatic fever, she had spent many months travelling the watering places of England, bathing and drinking the foul-tasting waters at Bath and Leamington, at Buxton and Matlock, and gathering a store of curious stories about the valetudinarian way of life that would last her a lifetime. The elegance that Brummel and his kind had once given to such places had been destroyed by Victorian respectability, and only a macabre pumproom comedy of hollow pretensions remained.

In 1910 an uncle in the United States invited her there to recuperate. He was the head gardener of Amy Lowell's estate at Brookline, near Boston, and there my mother stayed for several months, being patronized by Amy and defending her Protestantism against the Catholic bigotry of the Irish house servants, whose maximum concession to common humanity between them would be the remark: "And, indeed, isn't a bad Catholic even worse than a Protestant!" She was present at the great fire when the Lowell stables burnt down, the horses all died, and Amy wandered the grounds like a madwoman, wailing: "My poor Gazebo! My poor Gazebo!" in grief over her favourite mastiff which had shared the fate of the horses.

In later years I came to respect Amy Lowell as a writer and to appreciate her importance in the Anglo-American literary tradition, but I could never get my mother to take her seriously as a poet or in any other way. All she could remember was a ridiculous, overbearing fat woman, with a hysterical disposition and, of course, the Boston saying that: "The Lowells speak only to the Cabots, and the Cabots speak only to God." Because of her narrow but intense experience, she treated as completely mythical any talk of American democracy; for her, perceiving the great gulf between Amy Lowell and Bridget the kitchen maid, it seemed an aristocracy far more rigid than the easy feudalism of Edwardian Shropshire.

As Daisy Ashford might have done, she remembered the United States most kindly for the great variety of elaborate, delectable ices she ate there and the vividness of the early comics, so that my childhood vision of the great republic combined the flavourful richness of a Knickerbocker Glory with the wild humour of the Katzenjammer Kids in a semi-surrealistic fantasy given a sinister grimness by the refrain of a ragtime song my father often sang, "And the razors are flying in the air!"

My mother sailed the Atlantic again in the spring of 1911, this time to Québec, where she landed early in May and immediately took the train to Winnipeg. On the 17th of May she and my father were married at St. Matthew's Anglican Church. In after years, "Marry in May, you'll rue the day," was a saying constantly on my mother's lips, along with such sardonic maxims as, "We live in hope, if we die in despair," and "Blessed is he that expecteth nothing, for he shall not be disappointed."

She was a proud woman. She suffered and endured a great deal through my father's eventually fatal illness, which began not long after their marriage, and through his early death. For almost thirty years, half her life, she carried the burdens that normally would be borne by both partners in a marriage. But the essential bitterness of her view of life had perhaps evolved before her marital misfortunes. Once, at the height of one of those cruel liberation battles that son and mother sometimes inflict on each other, she told me how, when she was carrying me, one of her legs was immoveably locked with rheumatism. I am sure she spoke the truth; she was too proud to invent anything for the sake of an argumentative advantage.

Yet she had also the saving power of jesting under misfortune that I have inherited from her. I am never so humorous as when I lie sick in bed and suddenly see the world as a bizarre and comic opposite to the serious place I normally inhabit. I remember my mother talking through my childhood with a kind of acrid wit about Winnipeg, the timber town, with its wooden sidewalks and wooden buildings like the apartment block where we lived; about the Chinese laundrymen, pigtailed and in long blue gowns, who would come with their bills written in pictographic characters on bits of brown paper which they would interpret in pidgin so that they always seemed to add up to "tirty-fi ten" (35 cents); and about the Doukhobors in their sheepskin coats who would come into the city in winter to clear the streets of snow. Her most dramatically-told tale was about the Chicago gangsters, Lefty Louis and Zip the Blood, who fled north of the border and shot it out with the Winnipeg police from a burning streetcar in which they had been trapped and from which neither of them emerged alive.

Even the wry humour with which my mother looked at post-pioneer Winnipeg could not induce her to accept a second prairie winter. She left, with me, in October, 1912. Anxious to rejoin her and tempted by my grandfather's renewed offer of a partnership in the coal business, my father followed her on the first liner to leave Montreal after the spring breakup of 1913.

Neither of them would ever go back to Canada. Yet my father longed to resume his life there and as the years went by his memories of the country grew softer. When I was ten years old he was already trapped in the long illness from which he would die, yet he talked constantly of plans for that return. We would go far over the prairies to the Peace River country where the great white mountains would rise on the horizon; build ourselves a house of poplar logs and walk in autumn through our fields of wheat billowing in the wind; make beehives to catch the sweet honey of the prairie flowers; and grow melons in cold frames according to the pamphlets distributed by the Canadian immigration who one day in 1923 or 1924 appeared in the square of the little town of Marlow where we lived with a van full of propaganda literature.

My father died not long afterwards, as I shall tell, and it was I who returned to Canada, of which I had retained and treasured my father's memories as my own. I went beyond the prairies, beyond even the Peace River, and settled far to the west in the remoteness of Vancouver Island, within hearing of the Pacific tides. And if, in this first chapter of my memoirs, I have written at some length about times before I was born, it is because I have often wondered how far my life has been shaped to give a different and less pathetic end to my father's.

II

A MARGINAL INFANCY

WHEN WE RETURNED TO SHROPSHIRE, my mother first took me with her to live in Harry Lewis's cottage in Little Drayton. When my father returned, they moved into a cottage on Longlands Lane on the eastern verge of Market Drayton; the name, Longlands, carried a memory of the long strips in which this area was cultivated before the enclosures of the common lands. I have no direct recollection of living in this home, though I saw the house in later years with its thick red sandstone walls, thatched roof and long garden, brilliant with dahlias, and filled with old apple trees sprouting mistletoe.

Yet I do remember vicariously, as if I had actually seen it, an incident my parents often told. One of the great shaggy Shire horses that pulled my grandfather's coal carts was standing outside the cottage and I crawled under its belly. Fearing to make any sound that might cause the horse to lash out with his great and hairy hoof, they waited trembling until, with tantalizing slowness, I crawled back to safety. The horse clearly regarded me as of no account, and I emerged unaware of my peril.

It was after we moved to Frogmoor Road, nearer the heart of town, that my memories began to establish themselves. We lived in what was then called a semi-detached villa with a little white-paled flower garden in front and a long kitchen garden at the back. The other half of the structure was inhabited by Kent Godwin, my father's oldest friend, and his family. Kent was a massive and swarthy man, with the look of one of the dark Vikings; his roaring laugh fascinated and frightened me. He was always riding in and out on his bicycle, dressed in a hunting jacket and corduroy breeches, for he could not live on his income as a violinist and had to supplement it by selling Prudential Insurance — a few pennies a week — to the village people.

Kent Godwin's wife was a sallow asthmatic with a tongue as sharp as my mother's and sometimes they would indulge in duels of sarcasm. There were two boys. Cuthbert was a year older than I and Lance, a year younger, was an infantile attendant on the loud games Cuthbert and I would play in the echoing arched passage that ran between our two houses, until our parents, deafened by the tin drums we beat in accordance with the spirit of that belligerent epoch, would unite to descend in wrath and part us. Both Cuthbert and Lance will weave their ways through this narrative; Lance is still among my closest friends.

It was in Frogmoor Road, from which we set off to my aunt's wedding, that I began to experience, in an identifiable way, some of the grand human emotions.

Fear, for example. Down the road stood a large wooden shed coated with black tar that blistered and ran in the summer heat. To me, from the moment I was conscious of it, it seemed to harbour some malign power, so that I would never go past it alone. Later I learnt it belonged to the man known to his fellow townsmen as Skull Harper, because of the cadaverous face so fitting under the crepe-bound top hat he wore at funerals. Skull was the local undertaker, and though his black shed held only the furniture which he sold in his shop as a second business, I became convinced that it was filled with the bodies of the dead who any day might reach out and grab a small boy passing by.

I was early conscious of death and of its pathos as well as its terror. As well as her inclination to sardonic humour in adversity, my mother had a weakness for morbid ballads which she would sing rather well in a sombre contralto voice. Certainly I was no more than four when I became aware of "The Banks of Allan Water"; she rendered the closing lines with a superb melancholy:

> Now the miller's lovely daughter
> Both from care and grief is free;
> On the banks of Allan Water
> There a corpse lies she.

My mother also sang a ferocious little ballad about "Fair Lady Ida," who murdered her baby: "She stuck a penknife in his heart, fair Lady Ida,/ She stuck a penknife in his heart, down by the greenwood side-a." Fair Lady Ida was caught, and "They humped and bumped her against the wall, down by the greenwood side-a"; finally, "They took her off to Reading Gaol, fair Lady Ida." It was an interesting example of the way in which English folk songs tend to adapt themselves to current events, for it was then less than twenty years since Oscar Wilde had been taken off to Reading Gaol.

Both of these songs I accepted with innocent equanimity, and only later wondered at my mother finding them so congenial and so fitting to sing in an infant's presence. The song that actually awoke my sense of the pathetic was a mawkish ditty called, I think, "The Grandfather Clock," which told how the clock had kept time with it's owner's life, through all its vicissitudes, until he reached the ultimate solitude. It was the final refrain that I found so moving.

> O, it struck twenty-four
> As he entered at the door
>> With his blushing and beautiful bride,
> But it stopped short,
> Never to go again,
>> When the old man died.

I would burst into tears when these lines were sung, and so delicious did I find the emotion that I would immediately cry out for an encore, shouting, "More clock! More clock!"

Fear and pathos but also doubt and love made themselves known to me at this time. Part of the inevitable routine of each week was our attendance, at least once on a Sunday, at Emmanuel Church where we were welcomed with particular honour by old Brindley, the black-robed verger, and installed in my grandfather's pew, with the churchwarden's staff standing beside it. My grandfather himself was always to be seen in the choir, where he sang in a rumbling bass that made itself heard above all the other voices. His critics compared him with "the wild bull of Bashan," but I listened with pride and longed for the day when my infant chirp might be exchanged for such a thunderous organ tone.

As I have said, Emmanuel Church was a dissident establishment whose history is another among the rebel strains of my background. It came into tenuous being when a group of ardent Low Churchmen, including some of the local farmers and at least one wealthy landowner as well as my grandfather and other shopkeepers and merchants, revolted against the Tractarian antics of the vicar of St. Mary's, the big old parish church on the cliff over the Tern where my great- great-grandfather was buried. With candles and chasubles and gilded altar cloths and incense and wafers and processions they vowed to have no dealings. They represented a deeply Protestant tradition in the locality which had found expression as early as the seventeenth century, when old Colonel Clive of Styche Hall, the ancestor of Robert Clive of India, had joined the Roundheads of Wem and Nantwich to become a terror to the local cavalier gentry, who would sing:

> From Wem and from 'wich
> And from Clive of the Styche
> Good Lord, deliver us!

I imagine the vicar of St. Mary's prayed to the Good Lord to deliver him from my grandfather and his associates. After living for years in the figurative catacombs, holding services in schools and halls, sometimes conducted by visiting Low Church parsons but more often by one of the lay congregation, they at last gained recognition. I think our distant cousin, George Hamlet, the Archdeacon of Stoke, had something to do with it for, after his appointment, the Bishop of Lichfield became more understanding and allowed the wandering congregation to have its own church and to follow its own stark version of the rite, if it could raise the funds for building. And so Emmanuel Church rose up, a redbrick symbol of rebellion triumphant. It followed the Book of Common Prayer but gave it a rigidly Protestant interpretation, and I was once sternly reprimanded by my grandfather for pointing out that when we recited the Apostle's Creed we declared our belief in the Catholic church. All the decorative features of High Church rituals were dispensed with; the altar was called the Lord's Table and we took baker's bread at communion and denied transubstantiation. But in the plain interior of that church, under its barn-like roof, the hymns and psalms were sung with zest and the lessons were read with feeling because, apart from our beliefs, the Word was all we had.

My love of the Word sprang up there, yet for me it was never more than the word and the singing sound of the human voice. As the years went on, I found more and more satisfaction in the strong plain chants to which we sang the psalms and the hymns that sprang from the confidence of a church that felt itself still militant. Even today, when I am relaxed and feel the need to sing, driving in the country or walking on a secluded path, it is likely to be one of the grand old hymns of Heber or Wesley that comes unsummoned to my lips.

But for me the Word and the sound were not enough to make the faith, and I remember, as vividly today as on the summer morning I felt it, my guilty bewilderment when Mr. Thompson, the dour Scottish vicar who had brought his Presbyterian severity into the Church of England, stood in the pulpit sternly proclaiming the love of Jesus for the elect and the predestined hellfire awaiting those who could not return that love. I was perturbed, and I considered my perturbation with the peculiar rationality of a five-year old child.

I had already a very personal idea of what love meant. It meant Mary Sheppard, eight years old, red-cheeked, blue-tunicked and black-stockinged, whom I had seen climbing with incredible daring up the ropes of the swing down the street and balancing on the great limbs of the oaktree from which it hung, with her corn-yellow pigtails dangling to her waist. I knew, with that passionate certainty which life always dooms to be unfulfilled, that I would marry Mary Sheppard, and announced it to my smiling parents.

I knew, most important and disconcerting of all, that I loved Mary Sheppard more than I loved Jesus, and that it was impossible for me to love Him, since I had no knowledge of Him as a living person, an actual presence. If only He would appear to me, discreetly, among the rasp-berry canes where I would go to eat secretly on warm summer after-noons when the scent of warm fruit and the filtered green light induced in me a kind of regenerative serenity! But He never appeared, in any of those intimate recessions of life, and has not done so since.

At that time, with Mr. Thompson's solemn exhortations ringing in my ears, I certainly believed that I was doomed to hellfire. I dreamed of it: the gravel road outside the house would open up and I would go fall-ing down into a chasm among rocks that were burning with blue and purple incandescent flames. The dream recurred at intervals for several years. Curiously, I never had the sensation of being burnt by the flames, and this, I decided, was a sign that the Devil had indeed claimed me as his own. I accepted this conclusion with an extraordinary equanimity, and was certainly not nearly so frightened by it as I was by Skull Harper's black barn.

Memories of that early period lack contextual continuity. I remember episodes rather than a flow of existence; a scattering of places rather than a living community.

Shops, especially. The little sweetshop round the corner from our house. One stepped down from the Shropshire Street pavement that had risen up over the generations into a kind of cosy low-ceilinged cave in a half-timbered Jacobean building. The windows were leaded and dusty and the daylight shone in meagrely through tall glass jars of boiled sweets and barley sugar sticks, of mint humbugs and licorice laces, of aniseed balls and edible cigarettes. The dimness gave an alchemical mystery to each visit as the asthmatic little hunchbacked woman who kept the shop breathlessly weighed out one's twopence-worth and no more.

And the two toyshops, each with its special quality. One entered classy Miss Padmore's, kept by a clergyman's daughter who looked like Virginia Woolf, through a little wicket, like the bottom half of a stable door, which was always closed even on a summer's day against marauding children and piddling dogs. Here one found dolls and teddy bears, cuddly cats and puppies, brightly painted wooden toys and bricks; things that looked as if human hands had made them. Myopic old Totty Lyman's was the place for fireworks and mechanical toys, for Bassett Lowke engines and railway lines to go with them, for meccano and all kinds of clockwork oddities, a heritage of the pre-war years when Totty, who had come long ago as a refugee from some Polish pogrom, used to import his ingenious contrivances from Germany. Totty was at that time the only Jew in Market Drayton but when prejudice did mildly attack him, it was not for that reason. The rumour began to circulate that Totty was a German, but I have always found it to the credit of Market Drayton that nobody ever attacked him or smashed his windows. A few people stayed away from his shop, but most of them reacted like my father who detested gossip. A little later on when I heard the stories about Totty filtering down among the children, he gave me a clip on the ear for repeating them and asked me if I were not ashamed to be telling "women's tales."

The sweetshop and the toyshops were the haunts of occasional pleasures, but the shop that became a source of constant fascination was Billington's grocery on Shropshire Street. The age of packaging had not yet arrived, and the store was redolent with an extraordinary mixture of smells coming from its bags and bins and barrels, from its spice boxes and its hanging hams and sides of bacon, from its great wheels of Cheshire and Cheddar cheese and its aromatic piles of the crusty and pungent gingerbread that was a local Market Drayton speciality.

Everything in Billington's was measured out and packed on the spot in its appropriate kind of paper and tied with thin white string drawn from an immense spool and broken with a quick jerk of the hand. Tea was blended to the customer's taste from a series of large tin caddies painted in scarlet and gold with Chinese encounters. Coffee was fragrantly prepared from fresh beans in a grinder operated by a great hand-wheel; Java and Blue Mountain was the favourite mix, and I was entranced with the dream of strange places when I heard those magical syllables repeated. Another great hand-wheel propelled the cutter which sliced off translucent rashers of bacon prepared in the smokehouses of local farms.

The great Cheshire cheeses (of which we resolutely maintained that the best were made in northern Shropshire) were cut with a shining steel wire; the butter was squared and patted into cubes with ridged wooden paddles, always wielded with great bravura; the biscuits were weighed out of tins with glass lids; and the beans and rice scooped out of gunny sacks, the latter bearing the strange Hindi names of merchants in Patna and Benares. Sugar was tipped from the scale pan into blue paper bags and for spices and other things bought in small quantities a piece of paper was deftly screwed into a cone, twisted at the bottom and folded in at the top. Salt and soap one bought in great bars to be cut up at home, and broken biscuits, if one were hard up, came out of great wooden barrels.

When I went to Billington's it was the orgy of smells from the bins and baskets and the rituals of preparation that fascinated me; the bit of gingerbread slipped over the counter to me by Mr. Billington himself, great-bellied in his white apron, or a fragment of cheese offered on the tip of a narrow knife, would merely give sauce to the extraordinary pleasure I gained from every visit to his shop.

Perhaps the only regular experience of that time which rivalled our shoppings at Billington's was our walks down to the station. For there, in his signalbox, my grandfather Harry Lewis presided over the fates of the trains which passed through this busy little junction uniting the Potteries, on the old North Stafford line, with Wellington and Crewe on the Great Western. My mother and I would pick our way over the tracks, watching the signal lights carefully, and climb the stairs into a room that was exceptional in that era for being almost entirely window, giving a view over all the tracks and sidings.

Two rows of glistening levers, operating the signals and the points, immediately caught one's eye; they were painted in strong colours — red and blue and yellow and green — and the little steel release switch at the top of each lever would be polished so that it shone like soft silver. A smell of machine oil permeated the room, a kettle muttered and sang on the cast iron stove to renew the teapot that was always on the hob, and the bells kept on jingling. My grandfather, a severe-faced and bearded man with a touch of Gothic intensity in his deepset eyes, seemed to me like a magus listening to messages from another world as he ignored some of the bells, sprang to the telephone in response to others, and in reaction to yet others went immediately and without hesitation to one of the levers and pulled it out or slammed it back into place with a great metallic clang. Often, immediately afterwards, an express would go steaming and whistling past, its great green engine glittering with polished brass and the fireman red as a demon in the reflected glare of the firebox he was feeding. Two or three times, when one of these monsters was standing at the station platform, the fireman would lift me in because I was old Harry's grandson and I would stand there in the exciting smell of grease and hot metal as the driver let me stroke his wheels and levers and peer into the glowing depth of the firebox which reminded me of my hellish dreams.

THE TRUEST POLES OF ALL in my memories of those early years in Market Drayton are the houses of my two grandfathers. They stood on the opposite verges of Market Drayton, their positioning reflecting deep divergences in character and in their attitudes to life. Each had his four acres of land, but on Harry Lewis's well-cultivated radical holding stood a seventeenth-century cottage, half-timbered and thatched, and in the middle of Sam Woodcock's Tory fields a new brick house with bay windows which he had built only a year or so before I was born and which he named *Runnymede*. As his rebellion with the Church had suggested, he was rather near to what we would now call a Red Tory and he valued kings only because in his view they guaranteed freedoms more than republics could do. With its four bedrooms, its large dining room and drawing room, its lawns and rosebeds, Runnymede seemed to me then a veritable mansion. Later on the fields and the orchards and the big vegetable garden became my terrain of play and observation and fantasy, but when I was small the house and its denizens commanded all my attention.

My grandmother was then in her sixties and to me looked immensely old; a white-haired, sweet old lady, myopically peering through small spectacles like pebbles on gold wires, whaleboned into as near an hourglass shape as her plump and panting body would allow. She wore her skirts long enough never to show an ankle, Victorian bonnets with veils that were held tight by elastic under the chin, and lots of jet jewellery, so that she always seemed in semi-mourning, like the old Queen she had so greatly admired.

She spoilt me extravagantly, and among my sharpest early memories is sitting on a hassock before a high-burning fire in the dining room grate on a winter evening, dressed in a white cotton night shirt, eating raspberry tarts, and drinking milk out of a tall slender lager glass while she recited Victorian children's rhymes. My favourite was about mice, and I can reconstruct it like an ancient inscription, with only two lines missing:

> A little hole was in the wall.
>   Three baby mice were in it,
> And one, the babiest mouse of all,
>   Was playing every minute.
> One day mother mouse said,
>   "Come, Frisky, cease your gambols.
> It's time you earned your cheese and bread,
>   So start upon your rambles.
> "Go where you like, the house is wide,
>   . . . .
> . . . .
>   But don't go near the larder.
> "True, there are scrumptious things to eat,
>   Such piecrusts, cakes and biscuit,
> But, O, the traps for heedless feet!
>   I dare not let you risk it."

I tended, as children do, to substitute familiar for unfamiliar words, and "traps for heedless feet" became "traps for eagles' feet," which I still find more poetic.

My grandfather Woodcock was less a figure of the indulgent fireside than of the active world, a man at the height of his vigour, broad-shouldered enough to neutralize his tallness, bearded iron-grey, and proud of his sixteen stone and the belly which he called a "corporation" and which showed his thick 22-carat gold watch-chain to such advantage. There was a bear-like look about him and a bear-like unpredictability about his temper, so that he could be in quick turns gruff and snappish and gentle and generous. His appetite fitted his size, and he made something of a display of eating, being as stylish a carver as he was heavy a trencherman. In the Shropshire style, he ate his dinner at midday, and always, before returning to work at the coalyard, he would announce his intention of having "forty winks." The blinds would be pulled down in the dining room, and everyone in the house moved softly and talked in whispers until he emerged, precisely half an hour later. This procedure so fascinated me that sometimes I would gently open the door and steal in to stare in wonder at this great man stretched out in his easy chair, his head back so that his beard jutted forward, his hands folded on the great mound of his belly, and his breath emerging from his open mouth not in snores but in gentle blowing puffs that fluttered his long and tea-stained moustaches.

My grandfather had the physical vigour and the confidence my father had lost through sickness, and in some ways he became for me a kind of sustaining surrogate parent. I was devoted to him and in the end, because of that devotion, all the more shaken and disillusioned when I began to learn in adolescence that he was not so large-hearted as I had believed. But that was far in the future and what I remember most intensely from those early days, when I was still four or five, are the summer evenings with their silvery northern light when he would work diligently in his flower garden and I would play beside him, opening the leonine mouths of the fallen snapdragon flowers and clothing my fingers with foxglove blossoms. When we went indoors he would allow me to carry in to my grandmother a bouquet of sweetpeas or roses, or a handful of the great translucent golden and garnet-coloured gooseberries which he grew especially for dessert.

As for the third member of the household, it was a long time before my mother, who detested her, told me that Aunt Mary was not an aunt at all. Over the years I pieced together her story, not untypical of the Shropshire countryside of that period. She was the surplus mouth in a poor farm labouring family, and for a pittance in her early teens my grandparents hired her as a servant to live in. In one way it was a scandalously exploitative situation, for I later discovered that even in the late 1920s, when she was at least fifty, she was still being paid only twelve pounds a year, or less than five shillings a week, with her keep and a few presents of clothes thrown in. In compensation, she had a far more comfortable home than her siblings, she was not overworked since my grandmother was an active cook, and she ladied it over her relatives when they visited her and gaped at the size of the house she lived in. Yet her position gave her a never spoken bitterness that emerged in a combination of narrow piety and prim puritanism. She had a sharp vinegary smell that seemed to go with her nature and which I did not like; but then I felt that adults in general smelt rather disagreeable, except for doctors who whiffed intriguingly of medicaments and flighty aunts who used scent.

Again, out of the episodic pattern of my early memories, emerges an incident in which Mary is held framed. One day our big, red-haired, loud-voiced Scottish doctor McQueen came to the house and Mary, who was notably hypochondriac, complained of a pain in her chest. "Och, we'll tak' a luik at ye," he roared, opening his black Gladstone bag and pulling out an old wooden stethoscope. I was immediately interested. "What are you going to do to her?" I shouted. "Oot o' the room, young mon," he roared. "I'm takin' a luik for a hool in her stocking!" So out I went and listened through the keyhole to the muttered conversation, which left me no wiser.

My curiosity thoroughly aroused, I went downstairs and hid under the great tablecloth in the dining room, whose folds, reaching down to the floor, covered the table legs in true Victorian modesty. I was perfectly concealed and I knew that the ladies, my grandmother, my mother and Mary, would shortly gather there with their crochet and knitting. When they did come, I located Mary by her voice, crept towards her, carefully lifted the table cloth, and then gently raised her long skirt to peer at a thick and clumsy ankle. No hole could I see in that dingy lisle stocking and I had no time to look at the fellow ankle before I was detected, hauled out, and denounced as a saucy young wretch, lifting skirts at the age of four! My mother, aware that in my grandmother's eyes my mischief reflected the degeneracy of the Lewis blood in my veins, assumed her customary role of executioner, taking me out to the kitchen to slap my bare bottom. My grandfather, when he came home, listened to the tale of my crime with a twinkling eye, and that evening gave me an especially large piece of chocolate.

Runnymede had its special source of terror, visible as soon as one went in through the front door and past the tall mirrored clothes stand in the hall. The vastly-horned and hairy head of a yak, which my grandfather had picked up in a sale at the house of some retired Old India

Hand, hung over the first stair landing. Staring at me with its great jetty eyes, it seemed the embodiment of menace, and I feared that at any moment it would spring into destructive life. It was a long time before I would ascend those stairs alone, and even longer before I learnt how harmless a creature the yak generally is. I had no idea that one day my life would draw me very near to the yak's own country of Tibet and its people.

In the dining room and the drawing room I felt secure from the menace on the stairs. The dining room represented the megalomania of the Victorian mind; it was filled with massive pieces of mahogony furniture and, in the corner near the window, stood a tall old grandfather clock which my grandfather would solemnly wind each week, adjusting the pendulum weights within its abdomen. Its dial was painted with a bright, naive representation of the Battle of Waterloo, with the Iron Duke on a black horse, watching from a small hill. On the mantel stood a massive example of French bronze sculpture of La Belle Epoque; it represented the marvels of telegraphy, heroic figures, workers and women, raising high their cross-like poles festooned with wire. The motto underneath was the first French I ever read: "L'Union fait la force!" I found the dark wood, the bronze, the battle scene, sombre and awesome.

The drawing room was quite different, a white, light room that reflected the sentimental frivolity that was the other side of the Victorian mind. The furniture was light and fanciful: kidney-shaped walnut tables, chairs upholstered in petit-point, embroidered silk banners on brass stands, little glass-doored cabinets filled with porcelain and glass, bamboo constructions in the bay window to hold ferns and pendulous cacti, a polar bear skin as a rug (fortunately, given my terror-ridden imagination, lacking its head), and on the walls, looking down with thyroid-eyed surprise, the stiff portraits some intinerant artist had painted of my grandparents a generation ago.

The true focus of the room was the mantelpiece, an airy white structure of tiny shelves supported above each other by miniature Corinthian columns which rose up on each side of the fireplace. The great mirror above it almost touched the ceiling. The shelves were crammed with the lifelong accumulation of my grandmother's magpie taste: scores of miniature china vessels bearing the names and coats of arms of northern English towns and seaside resorts; dozens of tiny pottery and glass birds and animals; and legions of the awkward little figurines of human beings and animals that Victorian travellers brought back from India.

I would play for hours on end with these figurines, arranging strange encounters on the snowfield of the bearskin and inventing appropriate dialogues. Yet the object that so fascinated me that I can feel its weight in my hand as I visually remember it, was too beautiful and mysterious ever to become an object of mere play. It was an egg of cut glass, as large as a goose-egg, its surface trimmed to a vast number of tiny diamond-shaped facets. Perched on the egg was a life-sized grasshopper made of green-enamelled metal. I would carry this strange object around in my hand and lay it alone on the bearskin to contemplate the delicate shaping of the grasshopper and the way the light struck with prismatic iridiscence through the facets of the glass egg. It was perhaps my first intense aesthetic experience, but it also led me into primitive thoughts about meaning. Obviously the grasshopper could never have laid so large an egg or even hope to hatch it. So why was it there? What was the connection between egg and insect? Nobody could give me an answer.

HARRY LEWIS'S COTTAGE in Little Drayton complemented the Victorian complacency of Sam Woodcock's Runnymede with an image of peasant sufficiency. He was one of a few men I came to know in this north-western corner of Shropshire who still carried on a vestige of the old cottager tradition that by then had died out in most of England.

> But a bold peasantry, their country's pride,
> When once destroyed, can never be supplied.

My grandfather and his kind were perhaps the last of England's "bold peasantry." They often had modest jobs that were physically not too exacting — like my grandfather's work as signalman — and they used their summer evenings and their weekends and the daylight hours when they were on night shifts and the labour of their children to gain from their small pieces of land a basic self-sufficiency.

Harry Lewis might not be able to graze a cow, but he reared chickens and pigs and got many of his other necessities by barter, exchanging surplus eggs for milk, or giving a neighbouring farmer some pork when he killed a pig, in the expectation of getting cheese and butter. He grew all the vegetables and fruit the family needed, and had apples and potatoes for sale. At least two acres of the four were rotated like a farm, with mangolds one year and oats the next, to be sold to farmers for fodder; in the third year sheep enclosed in hurdles would graze on the fallow and dung it.

The front door of the cottage was in the south wall, espaliered with pear-trees and facing out to the Little Drayton village green, but that door was opened only for weddings and funerals. We entered always from the Shrewsbury Road, up through the lower orchard and in at the back door by way of a wooden leanto that served as a north-facing larder. Here were kept the great steens, as we called them, wide earthenware basins with handled wooden covers which held cool sweet water fetched from the well in the corner of the garden. Smaller steens held milk and butter standing in water to keep cool. The kitchen, the festive scene of my aunt's wedding party, was also the place where everyday life went on. It was spacious, spanned by long thick oak beams, and had a great round table, which I always thought King Arthur's must have resembled, and a wide-deep hearth with high-backed benches on each side where we sat on winter nights to keep out of the draught.

Here the bacon and ham were brought in to be slowly smoked after a pig was killed. I was once there at the time of a killing when the butcher arrived with his little bag of knives. I wanted to see everything that happened and was indignant when my mother, remarking that "Curiosity killed the cat!" kept me indoors while the pig's throat was actually being cut, though the terrible squealing which I soon heard dampened my eagerness.

However, I went out immediately the killing was over to see the pig's carcass being immersed in a bath of boiling brine, and my grandfather and the butcher scraping it pink and clean of bristles. I almost swooned at the sight of a big basin of blood standing beside it, for blood long horrified me. But I was quickly alert again, watching the extraordinary resourcefulness and economy with which Shropshire villagers dealt with sources of food. The butcher worked with speed and an accurate knife, cutting away the hams and gammons and flitches for smoking, and other parts of the pig for eating immediately, while my grandfather cleaned the intestines which would be eaten as chitterlings. Neighbours dropped in to receive the cuts for which an eventual return gift would be expected and Jack the dog got his customary scraps. Then for days we fed in various ways on that pig: roast pork and cold pork; boiled hocks and pickled trotters; sausages and black puddings made from the blood and brawn from the head. Since there was no refrigeration we had to eat before the unsmoked meat was spoiled and, like primitive people in a feast-and-famine economy, all of us were stuffed day after day until we were almost comatose.

The pig was killed in cold weather so that the meat would keep as long as possible, but otherwise the great gathering season was the autumn. Connected with it, was the country round of preserving and jam making that went on in both grandparental households and culminated, about three weeks before Christmas, in a period several days long when the kitchen would be aromatic with the mixing and cooking of the rich puddings and cakes and mincemeat, not for the current Christmas, but to be put away and matured — well laced with brandy — for eating just over a year ahead.

In his autumn garden my grandfather Lewis would pile his potatoes in long heaps and then put straw and earth over them to protect them from frost; these barrow-like structures we called *hogs*, and from this derived a local expression for hoarding, *hogging it up*. Smaller hogs were devoted to root crops like turnips, carrots and parsnips; onions were plaited into strings and hung on the south wall of the cottage to dry before they were taken indoors to save them from the frost; herbs like sage and mint and thyme were also dried; only the leeks stayed in the ground, for the first frosts were said to improve them.

The berry fruits had long been gathered, but now the late apples and the keeping pears were picked and stored on beds of straw in the loft above the west side of the house, which we reached by an outside staircase and not by the little winding stairs that led up to the stuffy small bedrooms at the eastern end. I delighted to climb up and see the rows of coloured fruit lit through the small windows by the pale winter sun, and to smell their heady fragrance.

But the loft was also associated with the most humiliating disaster of my childhood. One Sunday, on someone's birthday, my mother had taken me to Little Drayton in my brown velvet suit with its freshly laundered lace collar. My Aunt Jessie took me up to the loft to help her choose some fruit. She picked out one especially splendid red apple and gave it to me and I went down the stairs with it. But to reach the back door of the cottage I had to pass the mixen, where pig and chicken manure and any other rottable rubbish were collected until muck-spreading time. I dropped the apple; it rolled and I ran greedily after it. It fell over the edge into the mixen and so, slipping on the slimy stone rim, did I, to sink overhead in the nauseating morass and to be hauled out, stinking and screaming, by my eight-year-old cousin, Jack Newing.

The mixen was added to my list of terrifying places, but there was one benefit from the disaster; the brown velvet suit was ruined and I never had to wear it again.

Jack and his brother Stanley were the sons of my Aunt Alice from Colwyn Bay. Jack was four years and Stanley one year older than I, and they were the only playmates, apart from the Godwin boys, whom I can remember from my early childhood. Jack was, and remained until his recent death, a warm and generous being, wise without cleverness, whereas Stanley was the first naturally malicious person I ever encountered. We would play noisy games in the orchard, usually with me as victim, Stanley as persecutor and Jack as protector, until my grandfather would appear and shout in semi-dialect, "Pipe down, yo yung ulluts, or I bin goin' to teal yur bloody arses!" *Ulluts* were owlets, meaning obstreperous children, while *teal*, meaning *beat*, was a local word whose origin I have never discovered.

Harry Lewis must have projected a great deal of moral power, for I never remember that he tealed any of our arses, yet as soon as we heard the word *ulluts* we would stop shouting and retreat into the quiet corner of the garden where the tall raspberry canes concealed us, and there we would pee in competition, and I would admire the grandeur of Jack's fluid arc.

It was to the Newings that we went on the only journey I remember from those early days, when I saw the sea for the first time. Early childhood impressions are never extensive in time or space, so that I have no recollection of the journey we made from Market Drayton to Colwyn Bay, which must have taken us the best part of a day, nor do I recollect the sea as the vast glittering expanse, dropping over the horizon towards the Isle of Man, which I later saw from the same place. I see waves beating on a beach and threatening the sand castle which Stanley and I were building. I see pink shrimps being served for tea and my mother shelling them for me. I see a boy named Louis.

All my life I have in some way been involved with refugees, those sad, unwilling world citizens; Louis, when I was four, was the first. His family had come in flight from Belgium after the German invasion in 1914, and my aunt and uncle had taken them in. I cannot remember the parents, but Louis stays in my memory. He was a little older than I, but no bigger and a great deal frailer, with enormous sad eyes and a translucent pallor. He must have been precocious, for he talked enough English for us to communicate in a primitive way, and his great accomplishment was to make houses of cards.

He would lean his cards in pairs, and build them upwards until he had created a kind of narrow ziggurat taller than any of us. But the ziggurat never endured, for as soon as it was complete Stanley's malice would trigger off his rage and he would dash forward and sweep his hands through the precarious but, to my eyes, marvellous structure. Nor was I innocent of aggression. Sometimes, when Stanley shouted, "Fight him, George!" I would dash forward and pummel Louis, who would immediately weep copiously and attract grownup attention. But I loved his tall card castles and in one way or another have been trying to rebuild them ever since.

BELGIAN REFUGEES WERE only one way in which the Great War entered my expanding awareness. It was talked of constantly and vibrated in the air, as money vibrated in the air that D. H. Lawrence's small boy protagonist breathed in "The Rocking Horse Winner." At church Mr. Thompson would offer prayers for battles whose names, which he uttered in a voice of thunder, still echo in the mind's attic: Mons, the Somme, the Marne, Passchendaele. When naval battles were fought we would sing "For those in peril on the sea," and its surging rhythms evoked for me the menacing storm. At the slightest excuse we would break into "Onward Christian Soldiers!" as if it were a marching chorus. And as crisis moved over Russia in 1917 the sombre tones of the Tsarist anthem, "God the All Terrible," would echo with with heavy menace in our little church.

I could not yet read newspapers, but I remember cartoons and posters and particularly one, hanging in Dr. McQueen's office, that appealed to me because all the participants were animals, as in a child's fable. A great dog fight was proceeding across the coloured map of Europe. A German dachshund, bullying a tiny Belgian griffon, was being set upon by an English bulldog which had him by the snout, and a French poodle was savaging his flank; from the rear a great snarling Russian bear was advancing. Now it would seem to me a demonstrably unfair fight — four to one — but small boys are not inclined to weigh such matters; I knew that the bulldog was on my side and the dachshund was not. Yet why has that cartoon remained in my mind, while all the others have vanished, if it did not in some way disturb me?

In Shropshire we were remote enough to be spared the more dramatic effects of the war. We heard of the Zeppelins, but had only the vaguest idea what an air raid meant. We were country people who grew much of our produce on our own land and bartered our surpluses for what we had not, so that only a few exotic items like sugar were ever in short supply. No soldiers were stationed in Market Drayton and the closest thing to a military camp was the Royal Flying Corps training station at Tern Hill. This was near enough to Little Drayton to be taken in during an afternoon's walk and sometimes my mother would set off with me in the pushcart. We would go to the gate and stare at the sentry standing in his box with his bayonetted rifle, and then wander beside the tall wire fence watching the little Handley Page biplanes flying about and looping the loop, sometimes so near that we could see the pilot in the open cockpit. Grownups were always talking in my hearing about the crashes at Tern Hill, and the poor rash young men who tried impossible tricks and were burned to death for their folly.

But then the Australians came to Tern Hill and wandered slouch-hatted around the streets of Market Drayton on Saturdays; they had such a reputation for fighting and debauchery that my grandmother and other old ladies talked as if the arrival of the "Huns," as we always called the Germans, might perhaps be preferable. But I can remember only one Australian, a tall bronzed man who one day overtook my mother and me as we were walking home and insisted on carrying me all the way back, talking amusingly about his own family, and kangaroos, and sheep, and giving me a glittering new half-crown when he put me down outside our garden gate.

Inevitably, the war impinged on our personal lives, though we were less affected than most other families. My Uncle Harry had already vanished into his prison camp before it assumed its character of a great man-eating conflict of attrition, and though he never said so in public, my grandfather Lewis would sometimes thank God in the circle of the family that his son and namesake was safe. The three husbands of my mother's sisters all escaped military service, either because they were unfit or because they were indispensable. My uncle Harold, my father's brother, joined the Royal Flying Corps, but became a mechanic and never stirred from the base at Farnborough, whence he would arrive periodically in his grey-blue uniform, riding a motor bike with his wife, my rose-petal-pretty Aunt Ethel, in the side car. I looked forward to his visits, for he would throw me in the air and catch me while I screamed in delicious terror, and give me rides in the side-car, and bring silvery ball-bearings which made the best of all marbles, and little toys he had welded out of various metals in his workshop.

My father, who volunteered twice and then conscientiously appeared when he was called up for conscription, was always given the lowest possible rating by the medical board, which meant that he was never called up in any capacity. Since returning from Canada, he had begun to suffer from Bright's Disease. Thanks to the ministrations of a variety of doctors, orthodox and unorthodox, and to the ingenuity with which my mother kept him on a very strict diet, he survived for a whole decade a sickness that usually kills quickly. But he was living on borrowed time and he knew it, and so did my mother. And so, a little later on, did I.

III

GROWING UP POOR

T HE REASON FOR MY FATHER'S ILLNESS became a subject of bitter controversy within the Woodcock family. My grandparents, and especially my grandmother, blamed it on the extremities of the Manitoba climate. When he died ten years later, she would say, "If only he had never gone to that dreadful country!" and reproach me bitterly if I happened to claim, as I sometimes did for the sake of difference, that I was Canadian. My mother blamed it on his exposure to the damp and penetrating English cold when he worked in S. Woodcock & Sons' coal business; he often had to be out of doors in bad weather, supervising the unloading of coal wagons at the railway sidings and the loading of the carts that took the coal to the farmers who were my grandfather's best customers. It seems to me unlikely that either environment brought on the sickness, but there is no doubt that once it appeared he could no longer carry on the physically hard work at the coalyard. Besides, he was too proud and touchy to work happily as my grandfather's assistant, so some time in 1917 he left the business.

My father did not want to seek a job in Market Drayton; it would have given a public character to his break with my grandfather and he was too loyal for that. So we went to Altrincham in Cheshire, a remote suburb of Manchester, where he found work as a bookkeeper in a flour mill. We moved into a terrace of houses beside a main street where tram lines ran and there was a good deal of traffic, mainly horse-drays, steam wagons and a few early motor trucks. By this time I was almost five and I must have been allowed a certain freedom of wandering, for once I caused a great commotion when a blind man asked me to guide him across the street. I proceeded to do so as if the roadway belonged to me.

[47]

By the time we reached the middle there was a great shouting, a driver reined his dray horses to a halt, and, as the blind man and I reached the farther pavement, my mother and a woman neighbour came running to take me back. Relieved as she was, my mother's code of strict behaviour forced her to slap me, especially as my crime had been compounded by the fact that the blind man offered me a penny and I accepted it. I puzzled greatly over the fact that while it was wrong to take rewards for helping the unfortunate, there were also times when it was wrong to help them without reward. I do not seem to have taken very seriously the physical danger.

I was much more aware of the Great War in Altrincham than I had been in Market Drayton, for this was the centre for a group of military camps, perhaps because it was fairly near to the port of Liverpool. There were always columns of soldiers marching through the town headed by military bands, whose noise I detested so much that when one drew near I would run to hide in the cellar.

But one bandless march I remember very vividly. It was a long, silent column of prisoners of war on their way to a special camp a few miles out in the country; the authorities seem to have thought a Caesar's triumph would boost local morale. British soldiers in their familiar khaki uniforms marched as escorts. But it was the prisoners in their field-grey or sometimes navy-blue uniforms who drew everyone's attention. Their desperate melancholy, their sense of helpless defeat impressed itself on my child's mind, as I think it did on the minds of all the women and old men who came out of the houses to stand and silently stare.

I was a very fair child, with corn-coloured Saxon hair that in later years, perhaps as my Celtic ancestry asserted itself, turned darkish brown until, in my early twenties, I became prematurely white like most of my mother's family. On that day in the spring of 1917, as we watched the prisoners march by, my mother held me in her arms and one of the Germans looked at me with his tired eyes and suddenly smiled. He said a word to the man marching beside him and looked again and smiled a second time, with a great sadness. By an immediate intuition I knew that I reminded him of his own child, and I remember the incident more vividly than anything else from that period.

I do not recollect much about the house in Altrincham, where we lived too briefly for it to become a home in my mind, except for the great bath enclosed in a polished wooden surround, where I would play with celluloid fishes, and for the cellar where I hid from the military music. It smelt of earth and potatoes and coal dust, and had a long slate slab where, in those pre-refrigerator days, we kept perishable foods in the cool darkness. Fishes are linked in memory with the cellar as well as the bathroom, for it was here that my father gave me an early lesson in natural history by showing me the swimming bladders of some roach an angler friend had given him, and explaining how the bladders kept them upright in the water.

The passion for natural history that by the age of ten had me reading books like Darwin's *Voyage of the Beagle*, H. W. Bates's *Naturalist on the River Amazon* and W. H. Hudson's *British Birds* must have had its roots in this period, for I also spent a great deal of time with a brother and sister a few houses away whose names I have forgotten but whom I always think of as the Butterfly Children.

The Butterfly Children caught splendid insects like Red Admirals and Peacocks and Tortoiseshells and Hawk Moths, and kept them in large glass jars whose tops were covered with pierced paper to let in the air. When and if the butterflies laid eggs on the leaves put in the jars, they let them go, but kept the eggs and the caterpillars that hatched and the chrysalids into which they turned. I knew the Butterfly Children long enough to see the metamorphosis completed by another generation of insects struggling free of their pupal cases, and so, even before I went to school, I had witnessed and largely understood one of the great natural cycles.

Apart from the Butterfly Children, two people stand out with vivid clarity from those days in Altrincham. One of them is an old Scottish baker named Anderson who came each morning to the back door with his big square basket of bread. My father had done him some favour, getting him extra flour at the mill in the difficult wartime situation, and this gave a special flavour to my Saturdays, since when Anderson came that morning he would always add an iced cake, usually a brightly pink one, "For the bairn!" I was always present in time to receive it.

Mr. Skelhorn, the house painter who lived next door, held with no such offenses against nature as pink icing; in fact he was the first health food fanatic I encountered. He had a great belief in the therapeutic value of dandelion roots and sometimes fed me these bitter tidbits which I ate out of affection for this large and rufous man who treated a child as an equal, until my mother found out, was shocked, and put an end to it. Once I imagined I had discovered Mr. Skelhorn occupied in preparing something more delectable than dandelion roots and ran into our kitchen to shout: "Mr. Skelhorn is mixing blancmange in a bucket!" I had a passion for this dish, more for its intriguing wobble when it was taken out of the mould and carried on to the table than for its bland flavour. But Mr. Skelhorn was only mixing whitewash.

My father's job in Altrincham was only temporary, and he would have lost it if its former occupant returned from the war. Besides, he wanted to be taken back by the Great Western Railway, for which he had worked before going to Canada. He saw security there, and the alarming state of his health made security seem necessary. Influence, "pull" as we called it, counted then, and a boyhood friend who had risen in the railway service got my father appointed goods clerk at Marlow, almost two hundred miles south, beside the Thames. But he never won the security he desired. Unable to pass the company's medical examination, he never became a permanent employee with the right to a pension. He remained in a temporary status, from 1918 when he reached Marlow to 1927 when he died there, and this gave our life a curiously provisional quality that was enhanced by the matter of the house we lived in.

My father preceded my mother to Marlow and did his best to find us somewhere to live. The town, a little riverside resort place, was crowded with people who had come down from London thirty miles away to escape from the air raids. The good housing that remained available was beyond my father's income, for from this time onward his salary never rose about £200, which was then equivalent to $1,000. Eventually he did find a place that was cheap and near the station, but it was a small terrace house so modest, so positively mean in every way compared to our houses in Market Drayton and Altrincham that my mother wept when she saw it. Both she and my father regarded it as only temporary, and so in this way as well our life was provisional. Eighty-two Station Road was a camping ground; we were always going to move, but the will and the money were lacking, and there we stayed until both my father and mother had died, twenty-two years from 1918 to 1940. I finally left the house, then, and only once, in the long years since, went back to take a look at its crumbling brick exterior.

It was the eighth house of a terrace that must have been built early in the nineteenth century, with at the end a little shop, high priced as they always are where people are hard up. There were no front gardens, and people walking along the pavement passed before our window. Behind was a garden as narrow as the building itself, with worked-out soil that seemed to grow only coarse irises whose roots were inhabited by enormous snails.

Next door stood a long wooden building which when we arrived was a factory where a round jolly little man in rumpled tweeds named Joey Rumbelow made "antique" furniture out of oak from old ships, which was said to be beaten with chains and drilled with simulated worm holes to make it look authentically ancient. It meant that the sound of hammering and of circular saws continued for five-and-a-half days every week, and when it was closed at the onset of the Depression (there no longer were any American customers for Joey's fakes) it became an even worse source of noise, since children from streets around found their way in and made an incessant din racing over its wooden floors.

Eighty-two Station Road had two rooms below, a "front" room we entered right from the street and never had the heart to pretend was a drawing room, and a kitchen in which we lived most of the time, with an earth-floored pantry under the stairs, and a scullery with a lead sink and a copper for boiling clothes. Upstairs there were two bedrooms and a tiny room over the scullery that served as a box room and had space for a camp bed. There was no bathroom; the john was a little corner bitten out of the scullery, reached from outside through the coal shed.

The amenities we had known elsewhere did not exist here. There was neither electricity nor gas nor piped water. We cooked with coal in a Victorian cast iron range, and burnt sawn-up railway ties in the front room grate; I can never remember the bedrooms being other than bitterly cold in winter, with ice forming on the chamber pots by the morning. We lit the house with candles and a brass paraffin lamp which had a tall glass chimney that cracked or blackened when the lamp smoked, and a pearly white globe that gave a soft and harmonious creamy light. We levered away at a hand pump over the lead sink, always careful to have a full bucket beside us to prime the pump in case it choked dry. The water was hard from the Chiltern chalk that underlay the valley alluvium, and we kept a rainwater butt for soft water to wash our hair. It was also not very pure and often, in a glass, one would see tiny but visible translucent grey creatures and small vivid worm-like fragments of scarlet thread. God knows what microscopic menaces accompanied them in that water which tasted so fresh and cool as one drew it up from the depths on a summer day.

As a child I did not find all this so appalling as my parents did. There was a novelty which I enjoyed, and only when I was nine or ten did I really become aware of what troubled my parents most: that we lived in a row of houses where all the other residents were manual workers, and not even very high in the complicated caste structure of the English working class. In other words, we were isolated in a world outside our own class. All our shabbiness, by the pressure of circumstances, turned into a soured gentility. On a lower level, we were like the impoverished upper middle class of Orwell's world, and perhaps similar embittering experiences helped to induce similar outlooks, so that when I met Orwell we understood each other easily.

Our situation, and my parents' reaction to it, resulted in an almost complete atrophy of any kind of social life as a family. I cannot remember our formally entertaining anyone during the nine years from our reaching Marlow to my father's death. Once I remember our going to dinner in the house of one of his colleagues, but we never returned the invitation. My father had a wide circle of acquaintances, but I can think of only two real friends he made in Marlow, and each of them in his own way was an odd man out in the community who understood his predicament.

Artie Porter, a florid sporty man, ran a carrier's business, bred horses, and had a staggeringly beautiful wife who drank. Artie and his father, the most prosperous farmer in the area, recognized in my father a man who had seen better days, and did their best to recall them in minor ways by giving us partridges and pheasants in season, and chickens from the farm, and sometimes one of the great Thames eels they caught in their weir. The first of these eels caused an exciting kitchen drama: skinned and decapitated though it was, it began to leap about the table from the reflex actions of its dying muscles, thoroughly scaring my mother as she tried to put it into the stewpot.

My father's other friend was old Dr. Bath, the hunch-backed organist from All Saints' Church and a notable figure at the Royal College of Music, who was intrigued by my father's youthful links with Edward German and was the only acquaintance with whom he could talk about books and music and ideas.

However much they seemed like friends to my father, and in their own way were, the Porters and the Baths would never ask us to their houses and my mother would have been filled with consternation if they had done so, for how in our wretched cottage could she have returned their hospitality?

We were as surely isolated from our neighbours as we were from the people to whom we felt we really belonged, and though my parents could not stop me playing with the "low class" children in our street, they tried to restrict my contact with them as much as possible. I might pick up wrong ways of speaking and God knows what proletarian habits! Especially, I was not allowed to join them in the evenings, and I still remember being sent to bed in summer when it was still light, and lying there tracing the strange coasts and rivers delineated in the map of cracks on the bedroom ceiling while my playmates' voices sounded in the street below:

> Nebuchadnezzar, the king of the Jews,
> Sold his wife for a pair of shoes.
> When the shoes began to wear,
> Nebuchadnezzar began to swear . . . .

In a quite different way, when I went to school, the attachments I formed depended a great deal on the status of the other children's parents. A crisis would immediately arise if I were invited to a party at some relatively prosperous home. My mother would feel it shameful that, if I went, she could not possibly offer the same kind of hospitality in return; no birthday parties were given for me lest children from better-off homes should tell their parents how poorly we lived.

Yet when I did make a real friendship, a casual kind of in-and-out-of the house relationship was tolerated. My parents seemed to know the kind of boys to trust and so, I suppose, did I. I do not think I really lost through the situation, since the boys I did associate with tended to be outsiders like me. Gino Boscetti was the marvellously sunny Italian son of the chef at the Compleat Angler Hotel. George Nicholls had come from India with his parents and, as I realized only later, they must have been Eurasians, as we called them in those days. (The term Anglo-Indian, which now describes them, we then reserved for English people born in India.) In the untidy, curry-smelling Nicholls house my passion for India must first have awakened. Louis Heftel's mother was a French mystery woman, living in a glittering mist of town gossip against which my parents took it upon themselves to defend her.

It was at Madame Heftel's that I first listened to a gramophone, round about 1920, and heard emerging from the great horn a distant but sonorous voice singing in a foreign language. "It is Crusoe," I thought I heard her saying. I had recently read *Robinson Crusoe* and Defoe's matter-of-fact prose led me to believe that Crusoe was a real person.

Now I believed he was not only real but also alive, until my father told me that the man I had heard singing was really Enrico Caruso and explained opera to me. Afterwards he took me to a local performance of *H.M.S. Pinafore*, which was the nearest thing to grand opera that ever came near Marlow.

I cannot say I had a solitary childhood, but it was a childhood less populated than most, in which I learnt to play alone, improvising games out of objects that lay to hand awaiting an imaginary value and existence. I was always given more books than toys, which in the end I preferred, making do with little more than a wooden fort and some lead soldiers to populate it, a brass cannon that fired with a spring, a cap pistol, and a rag doll whom I named Victoria and put to live in the fort and queen it over my minute red-coated army. From learning to play alone, I came to prefer working on my own, relying on myself as I have done ever since. And certainly the untypical and often un-English households into which my few friendships led gave me an introduction to ways of life that I would never have acquired if I had moved only within the circles of provincial respectability and prejudice that despised the foreign as well as the poor.

Remembering the very first days in Marlow, when I was not yet six, I see most vividly the wide gracious sweep of the Georgian High Street, with its beautiful Regency houses and, at the bottom of the street, the smooth flow of the Thames, far broader than any river I had yet seen. On the day of our arrival we walked over the old Brunel-age suspension bridge at Marlow, with the water flowing blackly underneath in the early dark of a winter's evening, and the way across seemed endless. I could hear the thunder of the weir beyond the bridge and next day, when I saw the white water tossing and pouring through the open sluice gates, it seemed more stupendous to me than Niagara does today. Beside the weir was the lock and all through my childhood I would go there, particularly on luminous summer evenings, to see the water raised and lowered, and the boats going up and down with it. Later, I would help push the great beams that opened the massive gates.

I was fascinated by the river steamers which seemed to me as gigantic as liners, for I had never seen anything larger than the gaily-painted canal barges that Shire horses towed along the Shropshire canals. Not long after reaching Marlow, we went on one of the steamers down the river to Windsor and Eton and for the first time, among those grey and ancient towers and cloisters, I began to understand that history has its visible symbols which unite one age with another. And as soon as I realized that history lives outside books, it became a dominant interest and my favourite subject at school.

Other early memories still vivid? The rowing eights practicing on the river in their narrow shells even in winter, with the coxswains bellowing through megaphones strapped to their faces, and the regattas to which all this practice led. The first I attended must have been 1919, for these events were suspended during the war. I was caught in a crowd on the towpath, tall pressing bodies cutting me off from my father and pushing me towards the water until I screamed in terror. I was consoled that evening with the marvels of the fireworks and the river aglow with reflected light from the Chinese lanterns suspended on the swaying punts.

Armistice Day, 1918, when the sirens sounded and the bells rang in tumbling tunes from the tall spire of the church beside the river. We all went into High Street to see the parade of whatever aged soldiers were left in the neighbourhood, the local firemen and boy scouts, and anyone else who had a right to wear a uniform. I had just recovered from Spanish influenza, which almost killed me, with delirious dreams of foxes slaughtering white chickens, and I was a pale little shrimp, worn down to half my infant chubbiness, as I tried to see through the forest of legs. A tall man with a white hat standing beside my mother picked me up and put me on his shoulder.

I do not remember much of the parade, but I remember the man, for he was Jerome K. Jerome, and this, apart from the portentous backs of all the books in my father's shelves, was my first contact with literature. During the next few years (he died like my father in 1927) I would often see Jerome walking around the town, and for some reason he remembered and always greeted me. One winter, when I was perhaps ten, Jerome and L. H. Myers and Rebecca West, who lived up in the hills behind Marlow, decided to help arrange a series of literary lectures for the people of Marlow. One night Edward Carpenter came, and my father, who by this time had become very reclusive as if he were conscious of approaching death, broke his habit of not attending local functions, and we all went together.

Jerome was in the chair, but Carpenter was much the more striking figure, and I can still visualize his dignified but androgynous looks, the silky quality of his hair and beard, the powerful softness of his voice. He talked of some secular hermit, a man who had cut out from civilization, who had gone to live as North American Indians did, making his own garments from skins, gathering or cultivating whatever he ate, and, for the good of his spirit, living a life without any manufactured object. Most of the Marlow people in the audience were, I suspect, puzzled or bored, and louts guffawed in the back rows, but both Carpenter and his subject deeply impressed themselves on my imagination. I say imagination rather than memory because, curiously, I cannot remember the name of the man on whom Carpenter lectured, except that I think he had a French name which was certainly not Thoreau. Even more curiously, I have never since come across any hermit record that quite fits my memory of what Carpenter told. Yet it was one of the epiphanic evenings of my life.

SCHOOL WAS AN EXPERIENCE for which I was already prepared when I reached Marlow, in the sense that I knew my alphabet and had begun hesitantly to read before I entered a classroom. What school gave me, above everything else, was the negative gift of a sense of time; suddenly the days, which had seemed unbroken continuities, were divided into sections of time. The class periods and the school terms became prison sentences in which I would count, marking them on a calendar and even scratching them under the lid of my classroom desk, the days until the end of term.

Undoubtedly this preoccupation with time was accentuated by the fact that every school holiday, which meant a total of at least three and a half months a year by the time I was attending grammar school, I spent with my grandparents in Shropshire, still living a curiously unchronological country life so long as I was there. And so my years, from six to seventeen, were divided, in a way of which I was highly conscious, between life in time and life outside time. The two ways were so different that, writing now about my time-bound life in Marlow, I have to leave aside my timeless life in Shropshire.

I never wanted to go to school, and though I learnt quickly and enjoyed much that I learnt, I never liked schools as assemblages of human beings. I feared, disliked or despised most of the other children and most of the teachers; I loathed the organized sports that played so great a role in all English schools, and from the beginning I was a truant from the much exalted team spirit. If there had been any means by which, with a few kindred spirits, I could have acquired the power of expressing myself in words and a knowledge of subjects that interested me (English and history and geography), there was no time during my school days when I would not have chosen it in preference to what I endured. From the beginning it seemed to me that school, like any other massing of human beings, brings out more of the bad than of the good in them, and this in spite of the fact that though I was not sporty enough to be popular, I was never greatly bullied and had enough friends.

Though we lived on a poor street, or rather because we did, my parents believed they could not send me to the "rough" public elementary school attended by the boys of the neighbourhood. They could not even consider, in their own poverty, sending me to a boarding school, and I was fortunate at least to escape that special hell of English middle-class youth. I was sent instead to the only private school in our little town, a dame school which the Misses Illsley kept in the big tall-windowed Georgian rooms above the Post Office. One Miss ran the school, another gave courses in shorthand and typewriting in the evening as a local substitute for a business school, and the third Miss, the plumpest and most genial of all, kept the house.

A succession of young and not so young women earned wretched wages as Miss Illsley's assistants while they waited for something better to turn up. Most took out their frustrations on the children whom parental snobbery had put in their charge. I do not think Miss Illsley, who blinked benevolently like an old mole behind her thick glasses, really meant to exploit either her teachers or her pupils; she provided a good basic training in the three R's with painting and drawing on the side and, somewhat eccentrically, knitting for both boys and girls. After painful hours I did finish a wavy-edged scarf, but I never graduated to three-needle items like socks or gloves.

There were perpetual difficulties during the three years I attended the school, perhaps because we were living through the glimmering dawn of the British welfare state. Town councils were becoming conscious of standards of accommodation for schools and similar institutions, and before I had been there long we were expelled from the sunny and rather happy rooms above the Post Office, and moved around, like a clandestine English school in Quebec, first into the basement of the Wesleyan Church and then into the Baptist Sunday school.

I cannot remember a great deal that was actually taught during the fugitive progression from building to building, but clearly a great deal that characterized my later life was fostered by my encounters with Miss Illsley's acerbic assistants whose rulers were ever-ready to beat on errant knuckles, for most of the incidents I remember from that period have some flavour of deviousness or rebellion. I developed early, perhaps under my father's influence, an eye to the artificial in literature and when I was picked to recite Wordsworth's "The Daffodils" at a school event for the edification of the parents, I immediately recognized the silliness and falseness of the poem and developed a dislike for Wordsworth that I have never shed. I got my own back by reciting the poem perfectly in every rehearsal and then, on the day itself, playing the bumpkin, fluffing my lines clownishly to the amusement of the audience and the fury of the teachers.

I became a fluent liar and more than that. One day a girl who had spent a summer holiday in Cornwall brought into class a beautiful shell for which I felt a sudden and irresistible desire; when the opportunity came I quickly pocketed it and took it home, declaring I had found it on the road. I now regarded myself with a mixture of pride and perturbation as a thief and I felt a smug satisfaction the next time my mother brought out one of her favourite sayings: "You can lock up from a thief, but you can't lock up from a liar." I was both and, for a while, pursued the two careers to the point of rashness, which came when I passed off a watercolour sketch of snowdrops, which one of the young teachers had done hurriedly in class, as my own. It was a nice little piece of painting and my grandparents had it framed and hung it in their drawing room as a memento of my artistic powers. Foolishly, I allowed myself to be convinced by my own lies, and proceeded to do some more paintings — the great artist working on demand — which aroused such suspicion among my shrewder relatives that I retreated and reserved lying for self-defence.

This did not mean I retreated from creative fantasy; in fact, I carried it to the very verge of literary creation in connection with my truancies from church when I was between ten and eleven. My mother thought it would do me some good and my father felt it would do me no harm if I were sent off to church every Sunday morning, and I chose the village church of Bisham, about a mile from Marlow. I was going to school in the village (of which more later), so there was a plausible connection. I knew my father never went into a church except to look at the architecture, while my mother was too busy cooking the most elaborate meal of the week, the big Sunday mid-day dinner, to check on what I might be doing in a village church a mile away to which none of her acquaintances went.

I would pocket the pennies I was given for the collection, buy a surprise packet of stale sweets at the general store down the street, and spend three Sunday mornings out of four wandering in the woods around Bisham, munching licorice and gob-stoppers, and blowing the tin whistle that, if I was lucky, would be included in the surprise packet. On the one Sunday out of four I really would attend church, I would put my pennies into the plate and, when the sermon came, carefully watch the vicar of Bisham who was noted for his extravagent pulpit gestures, for his outlandish similes, and for the absurd anecdotes with which he illustrated his points. This would give me enough material to make up accounts of fictitious sermons for the rest of the month, which I would recount each Sunday on my return home, elaborating the oddities of the vicar's behaviour. My father would listen with a certain parental pride in my powers of expression and if he suspected I was romancing he never let me know. I was beginning to learn the power and joy of manipulating words.

My links with Bisham, the church and the school, were precipitated by an act of sheer rebelliousness at Miss Illsley's. This was some time in 1920, when there was a great deal of talk about strikes circulating among our parents and in the newspapers, whose headlines I was then beginning to read and understand. A new teacher had angered us with the capriciousness of her punishments and one day, when she had committed what seemed to us some intolerable injustice, news of it spread quickly from class to class, and we older boys of eight or so got up and began to shout "Strike! Strike!" Some of the more tomboyish girls joined us as we stampeded out of the school, bashing with our pencil boxes the monitors — goody-goody boys chosen for the task — who tried to stop us. Once we left the school we had no idea what strikers did, so we roved around the railway yards in a shouting gang, and then decided to go back to school to pick up the coats some of us had left behind. By this time the teachers had sent the small children home and closed the school, so we battered the door, running against it en masse to try and break it down. Then one of us broke a window and, appalled, we all ran away.

The strike did not last, for the parents applied divide-and-rule methods. My father had seen me from his office among the gang in the station yard and when I got home I was duly cross-examined and caned.

I imagine most of his fellow parents did the same, for the strikers all turned up at school next day, and neither we nor the teachers mentioned the incident, though the woman who precipitated it soon left. And so did I, for my parents decided I had outgrown dame-school teaching and needed a little manly discipline.

I was not yet old enough for grammar school, and they still did not wish to send me to the public elementary school in Marlow, so I was sent to the school in Bisham. Bisham was just over a mile from Marlow, on the other side of the river, a riparian village of thatched flint and mortar houses, with Bisham Abbey, a manor house said to be haunted by the ghost of Lady Mary Hoby who had smothered one of her children in Elizabethan days. A beautiful Gothic church with mediaeval brasses, contained a crusader's tomb with the armoured knight lying cross-legged, and a coloured alabaster monument to one generation of the Hobys, the father kneeling on one side with his sons in descending order behind him, and the mother with her daughters on the other. The churchyard, full of splendid old yew-trees, ran down to the river, and people buried there were lowered into water.

The school opposite the church was run by an arrogant and sharp-tongued little Welshman, Mr. Jones, who happened also to be a rather good teacher. He and his wife took the upper classes, and the lower ones were taught by two young women we called Teacher Sylvia and Teacher Dorothy. Teacher Sylvia was a pretty and sweet-natured woman, but I was too old for her to teach me and went immediately into Dorothy's class. She was a florid, genial, expansive woman who had the natural power of discipline that comes from being able to deal with any situation without allowing the equilibrium of one's good humour to be disturbed. There were some rough characters among the children from outlying farms, but it was never Teacher Dorothy who fell foul of them. She was the first teacher I really liked, and I used to steal flowers from the garden to take her. She set essays, compositions as we called them, on interesting subjects, and under her encouragement I began, at about nine, to develop a facility in prose.

Going to Bisham school would probably be regarded as a hard assignment by a modern child used to school buses and school lunches. It was over a mile from Station Road, and I would walk there, in all weather, for the first class at nine, walk home for the mid-day meal, walk back to school for afternoon classes, and then go home again at four o'clock. A group of us, boys and girls, went together, meeting every morning at the bridge over the Thames, earnestly hurrying on the way to school, larking and scrapping on the way home. Sometimes we would jump onto the backs of horse-drawn delivery vans, but often the drivers were malevolent and would flick at us with their long whips until we jumped off.

Again I cannot remember a great deal of what we were taught at Bisham, though I do recollect becoming strongly aware of history at this time, perhaps because it was in a way congealed in the neighbouring church and abbey, and also in the nearby site of Temple where the Knights Templars had built a priory, and where an old paper mill still stood which Defoe had mentioned in his *Tour Thro' the Whole Island of Great Britain* more than two hundred years before. Altogether, I remember the feel of the place and its look more than anything specific that was taught: the big room where the higher classes all sat together, boys on one side and girls on the other, a white room filled with sunlight; the long playground with the line of tall Lombardy poplars beside the main road; the corner where the small children played hopscotch under the thorn bushes; and the big area of grass where the older boys and the wilder girls played rounders and touch and some kind of improvized football.

There was a difference we all recognized between the town children like me and the foreigners like Gino Boscetti and Louis Heftel on one hand, and the country children on the other. They represented a different world of experience and values, an uncouth world to us, dominated by the rhythm of the seasons and close to the alien realm of animal existence.

More than anyone else it was a boy named Fred Rogier who personified that country way of life. He seemed to me the height of rustic barbarity, though his name, which we pronounced Rozha, represented that survival of degenerated Norman French gentlemanly strains among the rural labouring classes which George Borrow had noticed a century before. Coming from a distant farm, he always wore dirty corduroy clothes that whiffed of the stable and the byre; his red hair was always uncut and unkempt; and he spoke in a broader accent than anyone else when he talked about shit, which he constantly did. He was always inciting the other village boys to make the town boys eat horse dung, but nothing came of it.

Fred was partly responsible, with his exaggerated accounts of the behaviour of farm animals, for my dim awakening at this period to the facts of sexuality. There was, of course, no such thing as sex education in the schools of that period; even biology was considered too near the bone of frankness. And our parents, themselves bound by Victorian inhibitions, treated the subject with a worried blend of sternness and panic.

More formidable than Fred Rogier, because it was large and tended to act as a cohesive unit, was the Frith clan, a great interbred family of cousins who seemed to constitute half the population of Bisham. They were poor and tough, their parents mostly ordinary labourers and hard drinkers, steeped in Weathered's Ale. When I was at Bisham school the leadership of the clan had fallen to Ethel Frith, a loud-mouthed hussy with tousled hair who, like her sisters, wore the kind of long smocks, halfway down the calf, one sees in pictures of late Victorian girls. Ethel was beyond the control of any of the teachers, even Dorothy, and Jones, who was a great disciplinarian, decided he must take the situation personally in hand.

Jones caned one on the hand with painful skill, so that one's palms ached for hours after three of his best. But he had never before caned a girl. Girls were regarded as naturally more good than boys, and if Jones did not use his cane on them, it was due not to a sense that female flesh should be left inviolate, but to a knowledge that girls in general responded to less severe measures. Not so Ethel, who treated with contempt any ordinary kind of discipline, and finally Jones decided to break precedent by caning her and, to emphasize the lesson, by doing it in public, before the whole school.

It was a disastrous enterprise. The feeling was hostile to Jones from the beginning. The girls all supported Ethel out of sexual loyalty, and the boys out of a sense that what might be proper for them was not proper for girls. And then there was Ethel, who had no intention whatever of letting the occasion enhance the prestige of authority. Among the boys there was a code of accepting one's punishment and showing one's contempt by not flinching as the cane cut down upon one's flesh. Ethel recognized no such code. When Jones took her by the arm, she struggled, screamed, kicked and scratched, and Jones, in a whitehot Celtic rage, manhandled her across his knee, and beat her on the legs, the arms and the back with a fury that even to our innocent eyes seemed unnatural and perverse; I felt myself growing more knowing by inches as I watched. By the end of it all, Ethel was weeping, more dishevelled than ever, but still defiant. Jones was sweating and spent, with the red streak of Ethel's nails across his cheek. I think he was thoroughly aware of the silent disapproval of the whole school, including the other teachers, for though he declared that he hoped we now understood that nobody was exempt from punishment, he then turned and walked away with a blanched, set face, and was not seen for the rest of the day. Authority had shown its weakness to us and we fostered the lesson, while Ethel became a heroine, which she did not entirely deserve, for in fact she was just about as stupid as she was intractable.

MORE OF MY REAL EDUCATION took place in our house at this period than in any school. The kitchen, dominated by a great oleograph of Nelson's death on the deck of the *Victory*, was the place where we carried on the business of daily living, where our meals were cooked and eaten and in the evening I did my homework. The front room enshrined my father's interests, and it was a surprising room to anyone who happened to step from the pavement into that primitive cottage, for it seemed to throw into relief the desperation of our shabby gentility.

The furniture was the best kind of fake Jacobean oak, with marvellously turned spiral legs that even Joey Rumbelow admired. On the massive sideboard stood my father's collection of old English pewter, and on the marble mantelpiece and the tops of the two builtin cupboards on each side was ranged his collection of Staffordshire and Sunderland china. The cupboards contained his stamp collections, mainly from the Commonwealth; he spent a great deal of time with these, for he belonged to several exchange clubs and even made a little money out of speculating on rare issues.

The pewter and the pottery, and my father's books about them, gave me my first insight into the beauty of good craftsmanship and also into the way of life of the eighteenth century, to which most of his collection belonged. But the stamps were even more evocative, introducing me to exotic and primitive societies, to tropical scenes, to unfamiliar birds and animals and flora, and leading me into fields of interest that otherwise I would have ignored. Many years later, when I travelled in Asia and the South Pacific, the life I encountered was at least partially familiar to me from having pored over my father's stamp albums and the illustrations to Stanley Gibbon's catalogues.

Even more important were the books that filled one wall of the room. My father was a true bibliophile as well as an addictive reader. He coveted well-bound and well-printed books; he loved facsimiles and limited editions. A book for him was a sensual as well as an intellectual experience, a visual and a tactile artifact whose paper should please the fingertips as much as its type should please the eye. He had most of that splendidly printed turn-of-the-century series, the Tudor Translations, and would spend hours reading Florio's Montaigne and Urquhart's *Rabelais* and *Heliodorus*, the King James Bible and early translations of Machiavelli; *The Prince* and *The Florentine Wars* especially fascinated him.

He seemed, indeed, to have become a mental denizen of the Elizabethan and Jacobean ages for, as well as the Tudor Translations, I remember a collected edition of Sir Thomas Browne and one of Isaak Walton, a beautiful version of *The Closet of Sir Kenelm Digby*, and facsimiles of Nashe, Greene and other lesser Elizabethans, as well as Captain John Smith's accounts of the settlement of Virginia and William Lithgow's *Rare Adventures and Painful Peregrinations*. When I was very young I liked the wood block illustrations to Smith and Lithgow (and was particularly fascinated by the latter's lurid drawings of the tortures he endured from the Spanish inquisitors), and afterwards, in my *Robinson Crusoe* phase, I was fascinated by Smith's detailed practical accounts of his voyages and settlements. A little later, when I took to fishing, I spent a great deal of time reading Walton, whom I found more interesting as a pastoral writer than as a practical guide to angling, and stage by stage I read all the other books.

Outside the sixteenth and seventeenth centuries, my father's collection grew rather sketchy. Before I could remember them, he had sold to earn cash he needed urgently such things as his complete collection of Oscar Wilde. He was a great defender of Wilde, which took some courage in his time and place, though he characteristically never told me why Wilde had to be defended. But he had retained a good many books by Frank Harris, whom he admired; most of John Davidson's books of verse (which I liked as soon as I read them and still do); Clive Bell's books on art, from which I gained my first confused knowledge of Cézanne and modern painting; some Bernard Shaw; and the books of that rather good but now entirely forgotten Edwardian poet and essayist, Richard Middleton.

There were also novels by Frederick Niven, including *The Lost Cabin Mine*, which gave me my first idea of the terrain of British Columbia and a desire to explore it, and Maurice Hewlett's historical romances, which I devoured when I was twelve and have never read since. There were also the novels, which my father extravagantly admired, of George Meredith. These I found some of the hardest of his books to understand, which was unfortunate since I got my name from Meredith. There had been a great family row about it. My father wanted to call me George Meredith Woodcock, while my mother insisted that if I were to have a second name, it must be Henry, after Harry Lewis, and my other grandparents demanded that it should be Samuel, which was a Woodcock name. As a final compromise I had no second name, but the Meredithian George remained. Long afterwards my Welsh friend and fellow poet Lynette Roberts always called me Meredith, and even later I paid my debt by reading my namesake's novels with something approaching my father's devotion and editing *The Egoist* for the Penguin English Classics.

Apart from all these books that had survived from his more fortunate past, my father bought in a sale when I was young a set of *Chambers' Encyclopedia*, in an old leather binding that was falling away into dust, so that it must have been quite outdated. But for me it was a source of endless hours of fascinated reading when I established many of the mental clues I would put to use later on when I turned to historical writing. I did not read *Chambers' Encyclopedia* all through, as Aldous Huxley is said to have read the *Britannica*, but I made several efforts and became extraordinarily knowledgeable about aardvarks and Afghanistan, about beavers and bison and Bolivia and bos longifrons, but more sketchily so about entries after D, when I took to dipping with an eye to the more interesting illustrations.

I always enjoyed and still enjoy good reference books, since my kind of imagination thrives on a diet of widely assorted facts. Quite early in my boyhood I would read the county directories of Shropshire and Buckinghamshire from end to end, so that I had acquired by the age of eleven a good idea of the immediate regions in which I lived, their histories and geographies; I have kept the habit and it has undoubtedly fostered my inclinations towards regionalism.

More important in their ultimate effect than any of these compendia of actualities was the collection of issues of the *English Review* from the early days when Ford Madox Ford was editor which my father kept in a tin trunk in the box room. Especially after his death, I would dig them out and read them with fascination and a certain bewilderment, realizing often that I was encountering something hitherto quite unknown that stirred my mind more deeply than any structure of facts might do. Thus, when I most needed them, between the ages of fourteen and sixteen, I first encountered in those yellowing pages between the old blue covers of the *English Review* not only Ford himself, but also D. H. Lawrence, Norman Douglas, the Powys brothers, and a great deal of Joseph Conrad, whom I had first read as a narrator of physical adventures but now recognized as a guide to the adventures of the mind.

I do not think there was any medium of communication that impinged on my childhood in the way television does on the mental life of most children today. Because he hated the way the early sets distorted music, we never had a radio while my father was alive. I had to be content to listen in my friends' houses or when we visited my Aunt Jessie, for Uncle Joe was an early enthusiast and could do wonders with crystals and cats' whiskers.

Nevertheless, I was certainly aware from the age of five or so of the importance of newspapers because, particularly at serious times during the war, my parents would anxiously discuss what they read, and I was soon reading headlines and beginning to understand the news items, especially if they were illustrated. We took the *Daily Mail* and the *Sunday Telegraph*, and my mother would borrow the *News of the World*, of which my father disapproved on grounds of taste rather than morals, from our next-door neighbour. So, I followed with great interest the more sensational murders of the era, on which the English rather prided themselves, and shared the local excitement when a dairy farmer from the village of Little Marlow, a mile or so away, whom we all knew as the Whistling Milkman, was tried for killing his wife and boiling the flesh from her bones so that he could feed her to the pigs. Less comprehensible to me at the time were the hints I also gathered in the *News of the World* of strange crimes in public lavatories, often involving distinguished gentlemen.

I took my boyhood politics from the Tory *Daily Mail*, and from the age of ten or so believed in Empire Free Trade, the simplistic doctrine of turning the commonwealth into a closed, self-sustaining and self-contained federation, which Lords Rothermere and Beaverbrook had at that time combined to push through their powerful news empires. Perhaps my father's sustained interest in Canada, and my own pride in being Canadian-born (a point of difference from my schoolfellows which I cultivated), had a good deal to do with this imperialist attitude, which was fostered by my reading of the Canadian immigration literature that found its way into our house during the 1920s.

My father's political conservatism made him appear rather simplistic in his attitude to world affairs, as people were in those days before the totalitarian regimes that were beginning to emerge showed their real natures. Because he passionately loved Beethoven and Handel, and respected Wagner, he admired Germany, and always declared that in World War I Britain had chosen the wrong side; it should have elected to share the hegemony of the world with Germany rather than support corrupt France; especially it should not have allowed the American barbarians to gain a position in world politics which everyone, he believed, would regret. He thought Mussolini and early fascism were good for Italy, but I think he saw merely the trains running on time and had not the least idea what fascism meant in practice. He was like many people of that time who were appalled by the chaos of the post-war period and longed for a return to order, to the predictable world they had known in their youth, having no idea that the totalitarian creeds would lead the world into even deeper chaos.

He knew Oswald Mosley during the first part of his political career, for Oswald's mother, old Lady Mosley, had moved to Market Drayton and bought a house just down the road from Runnymede. Mosley's fascist phase was then far in the future, but my father was rather excited by his conversion to socialism and his emergence as a Labour M.P. The audacity of it stirred the maverick side of his nature, as did the intellectual audacity of Bernard Shaw. And he reserved judgment on the Russian Revolution, saying that Lenin must be given a chance to prove himself.

But this, I suspect, was said largely to annoy my grandfather, who was both scandalized by what he regarded as Mosley's apostasy and passionately incensed over the Russian Revolution, largely because he had been foolish enough to buy Tsarist government bonds, which the Bolsheviks repudiated. For a while, indeed, the Revolution loomed large in family concerns, and events in Russia were followed closely. Somewhere about the age of six I was taken to a lantern lecture on what had happened in St. Petersburg, in which the speaker denounced the Bolshevik atrocities. I retain clearly in my mind's eye two of the slides, one of dingily-clad Russian soldiers standing packed in railway trucks, and the other of fighting in a square, with people running and some lying dead on the pavements. I was introduced early to the realities of our time.

Apart from his own library and the books of biography and memoirs which he took out of W. H. Smith's circulating library and encouraged me to read, my father tried to direct my education by buying what seemed to him the right kind of books. He bought me books by Captain Marryat and G. A. Henty and R. M. Ballantyne, picking mainly those that told of adventures in distant lands, which supplemented the books of South American travellers, like Bates and Waterton and Belt, which he also gave me. I had *Alice in Wonderland*, but I was a very concrete-minded little boy, even in my fantasies, and only much later did I appreciate Carroll's rather contrived nonsense. I much preferred books on natural history, and this delighted my father, since my interest stemmed largely from our walks together. "Use your eyes and ears all the time," he would say. "There's always something interesting to be seen." He taught me to be constantly aware of the world around me, to observe and then to think about it. The lesson has remained throughout my life, and it has combined with my inherited curiosity to make me the writer I have become.

My father greatly admired Kipling, as I now tend to do, and he gave me most of his books. Strangely, these did not include *Kim*, which I read long afterwards when I finally went to the India, that has held its fascination for me ever since I first heard it talked of with nostalgia in the Nicholls' untidy home. I don't think India meant a great deal to my father. When he did think of foreign travel it was southward from the Canada he knew, into the Brazil and the Andes that the great travellers had described. I cannot remember his ever expressing a wish to see any European country and his literary interests were essentially English, for even in the Tudor Translations what really enthralled him was the resonant sixteenth and seventeenth century English through which the originals had been filtered. He began to see the world from his Morris armchair and he became more and more a recluse as he drew near to death in my early teens.

I can indeed remember him during our first years at Marlow, working on a summer evening in the allotment on railway land where he grew excellent vegetables which we would eat fresh in their seasons. I remember especially from that time the walks by the Thames to watch the fish swimming among the weedbeds, dace and bleak flashing silver through the clear water and sometimes the sinister shape of a pike, and the other walks into the hills and through the beechwoods to watch for birds. But from the last years I remember him mostly sitting in his chair poring over his stamp collections or, more often, over the *Florentine*

Wars or *Religio Medici* or Montaigne, whose search for self-knowledge he sought to emulate and whose stoicism increasingly influenced his view of living. He would often quote from the *Essays*. "One must always have one's boots on and be ready to go," he would say, and my mother would look pained and be silent. "The work of one's whole life is to build the house of one's death," he would continue, and she would look at me and say, "Arthur, the Boy!" And he would say, "He will learn, if he does not already know."

My father rarely went with the other men to the pub, for his doctors had forbidden him to drink, and he rarely attended any occasion when he would have to meet his species in numbers. He detested anything mechanical that had been invented since the steam engine, and, apart from his hatred of the wireless as we then called it, he never went to cinema. If I wanted to go, I would have to accompany my friends, buying fourpenny seats and slipping back into the sixpennies when the lights went off, or accompany my mother and sit in the eight-pennies, which was such a strain on our finances that it rarely happened.

As for his beloved music, he carried an enormous amount of it in his head, and in his later years he did not need to go to concerts. He even avoided going to church, claiming that the noise would bring on headaches from which he periodically suffered because of his glaucoma. I suspect the real reasons were his reaction against the sanctimoniousness of my churchwarden grandfather, and the fact that his own faith had worn to nothing. He never said anything, at least in my hearing, that positively expressed his Christian belief, yet he never said anything that categorically proclaimed his disbelief. I am sure that he was an agnostic but did not want to influence me by his own failure to raise a passion within himself for God or against Him. But he kept on his writing desk a card on which he had elaborately written two maxims. One was Montaigne's *"Que sçay je?"* (what do I know) and the other, which he attributed to Socrates though it was in Latin, was *"Hoc solum scio, quod nihil scio!"* (this only I know, that I know nothing!). But he never talked to me about these things; it would have been in his nature to wish me to reach my conclusions in this realm according to my own mind.

IV

TIME SUSPENDED

WHEN I WAS VERY YOUNG I would often ask my mother as I ate my porridge, "What are you going to do today, mammy?" And she, in her sardonic way, would laugh, and say, "Go out of my mind for change of air!" It was more than an inclination towards dark humour that prompted her. The combination of my father's illness, which required searching out and cooking special foods, our wretched, anti-labour-saving house, and looking after me, was sometimes almost beyond her endurance. She, as well as I, welcomed it when my grandparents offered to have me living with them at Runnymede for all my school holidays, which, when I went to secondary school, was three and a half months in the year, and before then about ten weeks.

What this meant was that almost all my childhood I lived in two alternating worlds. From the age of five to almost seventeen when I finally left school, I had two residences, two environments, two sets of acquaintances and friends. In my mind the division between them was so complete, that when I went from one to the other it was like journeying to the far side of a frontier.

My grandparents were motivated by something more than pride and devotion. Like most of the people who lived north of the Trent, they regarded southern England as effete and corrupt. Southerners were affected, unreliable, artificial, everything that could be summed up by the word *false*, whereas north country people, among whom the Salopians counted themselves, were straightforward, trustworthy, good-hearted, *real*. Southerners jabbered like Frenchmen; northerners spoke laconically, but every word they so deliberately picked made sense. Nothing distressed my grandparents more than to observe how, progressively, I began to speak like a Southerner, losing the flat *a* (Arnold Bennett's *a*) that was the mark of down-to-earth, honest folk. By immersing me in good Salopian country life, they hoped not only to strengthen me physically but also to mitigate the effects of life among people they regarded as no better than aliens. As for my parents, the fact that they did not have to feed me for a quarter of the year was a welcome financial help. I think also they were more at peace with each other when I was out of the way. For I had learnt early how to get my own way on occasion by playing on their differences.

No more than two days after a school term had ended, my mother and I would board the little local train known as the Marlow Donkey. We would change at Bourne End, a little way down the Thames Valley, and again at High Wycombe in the Chilterns where we joined the Holyhead Express that at the end of its journey connected with the boats to Ireland. As my father worked on the railway, we travelled on passes or quarter-fare tickets; otherwise we could never have afforded such excursions three times every year.

On these journeys I first really began to become conscious of space, as the wheels ran chunkety-chink north through the chalk hills scarred with neolithic emblems, past Basingstoke into the low rich Midland farmlands, through Banbury where we always stopped long enough to buy the flat spicy cakes of the locality, through Leamington Spa and Birmingham and Wolverhampton, until the Wrekin rose up above the plain. In the early days, we would get out at Wellington to catch the local train to Market Drayton; later this became unnecessary because the Crewe coach stopped at Market Drayton.

As the years went on I came to know all the landmarks along the way, all the transitions of landscape, and would await them with mounting expectation as the train chugged farther north. I was excited by the appearance of every remembered corner, which could be something as unspectacular as a farmhouse built in an unusual way, or a slow river white with crowfoot running through the meadows, or a stretch of woodland with its own special ferny character, or a bit of moorland with scattered birches rising among the vivid purple of the heather.

The most dramatic transition was between the pasture land of southern Warwickshire around Leamington and the Black Country which began south of Birmingham and did not really end until after Shifnal in southern Shropshire. A smoke-filled sky seemed to weigh down darkly that blighted country where the Satanic mills had killed off everything except sparse yellow grass and stunted thorn bushes; there was not a tree worth the name for fifty miles. On our early journeys I found it spectacular and interesting rather than shocking, as it always seemed to my mother. The slag heaps near the mines seemed like vast prehistoric earthworks, and I was to be reminded of them long afterwards when I first saw the long Mochica pyramids on the coast of Peru. The tall chimneys and the skeletal wooden superstructures that held the big wheels above the mineshafts had a dark grandeur; Piranesi would have admired them, and I still regard them as among the few architecturally interesting products of the Industrial Revolution.

Each journey I observed new aspects of this spoiled and sombre land; I began to see how grey and stunted the people were, how pale the children kicking balls around their cinder playgrounds; I began to recognize that though the rows of tiny workers' houses were perhaps no more cramped than our own aged terrace in Marlow, the grime that blackened them, and with which we had never contended, must have spread its darkness into the lives of their denizens.

After Shifnal it seemed as though we had at last crossed the border between the two lands of my childhood. The sky always cleared; the Salopian landscape seemed washed of pollutions, the pastures lush and green and the fields in summer a greenish gold from the ripening wheat which the wind billowed like a tide. We ran beside orchard-dense villages of white and black thatched houses and old mansions surrounded by rookeried elms; beyond the Wrekin the walls were of red sandstone, and in the ploughed fields the soil was the pinkish brown of my home country.

My excitement would build to a peak as we swept on through half-timbered Hodnet (named from Bishop Odo, William the Conqueror's half-brother) and Tern Hill. The train began to slow down through the red-earth cuttings of Little Drayton. By now I would have got over the train sickness that I so stoically endured, and would be quivering and stuttering with anticipation, standing at the train window to recognize the church tower and the brewery chimney which would be blotted out when we entered the next cut below the cemetery. The train eased itself past grandfather Lewis's signal box and into the station where grandfather Woodcock would be waiting to clasp me against his great comforting belly and rub my face in his beard.

We would work our way through the passengers bustling around the black and orange stagecoach that stood outside the station, an aged top-hatted coachman perched high in front. It belonged to the Corbet Arms, the old hostelry in the centre of town a mile away, and, since there were no cabs, anyone who lived in that direction was happy to pay threepence for a seat in its faded plush interior.

But Runnymede was hardly a quarter of a mile from the station. We would walk down Maer Lane, past the stalls and corrals of the cattle market, and in a few minutes we would be at the green iron front gate and see the open door at the end of the curved gravel path. I would be swept to my grandmother's cushiony and orris-smelling bosom, and we would go into the dining room where Aunt Mary had spread the table with a festive high tea: ham and sausage rolls, and pikelets and tartlets, seed cake and fruit cake, thin bread and butter with strawberry jam and lobster paste, and bottled plums or apricots. My grandmother's dearest friend, skinny old Miss Pearse with her grog-blossomed cheeks aglow and her breath smelling of Sandeman's Invalid Port, would arrive just as the tea was brewed, with a great bag of hard toffee and soft teeth-rotting fudge that she had made to celebrate my arrival.

My mother would stay a couple of days, but I never remember seeing her off on her lonely journey into the degenerate south, for by then I was looking forward to the laxer disciplines my grandparents imposed. The life I slipped into as soon as she had gone seemed an ideal and idyllic existence, so much so that throughout my school days my principal ambition, whatever else I might be choosing to do with my life was to arrange it so that I would spend all my time in Market Drayton, enjoying there all the seasons and months of the year, and belonging fully to the little town and the countryside in which it nested.

I WAS NURTURING, of course, the classic illusion of a great good place that would never change. Circumstances let me preserve it for an unusually long time and so completely that, even though the moment came when I could no longer live by that image, it was strongly-enough imprinted on my mind to allow me as I write, sixty years afterwards, to envisage that past as I believe it really was. It is a coincidence, to me an interesting one, that the only poem I know which faithfully recalls my own feelings about my vanished Shropshire life should be one of the less celebrated pieces in Housman's The Shropshire Lad:

Into my heart an air that kills
From yon far country blows:
What are those blue remembered hills,
What spires, what farms are those?

That is the land of lost content,
I see it shining plain,
The happy highways where I went,
And cannot come again.

To describe as idyllic the life I lived in Market Drayton is exact in so far as it conveys a pastoral and archaic quality. In Marlow, placed so near to London, I was fully aware, in my personal life and in my surroundings, that I was part of the quickly changing world of the 1920s, the world of flappers and fast cars and social unrest.

But in Market Drayton the pace seemed quite different. The people in my small circle of acquaintance there — family, church people, shopkeepers, the handful of friends my own age — changed very slowly, and images of them remained constant. They seemed the same as they always had been until the very end of the period when, at age sixteen, I began to change my attitudes to life and as a consequence to see people differently, because I, not they, had changed. I think the people in Market Drayton retained this appearance of not changing largely because their way of life evolved far more slowly than that of southern England. Indeed, I suspect that what my grandparents and people like them feared most about southerners was not that they were decadent, but that they represented the processes eating away at the Victorian world that for the rural middle class in the north country still represented, even after the Great War, emotional security, a predictable future.

In fact, the superstructure of that Victorian world had already crumbled away. Wartime taxes had forced the landowning squires to reduce their nineteenth-century establishments, and one by one, from 1918 onwards, the great Palladian and Georgian country houses around Market Drayton, with their large staffs and their populous stables, were deserted by their owners, to be taken over by war profiteers or Catholic institutions, or allowed to decay, or even to be pulled down for the building materials that could be quarried out of them.

My mother would talk nostalgically of the days when the grand Tayleurs would come riding in to church from Buntingsdale in their six-in-hand coach; but in my childhood the great hall of Buntingsdale was abandoned and soon it would be taken over by the Royal Air Force. Only a few of the more ancient and more secure families remained. The Corbets of Adderley (descendants of a Norman adventurer named Corbeau) still enjoyed their shadowy privileges as lords of the manor of Market Drayton and kept a pack of fox hounds. And up at Styche, from which Robert Clive set out for India, doddery old Lady Mary Herbert still maintained a skeletal establishment, letting half her gardens go to weed, and gently begging her gamekeepers not to expose themselves to the violence of the poachers.

But though the gentry had been more than decimated, northern Shropshire was still a country of substantial farmers kept prosperous by cheese and wheat; some aspired to take the place of the vanishing squires and rode to hounds. Market Drayton still lived on the farm economy, and especially on the markets and fairs for which it was named. All through the 1920s it was still the centre of a pre-mechanical little world of which my grandfather was typical in his reluctance to compromise with modernity. Until his death in 1930 he ran the most lucrative coal business in the town without installing a telephone or a typewriter. Each day he would walk around the town, greeting the shopkeepers and picking up their orders, and every Wednesday at market time he was to be found in the Corbet Arms, or outside on the pavement among the seed merchants with their portable desks, making sure that he got and retained the custom of the farmers. Anyone else who wanted fuel walked down to the coalyard or dropped a postcard to place an order. My grandfather communicated with the mines by letters handwritten at the rolltop desk in his little office at Runnymede, where he worked among spiked bundles of letters hanging from hooks on the wall, and trays of drying bulbs, beans and nasturtium seeds. It all went very efficiently because everyone knew the business customs of a traditional English market town and heads were still well-working computers.

When my grandfather died, my Uncle Harold took over the business and, as he had always been an enthusiast for automobiles, he immediately replaced the horse transport by motor lorries. But throughout my boyhood the coal always went out in two-wheeled carts if it was carried in bulk and in four-wheeled wagons if it was in sacks for delivery to houses. They were drawn by the same two great Shire mares, Daisy and Rosie. The fields of Runnymede, where I roved during the day, were theirs at night and on Sundays, and the harness room where their great collars hung among the scythes and pitchforks was one of my favourite haunts.

This conservative disinclination to accept the new machines my grandfather shared with the farmers who were his customers. All the ploughing around Drayton was still done by horses, and Hardy's "man harrowing clods/ In a slow silent walk" was a familiar figure of my childhood. The harvest was cut by a horse-drawn reaper-and-binder with a curious hexagonal frame that revolved as the twine ran, and the sheaves were loaded by pitchfork onto brightly-painted wagons drawn by geldings that glittered and flashed with polished brasses. When the farmers went to market they drove in their traps, often with a pig or two squealing in the back, and when they went home at evening the ostlers at the Market Drayton taverns often lifted them in, blind drunk, threw the reins into the trap and gave the old ponies a whack on the haunch to set them off, knowing they would find their way home through the country lanes where motor cars still so rarely appeared as to present negligible danger.

In town everyone walked, or rode a bicycle, or went by horse, and class did not enter into it, for even old Lady Mosley was driven about by her gardener in a dog cart, which was really a little pony trap. One of the most splendid sights to be seen in my childhood years was a brewer's dray loaded with iron-bound wooden barrels and drawn by a team of four great beribboned and brass-clattering Shire horses, black and lustrous with combing, their great hairy hooves striking sparks from the stones as the driver whipped them to full speed over the cobbled streets.

THAT WORLD, WHERE THE MACHINE was represented by polished green locomotives smelling of machine oil and coal smoke, a few cars speeding at forty miles an hour to scare the chickens in the country roads into squawking and fluttering protest, and even fewer early aeroplanes staggering into the skies over Tern Hill and drawing everyone out of doors to stare upward when they ventured over the town, was in my awakening consciousness divided, like the classic diagrams of the Hindu sacred mountain of Meru, into a series of concentric terrains through which I moved outward as my childhood progressed.

Central and constant was Runnymede itself. Living there day after day throughout my holidays, my experience differed from that of my earlier self, the infant visitor. I slept in the room that had been my grandmother's dressmaking workroom, and always before I went to sleep I would wander around examining its curiosities: the black seam-stress's dummy with its swelling Victorian bosom and narrow waist, the most unnatural image of woman one could imagine; the big gaudy oleograph pictures of imperial battles, Omdurman and Waterloo, and the little delicately-coloured Baxter prints of the imperial heroes, Nelson and Wellington; and the piles of patterns and scraps of cloth and reels of coloured cotton and boxes of beads and bugles scattered over the big table beside the trestle sewing machine of elaborately coiled and curlicued and gold-painted iron that looked as if it had been bought from the catalogue of the Great Exhibition of 1851.

I would sort and arrange the coloured debris on the table, and study the formalized atrocities of the battle scenes, which sometimes entered into my nightmares, and invent dialogues between Nelson and the Iron Duke. Finally I would sink deep into the goosedown mattresses on the little bed in the corner of the room and sleep long and luxuriously, with no morning school bell to interrupt my dreams. When I did awake late in the morning, I would be angry with my grandmother who, for the sake of my health, had indulgently let me slumber until the sun was high. There was so much to be done and seen in the world outside the windows, the world I would watch avidly as I hurriedly downed my breakfast in the kitchen, facing northward to fields where all winter long the lapwings wheeled in great flocks, screaming eerily as they swung in their marvellously co-ordinated patterns.

All day long, if I chose to stay around the house, I would be virtually alone exploring what then seemed to me the vastnesses of my grand-father's four-acred domain. There were two gardens; that to the west of the road into the stable yard was a kind of natural fortress, a magic domain, surrounded by a dense, thick holly hedge, a veritable green wall that must have been planted long before my grandfather bought the property. We passed through this prickly barrier by a tiny door, barely five feet high, so that grown people had to stoop. Inside one seemed entirely isolated in a quiet orchard of tall old apple trees, virides-cent with lichen, sprouting thick tufts of mistletoe, and loaded in summer with jewel-bright apples of many old-fashioned English varieties: Cox's Orange, Pippins and Worcester Pearmains, Newtons and Blen-heims and rough brown-skinned Russets, and others whose names I never knew or have long forgotten. There were big bergamot pears and red fleshy Victoria plums and gnarled damson trees heavy with black fruit and cherries, though they always ripened before I got there for the summer holidays.

I had an agreement with my grandfather that I could eat windfalls but must not pick from the branches and in general I kept it, for it provided a sufficiency of ripe and green fruit to keep my belly full and churning. But one tree Eden-like tempted me to casuistry, for it bore enormous red fruit that attracted me for their size and their luminous colour (the flesh was in fact rather mild and mealy), and I would make the wind's task easier by gently shaking the branches, though even here I never actually picked.

Among the apple trees grew crops well-manured from the stable dung: potatoes and roots and cabbage and peas and beans and always a brilliant and fragrant barrage of multi-coloured sweet peas from which all summer long my grandfather picked to fill the vases in the house. At that latitude (53°) the hours of summer sunlight are long, flowers are brightly coloured, rather as Arctic flowers are, and the northern vegetables are large and tasty, but we could never grow anything southern and exotic, like asparagus or peaches or grapes on southerly walls.

The eastern garden on the other side of the house was devoted largely to bush fruit: red and black and even white currants, gooseberries that ripened into fat translucent ruby or yellow gems, and long secretive rows of raspberry canes and loganberry briars where I could eat in perfect concealment. Here grew herbs of many old English kinds and, late in the season, immense tomatoes.

Between these two gardens, in front of the house, was the perfectly-mowed lawn, with its path of white quartz gravel curving up to the front door, flanked by great urns of scarlet geraniums. Beside the lawn lay deep, dense beds of roses and dahlias, delphiniums and foxgloves, snap-dragons and carnations and pinks, marguerites and sunflowers and poppies, so brilliant in their deep stable nourishment that people walking by would stand at the wicket gate and express such gratifying admiration that, if he were there, my grandfather would often plunge among the roses with his thin-honed clasp knife to cut them souvenir bouquets.

North of the holly-walled garden was the stable yard, with the stalls that always reeked with the sickly-sweet smell of horsepiss, and the harness room with its scents of leather and Propert's Saddle Soap, and the crushed oats in the great bins, and the fodder shed with its hay cutter whose sharp and dangerous curved blades were turned by a great iron wheel. The junk shed in the corner of the yard was filled with fascinating relics, decaying from year to year: piles of rusting abandoned horseshoes, broken bits of farm machinery, a great mound of pitch that each summer softened and spread out more widely, and a light racing gig that an unknown man had bought at a fair, left with my grandfather for safekeeping and never returned to claim.

Behind the stables stood the open cart shed, and two great iron cauldrons five feet across — relics of a primitive stage in the sugar industry — from which the horses drank rain water from the stable roofs when they came in from their day's work. There was also a pile of the trunks of oak trees which my grandfather had once bought when he thought of expanding into the timber business and had let decay. They were piled to leave a space in the centre which formed the impregnable fortress that I could defend with bow and capgun against invisible enemies. I would sally forth on the energetic trots around the fields which I regarded as knightly peregrinations or the stealthy walks in which I imagined myself the Last of the Mohicans pitted against the French of whom my father talked so contemptuously.

On the other side of the log fort were the chicken sheds, night homes of the Rhode Island Reds and White Wyandottes that in daytime fed freely in the stable yard and wandered through the fields. My one agreed task at Runnymede was to help my grandfather scatter maize to the chickens at their afternoon feeding time, and then go round the sheds with him searching out the eggs laid during the day, which my grandmother took into her charge and sold to visiting customers. The "egg money," which she kept in a tea caddy on the kitchen mantelpiece, was her special perquisite, from which I soon learnt to expect my share in tips and presents, particularly later on when I was given the responsibility of making sure the chickens were all in their sheds at nightfall and the doors were securely fastened. There were many foxes around Market Drayton, for the hunting interests were still powerful enough in northern Shropshire to discourage farmers from shooting them as vermin, yet the hunt itself was becoming less frequent as the old landowners departed.

The attachment to the land which my grandfather had inherited from his ancestors was expressed through horticulture rather than agriculture. He was a meticulous and productive gardener, but as the years passed his fields grew more neglected. The hawthorn hedges dividing them were allowed to grow up into tall dense thickets, and large areas of pasture were invaded by a tall, coarse tussock grass which the horses refused to eat. This made the fields a better playground, for the long, overarching branches of the thorn bushes created caverns of vegetable shade which I could imagine were Iroquois longhouses or even smugglers' caverns. Rabbits lurked among the tussocks, and would often start off, leaping away with white-flashing tails, as I walked along the long grass.

The rabbits burrowed into all the hedgerows of my grandfather's fields, and when they had their broods I would spend hours at the kitchen window watching the young ones playing outside the entrances to their holes. They had their natural enemies, for often I would see the narrow bodies of weasels snaking through the hedges, and Tom, the big stray tabby whom we fed and who kept the rats down in the stable yard, would sometimes lay a young rabbit on the kitchen doorstep as a kind of offering which we interpreted to mean thanks for his breakfast and dinner. Once, in a snowy January, he brought a winter stoat that was almost ermine white.

But in spite of such predators, the rabbits increased, eating a growing share of the lettuces and the young carrots, and when their numbers had become unmanageable my grandfather would call in the local rabbit catcher. This man, the most sinister figure in my childhood imagination, was called Charlesworth; I never heard his other name. He was tall and swarthy, with black eyes and a long black moustache that hung down like a Tartar's; local gossip insisted that he was at least half-gipsy. He cycled around the town with an enormous black cat sitting on his shoulder, the largest domestic cat I have ever seen, and gossip maintained that the cat acted as a retriever and enabled Charlesworth to poach with impunity.

Having read stories about witches, I thought that the strange relationship between Charlesworth and his cat meant that he was a warlock, and I tried to keep a safe distance from him when he came rabbiting in our fields. But always he directed those large dark eyes of his towards me and beckoned. I was drawn to his side, and stood there as he fixed the nets over some of the burrows, and sent his white, pink-eyed and rank-smelling ferrets down the other entrances. Soon the rabbits would come up in a rush, and usually they would get entangled in the nets for

Charlesworth to seize and strangle in his sinewy hands. But sometimes, by the sheer force of his uprush, one of the rabbits would tear out the pegs holding a net and streak free into the field; now Charlesworth's great cat would leap forward like a panther, and always he secured his prey.

At the end of the foray a pile of rabbits, a hundred or more, would lie in the middle of the field. Half would go to Charlesworth and his cat and we would later see them hanging from hooks outside the poulterer's shop in High Street. My grandfather took the rest and made a pound or two out of selling the skins to the gipsies, while we and all our relations and friends, down to third cousins like the perpetually drunken Larky Woodcock who lived in a tumble-down cottage over the railway lines, would live for days on roasted rabbit and rabbit stew. But Charlesworth was a cunning hunter; he always contrived it so that enough of the rabbits survived his white ferrets and black cat to increase and multiply and provide a new harvest in a couple of years. Nothing that Charlesworth did or calculated would have astonished me; I regarded him, like Skull Harper, as an incarnation of the diabolical, an agent of the realm to which my dreams of coldly-burning hellfire had told me that, whether or not I liked it, I belonged.

In spite of the many days I spent playing alone in my grandfather's fields and learning the resources of solitude, I was not in any real sense a solitary child. It is true that in the first few years of my holidays in Market Drayton, between the ages of six and ten, I had few companions of my own age in comparison with the many children I encountered in my schools in Marlow and Bisham. But I did have a great deal of the company of adults and in many ways tended to assume their attitudes.

It was not merely a question of my grandparents' friends and acquaintances. On the rare occasions when my father came to Market Drayton during my holidays, he would take me into the town and I would stand beside him as he exchanged recollections with the shopkeepers and lawyers, the accountants and cattle dealers, who had been his boyhood friends. Sometimes more disreputable acquaintances would stagger to his elbow out of the past, red-nosed and stinking of the beer for which they would cadge a shilling, and sometimes the encounters would be more exotic.

Once, while he was there, a fair came in grand and smoky procession past Runnymede, caravans and great wagons drawn behind puffing traction engines and a camp following of nondescript horse-drawn vehicles, establishing itself beside the racetrack near my grandfather's hayfield. My father and I went in as they were assembling the great roundabout with its painted prancing horses suspended on twisted brass rods and the many-piped calliope organ in the centre. A tall, dark man stood there supervising the work and as soon as he saw my father he came over and they embraced. His name was Greatorex. I never knew what bond united my father and this stranger whom he treated more warmly than his brother, but I do know that for years afterwards, whenever the Greatorex fair came to Market Drayton, I had only to find the swarthy bohemian wanderer and remind him that I was Art Woodcock's son, and I could ride the painted horses for nothing as long as I liked.

But I had to pay if I wanted to shy at the coconuts or the Aunt Sallies, or ride the ponies, or take a pot shot in the shooting gallery, or get some of the toffee that was made from great skeins of hot sugar looped and looped again and again over meat hooks in the glaring light of the Naptha flares. For the fairs were curious symbiotic organisms. One man had the capital to buy the big roundabout with its engine and calliope, which was the centre of the fair, and he negotiated with towns and villages for permission to operate in their territories. All the other operators, from the stallholders and the men who cranked the smaller hand-driven carrousels, down to the small sharpers who conned the yokels with three walnut shells and a pea on top of an open umbrella, paid their dues to this *primus inter pares*, and moved in his shadow, free to leave whenever they wished, for such is essential to the liberty of the road which the fairmen, like the gipsies and the didekoys (non-Romanies living a gipsy life), equally shared.

I loved the fairs, not only because my father's friendship with the great Greatorex gave me special privileges; I sensed a defiant difference between the fair people and the folk out of whom they made their living, and even as a small boy I felt a tingling response to the brazen insolence of the bold-eyed women in the stalls. In a strange way they were my own people, perhaps because of my father's unexplained relationship with Greatorex, and I would often envy their wanderings over the northern counties. Long after I was sent to bed on the nights when the fair was operating near the racetrack, I would sit in the dark by the open window of my room, listening to the birdlike voices of the people a couple of fields away and hearing above everything the strident squeals of the calliope's organ pipes and the clash of its cymbals, blasting out

William Tell and *Poet and Peasant*, *The Merry Widow* and *The Chocolate Soldier*, Sousa marches and the livelier airs of Verdi and Puccini. Carrousel owners were conservative in their choice of music, perhaps because none of the popular ditties of the twenties had the kind of operatic richness to which their steam organs could do blaring justice.

THE VISITS OF GREATOREX were rare occasions. More often when I wandered out as a small boy from Runnymede it would be with my grandfather to the coalyard, where I liked to visit his fellow coal merchants and collect a shining tribute of threepenny Joeys and sixpences. I would also watch his employees loading coal from the railway wagons into his carts. He paternalistically called them "my men," and even when I was a small child I always addressed them by their Christian names. Joe was a little, dark, sanctimonious Celt who played the tuba on a Saturday night in the Salvation Army Band. Tom was a good-natured, phlegmatic giant, a corn-haired Saxon with cheeks so red that they always looked congested — a common type in this corner of the Midlands. And one-eyed waspish Walter, with the black patch over his empty eye socket, spoke in a highfalutin parody of southern English, though everyone knew he had been born in the Town Well, as we called the quarter inhabited by poachers and peddlers and other marginal characters, and that on a Saturday night he got drunk and stood around the Salvation Army meeting in High Street, shouting insults at ever-forgiving Joe as the banner of Blood and Fire flapped in the wind and the soldiers of God marched off to the tune of "Oh, we'll gather at the river!"

To my grandfather's "men" I was "the little mester," as Shropshire pronunciation had it, my grandfather's small reflection, and they treated me with a mixture of grave politeness and jesting amusement. Once, to their consternation, I insisted on joining them in one of the railway wagons and hurling out lumps of coal into the cart drawn up beside it. Both my grandfather and I were in very bad favour when I got home that day, black from head to toe with coal dust, and I was hurried away to the bath. For a long time I was forbidden to go back, and this greatly annoyed me, for I had made friends with the fourteen-year-old boy in a blue uniform who operated the weigh scales. He boasted an unusual conformation of the windpipe which he claimed made him immune from strangling. He would lie down on the bench in his little brick office and invite me to throttle him, which I vigorously essayed while he would grin and breathe with ease as I squeezed my utmost. I never learnt his trick.

The other place to which I went often in those early years in Market Drayton — usually on my own even when I was a small boy — was my Uncle Harold's house about half a mile away; my grandparents had lived there before they moved to Runnymede. I liked my uncle, though my mother was always warning me that his Celtic nature made him devious. I adored my pink-and-white, chocolate-boxy Aunt Ethel, with her hoarse and marvellously insinuating voice; she was pretty and indulgent and flattering. She and my uncle had a real affection for me, since I took the place of the child they did not have until I was eleven.

I had the run of their house and their garden, where there were trees loaded in summer with the largest and juiciest Victoria plums I have ever eaten, and a workshop where my uncle carried on his secondary occupation, which was sieve-making. The sieves were made of horsehair, and used by the local farmers in preparing their Cheshire cheeses. My uncle employed a company of poor women to hand-weave the horsehair into squares on little looms in their own cottages. Afterwards he and my aunt would trim and bind the squares into circular shapes that fitted into wooden frames. I don't imagine anyone makes sieves in this way any more; it was the last phase of an old cottage industry. I still remember very vividly the peculiar dry smell of the long hanks of grey and black and chestnut horsehair that would hang in my uncle's kitchen.

But to me the most important thing in my uncle's house was the little library beside the fireplace in his living room. All the Woodcocks were readers, but my uncle's tastes were less purely literary than my father's; they ran in the direction of historical novels and travel books. My interest in history was developing, and from the age of nine or ten onwards I read avidly, one after another, the novels of Dumas and Bulwer Lytton, Victor Hugo and especially Harrison Ainsworth, who has now fallen into undeserved neglect. Through such books the empty streets and buildings of the past came to life in my imagination. I also read travel narratives like Darwin's *Voyage of the Beagle*, and J. H. Speke's and Livingstone's narratives of African explorations. Combined with my readings at home of the naturalists like H. W. Bates and Thomas Belt and William Waterton, these books not only whetted the desire for travel I would long afterwards have the chance to fulfil in Asia and

South America and Oceania, but also made me aware of simpler and perhaps, in their own way, more desirable societies than those of mediaeval Europe and the ancient world which the historical novels portrayed in all — or almost all — their violence and corruption. Not that I really minded the violence. Children rarely do; they formalize it in games and thereby neutralize it, as I did with my tin soldiers and my popgun cannon.

The books that made the deepest impression on me were not in my uncle's library, but in the bamboo bookshelf behind a screen in the sitting room at Runnymede where my grandfather took his forty winks. It contained a jumble of Edwardian and Victorian gatherings, including an early edition of *Robinson Crusoe* illustrated with wood engravings, scores of missionary narratives, and some big illustrated volumes on Queen Victoria's Golden and Diamond Jubilees.

But the books that most excited me on my grandfather's shelves, were Heinrich Schliemann's three masterpieces, *Ilion*, *Mycenae* and *Tiryns*. The intoxicating image Grandfather gathered from these books was that of the merchant, a German Sam Woodcock, who followed his hunches, read the texts aright, and confounded the scepticism of academic scholars by finding Troy where Homer said it was. For me the fascination lay elsewhere, in the strange mystery of that faroff past which the narrative of discovery evoked and also the line engravings of the Cyclopean wall and the Lion Gate at Mycenae, of the great hollow cone of the Treasury of Atreus, and of the golden mask Schliemann believed concealed the bony mask of Agamemnon.

Until I read these books between the ages of ten and twelve, Agamemnon was not even a name to me, but once I had absorbed Schliemann's enthusiasm I never forgot him and his world. I acquired, without ever being taught Greek, an interest in Homer that has grown with the years. The happiest time in my whole brief academic career was to be the six weeks in 1966 when I was able to lecture on the *Odyssey*. And I began, even as a boy, to realize how wide the world can be for the man of free intelligence. If I later became a professor without winning a degree, and learnt without any university training to beat the academics so often at their own games, it was largely due to my childhood encounter with the maverick archaeologist, Heinrich Schliemann, who proved in the teeth of the classical scholars that the *Iliad* was history as well as romance. Perhaps I did not yet understand this fully at ten or even twelve, but the tale of Schliemann and the strange things he discovered lodged in my mind. To this day I can see the gilt-edged pages of *Mycenae* with their subtle engravings, and the blue, gold-lettered bindings of the large broken-backed volumes over which I would pore for hours on end, sitting on the floor behind the lacquer screen that shielded the bamboo bookshelf.

THE GENTLE REGULARITY OF LIFE at Runnymede was punctuated each week by two special days, Wednesday and Sunday. Sunday was a day when we ate for the glory of God. We all went to matins and to evensong; church had not changed greatly since my early childhood, except that now we tended to sing hymns about harvest rather than war, and dour Mr. Thompson had retired to Aberdeen and been succeeded by comic Mr. O'Flaherty, a refugee from the Church of Ireland who replaced his predecessor's promises of hell with droll Paddy jokes about the kingdom of Heaven. The real ceremonies of the day were the enormous breakfast of sausages, served with my grandmother's personally-invented tomato sauce, and the great mid-day dinner, centred on the weekly roast which my grandfather carved always with theatrical pride. People in our part of England chose to regard Lent and any talk of fasting as Papist inventions and one of our folk heroes was a Methodist local preacher who, when he was preaching on circuit and had been given what he regarded as an inadequate meal in some farmhouse, would say as his parting grace, "O Lord, we thank thee for a good dinner, but, dear God, if there had been more, us could have etten more!"

Food excepted, we were good Sabbatarians. Cooking the gargantuan meals was the only work allowed that day, and one spent hours idling in the name of the Lord. I was forbidden to play with my toys and to read anything profane; this was how I gained my early knowledge of parts of the world like Oceania, south India and Africa, for I was allowed to read the reports of the Church Missionary Society which had a good deal to say about such countries. I could read the travels of Livingstone because he was a missionary, but not those of Stanley; the autobiography of the Reverend John G. Paton, the Presbyterian apostle to the New Hebrides; but not Cardinal Newman's *Apologia Pro Vita Sua*, which was regarded as worse than paganism.

WEDNESDAY, THE OTHER GREAT DAY of the Market Drayton week, we spent in the community, for this was market day, and it not only embodied the name but also indicated the reason for the existence of our town, which had grown up early in the Middle Ages as a rural trading centre, operated by the Corbets, the lords of neighbouring Adderley, who still in my boyhood drew a great deal of their income from Drayton's markets and fairs.

The high point of the Drayton trading system was the Dirty Fair, held in November, when great herds of cattle and sheep and ponies were driven in from all over north Shropshire and even from across the Welsh border in Montgomery, and bought by the cattle dealers from the Black Country and the Five Towns. In a wet year the streets would be deep in mire, which gave the Dirty Fair its name, and in any year they would be full of wild and ragged drovers from the Welsh hills, gipsies plying their various trades, fair people including the great Greatorex, and, at least in my parents' childhood, ploughmen, shepherds and dairy maids lining High Street to be hired by the farmers for the coming year. At the Dirty Fair the lord of the manor's rights would be proclaimed at the annual Court Leet, presided over by the lord's steward. This mediaeval survival continued to the end of the 1930s, though I never witnessed it, since the Dirty Fair took place during my Marlow months each year.

But I was there for the Wednesday market, the real market from which the town was named and around which it grew from the clump of houses mentioned in the Domesday Book. I looked forward to the market for the whole week, and lived every moment of it with excitement. It would begin as I awoke in the early morning with the lowing of cattle, the bleating of sheep and the squealing of pigs as they went past Runnymede on their way from all the easterly farms and villages to the cattle market up Maer Lane.

I would dress and wash quickly, so that I could spend an hour before breakfast at the landing window which gave me such a good view of the road. It would be jammed with little herds of cattle and flocks of sheep, whacked on with blackthorn sticks by shabby and red-nosed herdsmen, most of them local derelicts who lived for this one day of employment and free booze, and cadged through the rest of the week. Through this river of beasts, the carts and farm traps pushed slowly, carrying pigs and calves under rope nets, or crates of chickens or ducks. Sometimes a great bull, as massive as a statue, with a glistening nose ring, would have a cart to himself. Occasionally a mare and her foal would trot past, or a great Shire horse, his brow glittering with freshly-polished brasses and his mane and tail plaited with coloured ribbons. I would bolt my breakfast and hurry up again, for it would be ten o'clock at least before the lane would be empty.

By then it would be time for me and my grandmother to sally forth to the market in the centre of the town. She would put on her best black coat, glistening with jet bugles, and reaching to within six inches of the hem of a skirt that always reached within an inch of the ground. She wore laced-up boots to the day of her death, and always went out in hat and veil, her hands gloved, and an ivory-handled umbrella, or a mauve parasol in summer, in her right hand. Her handbags, which always contained a tiny lace-trimmed handkerchief and a green phial of smelling salts, were of petit point or Victorian beadwork, and each of them would probably be worth a small fortune today.

We would walk up Maer Lane, Granny slowly and me fretting like an impatient dog. We would pass the cattle market, crowded with men in corduroy breeches and polished leather leggings, and hear the high-pitched voices of the auctioneers echoing above the chorus of lowings and bleatings and squealings and cacklings. Then, entering the main street from the station to the town, we would join a stream of people walking, and riding in traps and on bicycles, and sometimes even on horseback, towards the heart of the town where the market had taken over the streets like a small revolution.

Cheshire Street, where the market began, widened out into a bell-shaped plaza dominated by a building which we called the Butter Cross. In fact, there was nothing cruciform or Christian about it, for it was an eighteenth-century neo-classical collonade like a Greek temple without walls. Among its fluted Ionic pillars the farm women sat with their pats of pale fresh butter spread out on leaves before them.

Among the edges of the pavements that faced the Butter Cross, hundreds of farmers' and labourers' wives stood with the produce of their gardens and pens, each with two great square wicker baskets; for the privilege of displaying them she would pay a penny to the agent of the lord of the manor. My grandmother and the other women of the town moved to and fro, in a perpetually changing seasonal harvest festival, looking and touching, greeting and tasting, gossiping and bargaining, as they bought country produce for the rest of the week.

A skirmishing band of furtive-looking men, whom we called higglers, bought up produce which they later sold to the shops in the nearby industrial centres, mainly the Potteries and Crewe. The higglers usually waited to see how the produce was selling and then made offers to buy the stock of market women whose wares were selling slowly. In glut years the sellers would be at their mercy, and once I remember my grandfather letting a higgler have his apples at a halfpenny a pound and finally, when he could not sell them even at that price, dumping the rest in the field for his horses. But usually the higglers would have to bargain quite hard for the goods they carried away with them in their traps and their decrepit motor vans.

Townswomen and higglers alike had fruits of many kinds to choose from, from strawberries and cherries in early summer to the autumn medlars, which were ripe when they began to rot, and the late apples that were best at Christmas, as well as wild bilberries and cranberries and blackberries. One of the pleasures of that age, which nowadays we have almost lost, was getting the first fresh fruit of each kind ("*Les primeurs*," as the French call them) at its proper season, and knowing when each would attain its finest flavour. There were vegetables of many kinds and, particularly, new potatoes and fresh peas and beans (always offered as "morning gathered"). There were products of the woods like rabbits and partridges, wild nuts and mushrooms, though Shropshire people did not take risks with other kinds of fungi, which they regarded as universally poisonous. There were eggs, pale green duck eggs and brown chicken's eggs always selling at a slightly higher price than the white, and the chickens and ducks themselves, alive and lying in baskets with their legs tied together. When a customer wished to inspect one of them, the market woman would lift it up so that its breast could be judiciously probed and pinched, and I would feel a strange combination of guilt and sympathy as the bird quacked or squawked its protest.

So far as our establishment at Runnymede was concerned, we grew almost everything the market women had to offer, but this did not deter my grandmother from her weekly ritual of inspecting goods and comparing prices, and stopping for a special chat with the women she knew. The one she knew best, and whom I liked most, was our distant cousin Lizzie Morris, related to us in some complicated way I could never clearly determine, who had a little holding out at Longslow, the village that lay to the lee of the Clive estate at Styche.

WHEN I REMEMBER LIZZIE MORRIS, dead these thirty years, I can do no less than pause to write about that excellent woman whom my father liked the best of all his relatives. She was a tall, heavily-built blonde who projected an extraordinary serenity that affected everyone who knew her. When I was very small, and had to be carried half the way, my parents would take me over the fields to Longslow, a tiny hamlet where the cottages stood in a circle around the green, each with its spring and the clear water swelling up into a stone basin. Lizzie's husband Dick was a hedger and ditcher in grow-ing demand even as his craft fell into decay like that of the thatchers. But Dick died in his late forties. With a bit of money that had been Lizzie's dowry they had bought a small holding and when she was widowed Lizzie set to cultivating it with the help of her son Arthur, who worked in the day as under-gardener at Styche Hall. In the long summer evenings of our northern latitude he helped his mother to grow the produce she would bring in each week to the market and the field of oats or mangolds she would sell each year to one of the local farmers.

Lizzie never complained; if she had bad luck one season she tried something new next year and usually it worked. Apart from being a natural gardener and having a way with small livestock from bees to geese, she was something of a country wisewoman, knowledgeable in simples if one were suffering from a minor ailment and expert in elixirs. When I was a small boy we would sit in her parlour, filled with a green-golden light that filtered through the geranium plants in the windows, and she would offer us her homemade wines. There was a pleasant con-vention in Shropshire that such brews were harmless and to all intents and purposes unalcoholic, while bought wines were dangerously intoxi-cant and conducive to wickedness.

Lizzie's elderberry wine was densely purple and headier than any port but it was her straw-pale dandelion wine, dry and insidious, that was the most potent of all her drinks. I think the first time I felt real intoxica-tion was when I was about nine and had downed a glass each of Lizzie's elderberry and dandelion wines, and sat, giggling and swimmy-headed, watching the strange amorphous fungi which we used to call Australian Bees going up and down in their large glass jars; the yellow liquid in which they swam also became a potent booze which Lizzie dispensed as bee wine. She also made the real Welsh bee wine, *metheglyn*, from the honey of her own hives, and, since Longslow had no pub, she made an excellent beer from malt and hops which she dispensed secretly to her fellow cottagers and trustworthy friends.

GRANNY AND I would walk on from cousin Lizzie's baskets of beans or poultry to the stalls which the small dealers had erected around the Butter Cross and farther on, down the centre of the High Street. Some of them were run by merchants from the towns, trying to sell cheap clothes and flashy jewellery and shoddy household goods to the rustics. Others were run by the town shopkeepers as branch establishments to catch the country women too shy to go into the shops. But, as in the small towns of Mexico or the Andes, there were also sections of the market devoted to special needs. Along the quiet cobbled street outside St. Mary's Church, where little traffic went, men with broad flat accents from the Potteries spread out their "seconds" in china on the ground, and with a little luck one could pick up passable Minton or Wedgwood pieces for a few pennies. West of the High Street was a macabre arcade which, with rustic directness, we called the Shambles. It included not only butchers' and fishmongers' stalls, but also the rough restaurants where the country people would eat at trestle tables. I would look enviously at fat rustic infants, in linen bonnets and grimy imitation ermine coats, eating shrill pink and arsenic-green iced cakes that I was forbidden to touch. My parents and grandparents did not foresee the synthetic horrors of late twentieth-century food manufacture; the remembered scandals of Victorian adulteration were enough to instil in them the sound idea that the less like real food anything looked the more detrimental to health it was likely to be.

Somewhere between the Shambles and the Butter Cross was the line of cheesemongers' stalls. Cheese, because we made so much of it, was not merely an important item in the North Shropshire diet. It was also the local product in which we took most pride. My grandmother always headed for the cheese stalls, and went from vendor to vendor, each time lifting her veil up from under her chin and lodging it beneath her nose so that she could delicately nibble the fragments of their best cheeses that, one by one, they offered on the tips of their pointed knives. She never bought and they did not expect her to do so, for they knew that old Sam Woodcock would be there during the day to do the real judging and to buy the two grades of cheese we always ate, the sharp and old for eating and the new and mild that we used for cooking. But they never thought of refusing my grandmother her weekly tastes, for by that time, in her garb that was already half a century antique and with her dour mid-Victorian manners, she had become almost as much a Market Drayton institution as the market itself.

Some aspects of market day we strategically avoided. We hurried past the taverns from whose open doors the stench and the sound of incoherent voices flowed with equal strength, and from which a drunken man would sometimes come staggering out, all limbs flailing, to collapse cursing into the gutter. We would head home quietly down the short cut of Bell Lane, a fascinating odorous thoroughfare because of the big cattlefeed depots which smelt so pungently of oilcake and the smithy where Bill Hughes would be sweating away at the high point of his week's business with a queue of carters and ploughmen waiting for their great horses to be shod. I always begged my grandmother to wait a little while so that I could see the red-hot bars taken out of the flames and brought to the anvil, the shoes deftly shaped out of the dulling metal, the showers of sparks as they were hammered, the hissing of steam as they were dipped into the water trough for annealing, and then the puff of smoke and the whiff of pungent burning as they were nailed onto the horse's trimmed hoof which old Hughes always held gently between his knees, resting in his worn leather apron.

I found the market so fascinating that often, when I had seen my grandmother home, I would slip away over the fields and return to stand watching the quacks and hucksters who set up their pitches outside the Town Hall to conn the yokels with their magical remedies. There was a Barbadian black of great girth and marvellous glibness who would deliver a weekly oration on the mysterious virtues of the powder of Taraxacum which he offered as a specific for digestive troubles and masculine weaknesses; it was, of course, none other than the dandelion root which Mr. Skelhorn, the friend of my infancy, had fed to me in another form. And there were always the two men who sold mandrake root, illustrating their spiel with elaborate scrolls like those of a mediaeval medical treatise, expounding the plant's strange humanoid resemblances, telling how they had been half-deafened by the screams it emitted when gathered, and guaranteeing that they offered us the best quality of all, grown in the lonely places where long ago highwaymen had hung from their gibbets. It was, we were assured, an almost universal panacea but of special value to the infertile. Mandrake sold well in Market Drayton.

Often I could not resist breaking bounds, slipping into the Shambles to buy with my pocket money an especially gaudy kind of cake covered with carmine-died shredded coconut, and then wandering over to the Corbet Arms, to stare at the seed merchants shaking out their little bags of grain into the farmers' hands and sometimes catching a glimpse of my grandfather in companionable discourse. By about three in the afternoon the market would begin to break up, the pavement-side women would pick up their empty baskets or throw their red bandana kerchiefs over anything they had left, and head for the innyards where decrepit country buses or shabby horse brakes were waiting to take them home. The dealers dismantled their stalls, and the drunken farmers were loaded into their traps. Then I would start back for Runnymede and with luck might earn a couple of pennies carrying a basket for a townswoman going in the same direction.

I always managed to get back before my grandfather returned in a dense olfactory aura which I very soon learnt was the smell of beer. A Sunday pillar of the Band of Hope, dedicated to persuading young people to "Sign the Pledge" that would redeem them from the evils of drinking, grandfather on market day surrendered to the compelling dictates of Mammon, and justified himself by blaming the farmers with whom it was difficult, he claimed, to do business if they were completely sober. He was a man who could fulfil the urge for martyrdom in the most unlikely ways.

V

TIME THE ENEMY

CHRISTMAS WAS THE MOST COMPLETE of our family gatherings. My father would usually get to Market Drayton for at least three or four days and the family would be reunited in a rare harmony that left no room for strangers. Little was made by the Salopians of Christmas Eve except to walk around the town where the shops were open long, making last purchases and admiring at the lavishly-decorated shop windows. Late in the evening when we had all come home, the children, and in lean years even some adults, would arrive to sing carols and Christmas hymns; the favourites in Market Drayton were "God Rest You, Merry Gentlemen," "Once in Royal David's City," and a strange lilting version, rather Welsh in tone, of "While Shepherds Watched," which I have heard nowhere else and which I suspect came to us with the drovers from over the Montgomery border. Occasionally a mischievous group of boys would perform a parody by singing "Hark the Herald Angels Sing, Beecham's Pills are JUST the Thing," but, Beecham's Pills or not, the visitation would always end with the refrain:

> God bless the mester of this 'ouse,
> God bless the missis too,
> And all the little children
> That gather round of you.
> We wish you all a Merry Christmas
> And a Happy New Year.

A thunderous knock would follow, and we would stream to the door to dispense pennies and hand round the great tray of mince pies my grandmother had prepared. Each of us was supposed to eat at least twelve over Christmas, since every pie, in Salopian lore, promised a "happy month."

Though we never had a Christmas tree, since the custom was then new in Shropshire and regarded as rather Germanic and heathen, we did observe the paganism of our Celtic ancestors to the extent of having plenty of homegrown mistletoe hanging around to kiss under. The myth of Father Christmas was zealously promulgated; indeed, my grandfather himself, with cottonwool beard, impersonated him annually at the children's ball.

Our Christmas Day was devoted to even greater eating feats than our Sundays. I would begin, at first light of dawn, stuffing the dates and sugared figs and chocolates I would dig out of my pillow case. Then there would be a monstrous three-decker breakfast with porridge, kippers and kidneys, at which the adults would exchange their presents. By the time we had walked back from church after a noisy service, hollering "O Come All Ye Faithful" with clamourous zest, we were primed for the vast Christmas dinner. A quartet of capons or a large goose would be demolished; turkey was regarded as American and at least half-pagan. For dessert there would be the year-old Christmas puddings flaming with brandy, and the mince pies, and the Valencia oranges that had arrived just in time for the season, and the Cox's Orange Pippins specially stored to be ripe in December, and the nuts and preserved fruits. Toasts were drunk in fine crusted port (the Band of Hope conveniently forgotten for the next few days), with each time a tiny glass as big as an acorn shell for me.

While my grandfather took at least a double dose of his forty winks, the rest of us would trudge out on a long and necessary walk. By four o'clock we had to be back to receive the close friends who were the only visitors on Christmas Day and who had to be entertained with the stored-up richness of year-old cake and as many other sweetmeats as they could consume. Miss Pearce would always be there accepting diffidently an endless series of half-glasses of sherry and port, and Mr. Knight the postmaster, the other warden of Emmanuel Church, a leering jolly man with an eye that rolled as eloquently as Groucho Marx's. Once I remember Harry Lewis appearing to refuse all drinks and to sit in such austere and disapproving silence that even my mother was glad when he left. He was, I suspect, getting his own back in some obscure way on Sam Woodcock, since I cannot remember the gatherings in his cottage were ever killjoy occasions.

The other regular visitors were my Aunt Ethel's family, whom my mother regarded as raffish and vulgar. And indeed Ethel's younger sister Polly, who kept a hat shop which she regarded as chic, was loud and outrageously funny and liked to give the impression of being fast. But nobody could have seemed more stiffly respectable than her brother Alfred, the town's leading plumber, a pompous, slack-mouthed man with a slow voice and a considerable facial resemblance to Arnold Bennett.

Most interesting to me was Alfred's daughter Vera. She and I were not, of course, blood relations, but we were thrown together so much that we talked of and thought of ourselves as cousins, and I knew her better than any other girl until I reached my late teens. She was almost two years younger than I, and at first I dismissed her as a rather pudgily impertinent infant. But by the Christmas of 1923, when I was eleven, I began to realize that she had grown into a little girl of strong character and very good looks. She was an arrogant natural blonde, with clearly-cut features, glittering blue eyes and long corn-yellow braids.

That Christmas we began to challenge each other and formed a strange relationship. Against our elder relatives we were in close alliance, ready to lie if not die for each other; when we were alone together there was a curious kind of *noli-me-tangere* on both sides, tantalizing and often aggressive, for Vera was an expert flirt while I was in the stage of thinking girls idiotic even when they were beautiful, a manifestation of my abysmal shyness. In our later teens we would get on very well, so well that my Aunt Ethel had thoughts of marrying us off and my mother was alarmed. It might well have happened, for Vera grew steadily more fine-run and handsome, and by the time she was eighteen she showed every sign of growing up to be a classic Saxon beauty. She was also intelligent, the only person in the family after my father died to take seriously my growing ambition to become a writer. Though in my teens I was infatuated with other girls (I knew Vera too well ever to be merely infatuated with her) her image had a place in the obsessive vision of returning to live always in Shropshire that haunted me until I was twenty.

But then, just as that vision began to fade, Vera was herself transformed as if by some malign magic. As happened so often among the handsome Saxon blondes of Offa's Dyke, she began to put on weight, until soon only those splendid sapphire eyes looking sadly out of a moon face reminded one of the slender beauty of two years before. As a young girl Vera was one of the few people I have known who really seemed to burn with a hard, gemlike flame. But a psychological trans-formation accompanied the physical, and the flame died down. I did not see her again after she was twenty, for circumstances parted us. I have often thought of her with a painful regret.

During that Christmas of 1923 Vera and I were especially thrown together, exciting and tormenting each other, while the family was solemnly discussing my future. Since nobody thought of Bisham school as being the end of my education, I had to go on to some higher school. My parents, however, could not afford the fees and books and sports kit. My father argued I had done well enough at Bisham to win a scholarship; my grandfather, sensitized by his own poor childhood, insisted no grandson of his would be educated by charity. No matter how my father urged that scholarships were related to ability rather than need, he was too much the ardent self-made man to swallow the argument. Sam Woodcock's grandson would be becoming to no one outside the family, and in this my mother, as touchily proud as he, concurred entirely.

Once it was agreed he should pay for my schooling, there came the question of where I should go. Fortunately neither my grandfather's generosity nor his pocket ran to a boarding school, for which I have always been grateful. It was finally decided I should go to Sir William Borlase's, the old grammar school in Marlow. Now that a decision had been made everything suddenly seemed urgent, and my father said that he would go back immediately to make sure I got in after the holiday.

BORLASE SCHOOL, AS WE CALLED IT, was already a notable place in my mental map of Marlow. The part of it one saw from Oxford Street was one of the oldest buildings in the town, a structure of mellowed rosy brick that dated from Queen Anne's time or even from the late seven-teenth century. Stone tablets were let into the facade and the messages they carried in their old worn Roman lettering, had already impressed me with their stark sternness. "He that will not work, neither shall he eat," said one, and another, "By the sweat of thy brow shalt thou eat bread." I took them very seriously even before I entered the school. It was not merely that the puritan work ethic was strong even among children in those days; given the poverty in which we lived, I knew I would have to work for anything I wrung out of life.

Borlase School was in an historic quarter of town, full of curious relics. Beside the football field, surrounded by a wrought iron fence, stood the elaborate tomb which a Napoleonic war general had erected to the horse he loved as much as Alexander loved Bucephalus. Across the street was a large Regency mansion, called Remnantz, with large gardens and a paved court; it had once been the Royal Military College, a predecessor of Sandhurst. Next to the school was a long, low building, now divided into a number of little dwellings, which was called Shelley House. Shelley had indeed lived there with Mary, had composed *The Revolt of Islam* largely under the great cedar of Lebanon that still towered in its garden, and had been host there to Thomas Love Peacock and William Godwin. These associations were to become very important to me by the time my years at Borlase came to an end.

Borlase's own traditions went back much farther. The year I entered, it was celebrating the tricentenary of its foundation in 1624 by Sir William Borlase, a Cornish member of parliament in the reign of James I. It was Sir William's motto — *Te digna sequere,* Follow things worthy of you — that we sported on our blue and white school caps and celebrated in our school song, "A knight there lived in days of olde . . . ." Borlase had begun as an endowed school for the sons of impoverished gentry much like Eton and other charitable schools which later were to become public schools. But, Borlase fell on hard times between its foundation and the late nineteenth century; it moved elsewhere for a period when the old building fell into disrepair, and then was revived to become a good grammar school with, when I arrived, new classrooms arranged around the cloister and even a Gothic revival chapel.

In their more euphoric moods, its masters referred to Borlase as a "minor public school," and it is true that the better-known foundations paid condescending tribute to our age. Our first eight would row against Eton's third eight at Henley, always to be defeated, and in cricket our first eleven would play against Harrow's third or fourth, with similar results. We kept up pretences to the extent of having twenty or thirty wretched boarders who constantly complained about the food they got in the School House and who would be marched *en crocodile* to church every Sunday in bumfreezer jackets and toppers like Eton boys. They were a ragtag lot of sons of minor Indian officials and boys who had been expelled from better schools and very often did not last long with us, like the wild Irish boy Tyoran whom we rather admired for achieving his seventh expulsion by shitting in the boarders' wash basins. The other hundred odd boys were divided between the day boys, who came from the town itself, and the train boys from other places who tramped up from the station every morning and occupied the lowest rank in our pecking order. It was, on the whole, a good school, small enough for its staff of eight masters to teach with some effectiveness, so that in my day I am sure no boy who had some talent and wanted to learn went without encouragement.

The school's orientation was deliberately imperial. The headmaster, whom we called Baggy and who, well-primed with Scotch, conducted hilarious French lessons for the higher classes, came of the English side of the great Anglo-Indian clan founded by the famous Skinner of Skinner's Horse. His brother, one of the gentlest and most naturally courteous men I have ever met, was a colonel in the Indian army. Under Skinner's dispensation the school's main intent was to train young men for India and the colonies and the Board of Governors, presided over by the ancient General Sir George Higginson who had fought at Alma in 1854 and who became a centenarian during my boyhood, solidly supported his efforts. The hymn we sang with mock tears at the end of term closed with the verse:

> And now for those our comrades
> Whose schooldays now are o'er
> As boyhood's haunts are fading
> For some far distant shore,
> Give them thy strength, O Lord this day
> To fight the fight and work and pray.

Indeed, far more Borlasians went to India and the colonies than went to the universities, but there were still plenty who became clerks in the City of London. Most of those who did reach the far distant shores went into the minor services, like the police and railways and forestry, or into planting; I have never encountered in my long studies of imperial history the name of an Old Borlasian who held any influential position in the empire. Sterling mediocrity would probably describe the quality of our collective achievement. The only famous man I ever knew who went to Borlase was Hugh Walpole, and he was there for a very short time and did not like to talk about it.

Imperial ambition greatly affected life at Borlase. A fanatical stress was put on sports and we were encouraged to be fiercely competitive, among ourselves, between the houses into which we were divided in imitation of the real public schools, and against other schools. A victory over some minor establishment like Lord Bertie's in Thame or Dulwich College was treated like Waterloo or Trafalgar. Team spirit mingled with the traditions of schoolboy solidarity to produce a kind of adolescent orthodoxy. One did not sneak on one's fellows; one did not let the school down. The endless guerrilla war between boys and masters became, in its strange way, a preparation for the greater struggle to maintain the school's prestige against its rivals. To break ranks on either front was perilous. I have always felt school life of this kind would be a good preparation for life in prison, since schoolboys, at least in my childhood, have a morality very similar to that of convicts.

Entering Borlase in mid-term as a member of the Shell, as we called the First Form, meant joining a company of boys who were already four months wise in the school's ways and I realized immediately that I had to move with circumspection. I had to endure the verbal aggressions, the sneers at appearance (my big unshapely nose) and name (Woodcock: Timberprick). I had to put up with other urchins seizing and trampling on the halfpenny buns I would buy from Mr. Tidy, the baker who came into the quadrangle with his basket every mid-morning break. But, rather to my surprise, I had no difficulties in the classroom. My preparation in history and English, geography and basic mathematics, was good enough to take me to the head of the class within a month, and I was quick at the academic uptake so that I did not have to labour at learning. This meant that I fitted into the peculiar code of the boys who did not resent success so long as it was won with ease and style but who despised the swot, the boy who had to take time and trouble preparing himself.

The physical side of school life was less easy to accept. I disliked sports and any kind of exercise other than walking, which I have always enjoyed. And I had not become adept in the art of self-defence, which was something of a disadvantage in a school where a great deal of bullying went on and was usually practiced by the sportier boys. So I quickly accepted the virtues of evasion. I meticulously carried out my First Form fagging duties, which consisted in little more than taking my turn sweeping and tidying up the corrugated iron shed which was the Sixth Form common room. Thus I gained the good will of some of the senior boys and, on the rare occasions when I faced the prefects' kangaroo courts, I usually had a well-wisher on the bench who vouched for me as "A good kid" and saved me from the painful beatings with spiked running shoes that were often administered. I evaded combative situations wherever I could and learnt the soft answer that turneth away wrath, so that I rarely got involved in serious fights.

This did not mean that I went unscathed. I endured a good deal of minor persecution, and there are certain sensory stimuli that still bring back that time and its sick sense of fear. A strong smell of dog's piss, for example, will remind me of the changing sheds where on wet days Old Chiz, the school handyman in his green baize apron, would exercise the wirehaired terriers Baggy bred as a sideline. The changing sheds were the places where one was most likely to endure such indignities as frog-marching, arm-twisting, beating with wet towels, or merely pummeling in a corner. It was only when I reached the haven of the Sixth Form that I ceased to be fearful.

Since sports were compulsory, I made evasive obeisance. I would be seen on the cricket field, usually idling at long stop or clumsily knocking down my own wicket because I was mortally scared of fast bowlers. I trotted tentatively on the edge of fierce action on the football field, but never near enough the centre to become one of Kipling's muddied oafs. I became modestly good at gentler and more individualistic sports like running and long jumping.

This was the negative side of school; it was bad enough but not nearly as bad as the life endured by boys in boarding schools. What I gained was much more important; a good deal of knowledge, some excellent friendships and a growing sense of what I really wanted to do with my life. At first I thought it was to be a naturalist but later I realized it was to become a writer.

Good small schools tended to gather masters who were strange or eccentric. Stokes, the mathematics teacher, was so deaf that one day when a boy farted in class, he turned round to see the laughing faces, rapped his pointer on the desk and shouted, "Somebody has made a rude remark! Will you please repeat it?" To Barnes, the less than competent French master, I owe an accent that makes me ashamed to speak with Parisians, yet I still remember our delight when, on his last day among us, he declared, "Boys, I'm going out to Poona, where all the little boys are bwack!" Jones, the irascible Welshman who taught English to the lower forms, was moved to physical fury by stupidity or inattention and when he was out of patience would crack boys on the head with the long pole used for opening windows. And there was Baggy himself, a fierce canesman, whose sixes on the bottom one remembered ruefully.

But he was also an almost softly affectionate man; when he was old and blind and retired at Brighton he would like to be visited by his favourite pupils and would pass his hand gently and reminiscently over their faces.

Some of these men were in their own way excellent teachers. Primed to a bawdy daring by his lunchtime nips, Baggy could bring writers like Daudet and Hugo so much to life that ever since I read French books with pleasure and easy understanding. Stokes was a superb mathematician who never seemed able to communicate his knowledge to a class but became a greatly respected tutor when he took up a fellowship at Oxford. But for me the finest teacher of all was a dour-looking Welshman whom I feared at first and later came to love. His name was J. C. Davies and, because he never told us what the initials stood for, we called him Junk; he taught History and English from the Third Form upwards. Junk completed what my father had begun in fostering the enthusiasm for literature that has shaped my life. He was a man of dark moods, and I suspect he carried a deep mental wound from his experiences as a junior officer in the Great War. Once, when a boy repeated some of the militarist cant that was part of the school's conventional wisdom, he burst into a long and passionate denunciation of war as he had seen it in comparison with the myth that we were being taught. He finished by quoting Siegfried Sassoon's "The General," which he had by heart.

> "Good-morning; good-morning!" the General said
> When we met him last week on our way to the line.
> Now the soldiers he smiled at are most of 'em dead,
> And we're cursing his staff for incompetent swine.
> "He's a cheery old card," grunted Harry to Jack
> As they slogged up to Arras with rifle and pack.
> But he did for them both by his plan of attack.

We were stunned into silence by the passion with which he spoke, and by Sassoon's verse, which was unlike any poetry that had been read or spoken in the classroom before. He had touched on experiences so far outside our own that I do not remember our discussing the incident afterwards, but it is significant of the impression he made on us that no boy carried the tale. Certainly if it had come to the ears of General Higginson, Junk's appointment would have been quickly terminated. But he remained among us to transmit the natural enthusiasm for the rhythms of poetry and prose that would illuminate his saturnine face and fire his singsong Welsh voice as he revealed Milton's resonances and strayed from the reading list to bring us under the spell of Donne and Marvell.

Even the best of our teachers was circumscribed by the way our curriculum was directed towards key examinations, the Oxford School Certificate for which we sat in the Fifth Form and the London Matriculation for which we sat in the Sixth. For the very few who continued into the Upper Sixth, there was the Oxford Higher Certificate, which carried a modest university scholarship. But for most of us the London Matriculation, which gave access to many minor jobs, was the ultimate goal, unless we were in training for one of the imperial service examinations. The essential subjects were History and Geography, English and French, Mathematics and Chemistry, and an odd apology for Physics called Heat, Light and Sound. These subjects we required for both the Oxford and London examinations, and we studied them throughout our school careers. Music, mainly singing and a small amount of theory, we learnt only in our first two years, and the same, strangely, applied to Latin.

Not only were the general areas of our learning circumscribed. The custom which the examiners had of working in restricted periods or areas further narrowed what we learnt when the curriculum was strictly adhered to. In English, for example, we started with Chaucer and studied nobody after Hazlitt. History was strictly British and extended only from the Norman Conquest to the Battle of Waterloo. French, indeed, was somewhat broader; we were taught both Stendhal and Hérédia in the Fifth Form. Art from beginning to end consisted of the theory and practice of composition according to the inexorable laws of perspective. We never used any medium but graphite pencil, and spent endless hours doing shaded drawings of cubes and cylinders, of plaster casts and very occasionally vases of flowers. We never took a brush in hand or modelled even plasticene, and we were taught nothing of the history of art, whose rudiments I picked up from odd books in my father's library. As for science, we were officially taught nothing of the developments in physics that were taking place at that very time, nothing of astronomy or geology, and certainly nothing of biology. As for sex education, it was ignored by our teachers, except for occasional veiled admonitions against unmanly habits that could lead to insanity, though it went on underground in the sharing of our bizarre lore about female anatomy and, somewhere about the Third Form, in the furtive masturbation sessions in which we tried, at first not very successfully, to prove by ejaculation our entry into the world of men.

Fortunately some of our masters felt their own frustration at the limitations of the curriculum, and sometimes they would break away from it to open new windows of knowledge and interest. Junk would always find three or four periods a term to tell us about modern books we should know about, particularly those that had aroused his own enthusiasm, like the novels of H. G. Wells and Samuel Butler, Shaw's plays and the poems of Yeats and Walter de la Mare and Wilfred Owen. Stedman, the dry-witted Anglo-Indian science master, would sometimes break off a chemistry lesson early to give us at least an inkling of the ways in which modern atomic theory was modifying everything he taught us.

And I remember how, the day of Thomas Hardy's death, Baggy preached a long obituary sermon and actually wept in the pulpit at the departure of so great a man. I was not only stirred by the strange access of emotion on the part of a man so given to teaching the virtues of the stiff upper lip, but also impressed that a writer living in my own time could command such fame and feeling, and this was undoubtedly one of the events that nurtured my desire to become a writer.

Still, the range of what we were taught, though it was well taught, remained extremely narrow and our education was intensive rather than extensive. Such an approach need not be despised entirely; it was concerned with the method rather than the matter of learning and, like the vaunted classical training of the old public schools, it turned us out reasonably well-equipped to absorb and understand new areas of knowledge when we encountered them.

I immediately found myself moving easily among the subjects. My interest in history, geography and English grew rapidly, and one of the reasons I enjoyed them was that they enabled me to write a good many essays (compositions as we called them) and to discover the process of making words do just what I wanted. In midsummer 1924, at the end of the school year, I was first in the Shell, but according to a strange rule that prizewinners must be a full year at school, I did not get the prize.

The next two years, in the Second and Third Forms, I was again first and went up on Speech Day to take the form prizes from the shaky hands of the General, by now withered to the wispy remnant of the vigorous young officer who had fought in Crimea. Then Alma was only a little over seventy years away, and I did not find it extraordinary to shake a hand that had wielded a sabre there, but now that I am myself seventy I find myself looking back with surprise, not at the span of time, but at the vastness of the changes that have taken place within two lives, those of the old General who was born in 1826, eleven years after Waterloo, and of the boy, still vigorously working in 1981, who in 1926 received from his hands the volume of Shelley's poems that helped lead him to a philosophy of life far removed from that of most Victorian generals.

Since I had done so well in the first three forms, Baggy decreed that I should skip the Fourth, which greatly disturbed my father's sense of orderly progression, and he may have been right, for in the Fifth I had not only to make up for a missed year but also to face intensive cramming for the Oxford School Certificate. I kept my head well above the water of failure, but I could no longer sustain the impetus of the earlier years and dropped away to seventh or eighth place. In fact, I slipped rather willingly into this position of respectable mediocrity, since I was no longer possessed by the urge always to do better than the other leading students, and this meant I had more leisure to gather friendships, which was becoming important to me, and to appreciate the books we studied for their own sakes.

That year Stendhal and Hazlitt were both on the examination lists and reading them at the age of fourteen, I began to develop a clearer sense of form and style in prose. Junk was a devoted admirer of Hazlitt, for his politics as much as his prose, and when we came to study the great essay on the conversation of poets, he would act the whole tableau out in class, playing Coleridge and Wordsworth as he imagined them to have spoken, and then impersonating the taciturn and mainly silent Hazlitt as he listened. Junk told us of Hazlitt's wretched existence and lonely death, and of his astonishing last remark, "Well, I've had a happy life," so that we could wonder at the difference between the inner and outer perceptions of any man's life. And then he recited Hazlitt's boast, "I never wrote a line that licked the dust," and looked at us directly as he remarked, "That is an enviable thing to be able to say." Hazlitt's phrase stayed in my mind, and ever since I began to write it has been there as an exemplary exhortation.

AS I WENT FROM CLASS TO CLASS, I gathered a cluster of friendships that did as much to shape my mind and my life as any of the subjects I studied. At the beginning especially, I carried over from Bisham School my habit of forming friendships with boys who also were in some way outside the ordinary run, which at Borlase consisted of the budding imperialists. The two boys to whom I came closest at this time were a mentally and physically uncoordinated slow learner we called Weary Wellicome, and a fanatical butterfly collector, Joe Ford, who shared my passion for natural history.

Ford, whom I had known already at Miss Illsley's school, was marked off by being a Catholic; he always dropped out of the ranks of our morning drill parade when the rest of us marched into the chapel for our Anglican morning prayers, and sometimes boys would jeer as they passed him. Catholics in the England of the 1920s were still regarded as peculiar and not entirely trustworthy. For an Irishman to be a Catholic was all one could expect, our stereotyping minds told us, of a bog-trotting Paddy. But for an Englishman it came, if we were to believe all our history books told us, very close to treason. Even on a popular level, the dances on misty nights around the November bonfires kept alive the memory of the Catholic terrorist Guy Fawkes, whose image we carried through the streets — "Penny for the old guy, mister?" — before we tied him to his stake and burnt him as the golden-sparked rockets soared into the sky.

So Ford had his own reasons for being on the edge of things, and so did Weary, who was a three-year veteran of the Shell when I arrived, and never got higher than the Third Form. It was not that he was stupid; in fact, he was the victim of inflexible educational methods. He was enviably deft with his hands and extremely quick to learn processes from watching other people do them, so that after he left the school, in which he wasted his life for several years, he became an excellent and resourceful mechanic. But at Borlase he was a target of scorn. Sizing up a possible ally, he began to talk to me of his problems. There was no way I could turn him into a writer of serviceable prose, but I did my first and I sometimes think my best piece of teaching by finding a way of showing him rather than teaching him how to solve simple arithmetical problems, so that he was able to scrape up enough marks to emerge finally from the Shell and accompany me into the Second Form.

After this, Weary developed towards me an attachment that touched and flattered me, and when he asked me to his home, I went. His father was a small builder who owned half a street of working-class cottages like our own. He lived in a large old house near the school with French windows opening onto a lawn with bright herbaceous borders, an orchard full of big old apple trees, and a greenhouse full of exhibition chrysanthemums with flowers as big as a boy's head. Weary's mother was grateful for the help I had given him, and made me welcome with cakes and good nature. This meant a great deal to me at age twelve, since it extended the limits of life in our wretched cottage by providing something rather like Runnymede transported to Marlow. The Welli-comes had a big barn, splendid for invented games, a billiard table where Weary and I played long defiant games, and a good radio, which to me was a special delight, since my father still stood against owning any kind of wireless set. I now began to hear a great deal of music; it was on the Wellicome radio that I first heard an orchestra, and developed a passion for Handel.

It was now I began, sometimes with Weary and sometimes with Ford, to explore the countryside around Marlow far more widely than I had ever done before, so that soon I knew every lane and wood and hamlet in a triangle pointed by Maidenhead, High Wycombe and Henley-on-Thames, with Marlow roughly at the centre. It was excellent and varied walking country, with the water meadows along the Thames, and the escarpments of the Chilterns rising on each side of the river to sparse-grassed chalk hills penetrated deeply by dry valleys which we called bot-toms, and crowned with beechwoods. Beside the river the woods were smaller, more varied and denser, sometimes so tangled with wild clematis vines that they looked like bits of Amazonian forest. Around the little villages of flintstone or half-timbered houses — Medmenham and Hurley and Cookham — or in the folds of the hills — Fingest and Frieth and Skirmett — there were still fine stands of elms, homes for generations of rooks.

At Borlase there existed a cult of cross-country running which, it was held, would toughen us in body and character. Monstrous levels of endurance were expected of us. I remember with bitter clarity one of these runs in a freezing January. We were sent off in thin cotton singlets and shorts, panting over the hard-frozen lanes into the hills. We came back, exhausted, plunging through waterlogged meadows covered with thin ice, our ankles gashed and bleeding from the sharp glittering edges. On this stretch, the prefects and the athletic fifth-formers herded us along with shouts and kicks, and mocked those who complained. I hated these occasions for the way they depersonalized us into a pack of wretched juveniles who half-believed in the absurd cult of manliness that made us undergo such odious trials without even complaining to our comrades. We victims shared the code of the stiff upper lip that made it a crime either to whine or to tell.

My hatred of cross-country runs was strangely balanced by the passion I developed for great striding cross-country walks. Weary, who belied his nickname as soon as he was outside the ancient and inhibiting walls of Borlase, was as fierce a strider as I. I see as I write his tall and stooping figure, growing out of his clothes constantly so that his ankles and wrists were always rawly exposed, loping along with the wind blowing his hair into a strange Iroquois crest on the top of his head, and gasping out the outlandish ideas he picked up from old Wellicome, who was a British Israelite. Weary had a strange generalized love of the countryside. He looked with amused tolerance on my botanical desire to find Heaven in a wild flower, and was most elated when we were tramping on some exposed hillside where the wind blew pure ozone into our lungs. He would laugh and caper and shout from sheer pantheist ecstasy.

Weary also had a great aquarian affinity and, as the Wellicomes owned a handsome four-oared skiff kept in a boathouse under Marlow Bridge, he was able to satisfy his water urges all through the summer months without getting involved with the young snobs who joined the Boat Club across the river. Every Sunday, and on many of the long June and July weekday evenings, the two of us would take the boat out. For me this was an unexpected source of delight. My parents could never have afforded to buy a boat, and I would have continued to observe the life of the river as an outsider if it had not been for Weary and his skiff.

Sometimes we would idle in the backwaters behind the long willow-clad islands and swim in the already polluted and dank-tasting waters of the Thames, and sometimes we would row as vigorously as we strode on land to reach Henley-On-Thames on regatta day. On swan-upping day in Cookham, Mr. Turk, the father of one of our fellow Borlasians, would abandon his role as boathouse-keeper and put on the braided coat that identified him as Keeper of the King's Swans, and herd the grey cygnets in from the Cookham Reach to be branded, half of them the property of George V, and half of them dedicated to one of the City of London Livery Companies. Often, on a Saturday or a Sunday, we would stay out until dusk had deepened into darkness, drifting down the river between the moored boats lit by faint lanterns, and absorbing

without recognizing them the erotic intimations of the evening in ways
that came out years later in one of my earliest published poems,
"Thames."

> And in the evenings the gramophones
> Sing through the clotting dusk in metal tones
> The amorous laments of stones and towns.
>
> The anglers boast of escapades on cliffs.
> Under the branches, from the swaying skiffs
> Are heard the virgins' protests and the throaty laughs.

Perhaps it is characteristic of living on a fringe, whether in boyhood
or adult life, that one's friendships tend to be individual rather than collective. I rarely went anywhere with a group of boys, and I cannot
remember Ford having come on a walk with Wellicome or vice versa.
Indeed, they were so different in nature that I realize my friendships
with them revealed the divisions in my own nature. Ford was a punc-
tilious scholar, and had taken advantage of his religion to become the
school's only real Latinist. What attracted me to Ford was not his personality, which was stuffy and pedantic, but the fact that he was the
only other boy in school who was interested in natural history. And
while, on my walks with Weary, we responded to grand vistas and
views, to the wind on the heath and the waves on the river, testing our
bodies in the kind of physical exertion we enjoyed, with Ford it was
much more a matter of searching out the intimacies of the countryside.

Ford's interests tended towards entomology; he amassed great collections of moths and butterflies. My interests now were flowers and birds.
But we were happy to learn from each other and combine our forays
into the woods and hedgerows, the close groins of the chalkhills, the
watermeadows and the riverbanks — anywhere that insects gathered,
birds flew and flowers bloomed. Sometimes there would be an evening
expedition to sugar trees on Marlow Common, which was a good place
for night moths; sometimes a tramp to Munday Dean, one of the
Chiltern Valleys, the only place where marbled white butterflies bred
for many miles. But though I shared Ford's interest in lepidoptery, and
gathered a great deal of knowledge from him about moths' life cycles, I
never came to share his passion for collecting them as dead specimens. I
hated putting them into the killing bottles or boxes of crushed laurel
leaves which he carried, and became quickly bored with the process of
pinning them out so that their wings were neatly spread as they dried

into rigid forms. Watching the live insect, in repose or in flight, with its colours vibrating in the sun, attracted me, and I now realize that my boyhood passion for natural history, which I have largely retained, was aesthetic in impulse.

Perhaps this was why, after a while, I went less often with Ford and his butterfly net, and began to find my own solitary routes where I could encounter the wild flowers which, without then having read more Blake than "Tiger, Tiger, burning bright," I felt had most to tell me about the world of nature. I can still remember vividly the delight of finding flowers that were both rare and beautiful; a clump of tall summer snowflakes dangling their large green-edged white bells in a wood near Temple; the bee orchids that would come up every year in a hidden fold of the ground at the bottom of Winter Hill.

On these lonely walks I realized how much more intensely one responds, not only to the intricate beauties of plants or birds or insects, when one is alone, but also to the atmosphere of places. I went often to the beechwoods, not for the flowers I found there, since little more than wood sorrel or dog's mercury ever bloomed in them once one passed the wood's edge which might be rich with primroses and bluebells and windflowers, but because I loved the luminous, cathedral-like gloom of the inner groves, with the sun filtering thinly down through the delicate tracery of leaves and greenly lighting the smooth, pachydermatous trunks of the birch trees.

But there were times, in some of the woods, when the sense of awe would suddenly darken, the birdless silence would grow ominous, and an indefinable terror would seize me and impel me to run back into the light. It was not until long afterwards that I identified my feeling as authentic panic: the fear that the god Pan was supposed to instil in woodland travellers passing through Arcady.

I RARELY ENCOUNTERED ANYONE on these walks in the beechwoods, except occasionally a party of gipsies on their way to gather the mosses which they sold to florists for making wreaths, and the wild belladonna which they sold to drug companies. I usually gave them a wide berth when I saw them, for the fear of gipsies had been taught me from childhood, and it was kept alive by the presence of a large Romany encampment on the northern edge of the town, whose inhabitants I regarded with the same kind of apprehension as Charlesworth the rabbit catcher.

Fear, for me and the other boys, mingled with fascination for these people who kept themselves so proudly apart; we never saw in our schools their arrogant swarthy boys or their dark-eyed handsome girls. The encampment, sometimes almost deserted for months on end, consisted of an untidy collection of shacks whose obvious lack of sanitation the town council chose to ignore. There were always piles of bottles and rags and the other oddments that gipsies collected, lying among the huts, and when the greater part of the clan was on the road, it looked as desolate as a battle field. But over the winter and at midsummer in the regatta season when there was money to be picked up, they would be back, the camp filled with brightly painted horse caravans and lean horses grazing in the fields.

At such seasons the townspeople kept a sharper eye on their chickens and rabbits, and the Romany women fanned around the town, knocking on back doors to sell the wooden clothespegs they made, and nabbing visitors ("Cross my palm with silver, dearie") to tell their fortunes. Our gipsies had long given up the traditional garb still worn by continental Romanies, and except that they always wore a good deal of gold — earrings and bracelets — and generally went in for gaudy colours, there was not much in their dress to distinguish them from ordinary Marlow working-class people. Yet we could always tell a gipsy, and not only by the dark complexion and eyes and the sharp-edged hawkish nose; there was an arrogance in the strut of the men and even in the wheedling whine of the women.

The chief of the Marlow gipsies, who belonged to the Buckland clan, was an aged man named Plato. Tall, gaunt and stooped, Plato Buckland would wander about town in a black cutaway frockcoat and bowler hat, both of them green from age; his face was dark, not from complexion but from dirt, except where the tears from his rheumy eyes formed white channels beside his nose down to the corners of his mouth. Sometimes one would see him behind one of the greengrocers' shops, picking over the castout fruit and vegetables.

In fact, Plato was a man of great hereditary status among the Romanies, and Marlow people knew about this; sometimes they would say contemptuously, when he came tottering grotesquely along the street, "There goes the king of the gipsies!" Nevertheless, they were all impressed when Plato finally died, and the trains of caravans began to come winding down the roads out of the Chilterns and along the Thames Valley, and scores of dark strangers arrived by train from all over the south of England. The whole town stirred with excitement, and early that Saturday morning I swallowed my breakfast hastily to set off with a band of other boys for the big chalkpit near the gipsy encampment where Plato's funeral would begin.

We climbed up the hillside to the top edge of the pit, where we could look down through a screen of broom. The pit was crowded with gipsies and townspeople, except for the centre, where a great flat-topped pile of logs and brushwood had been built. "They're going to burn him," said Weary. "That they're not. You wait and see," said Tipper Sendall, whose mother was half-gipsy and who passed for an authority on Romany customs.

Newspaper photographers found good viewpoints on the side of the pit. A couple of policemen also joined us on the pit's edge; they were obviously keeping low. Then, to much shouting, the crowd parted and a dozen gipsies appeared, pushing and pulling Plato's caravan, glittering with new red paint and gilt. They dragged it to the top of the pyre. A procession of young men came with bits of furniture and other possessions and piled them beside the caravan. An old man led Plato's white horse, and harnessed him between the shafts of the caravan.

"Going on his last trek," said Tipper. The gipsies began to sing, the women's voices high and harsh, in a shrill oriental chant. "That's Romany," said Tipper. "I know all about that; I've read George Borrow," Ford smugly remarked. Then, as the singing rose to a crescendo, the crowd parted again, and a bier was pushed forward. The coffin was open. "He's got a new suit," said Tipper. "They've washed his face," said Ford. "Go on, you can't see that far," said Tipper. "I told you they were going to burn him," said Weary. It was the first corpse I had seen. My principal reaction was curiosity. "How would he burn?"

But in fact that last phase of the ancient ceremony which the gipsies had carried all the way from India to a Marlow chalkpit did not occur. Plato remained the only silent spectator as one of his sons went up and expertly shot the white horse which, with a strange great gasp from the spectators, partly horror and partly admiration, sank slowly down between the shafts. The young man sprang down and immediately others ran around the pyre with torches; the kerosene-fed flames rose high around the caravan and wafted the hot air up so that we had to retreat from the edge of the pit higher up the hillside. The caravan burnt quickly into a Gothic skeleton of glowing embers that finally collapsed. The body of the horse disappeared when the centre of the pyre fell in. Then they closed the coffin and wheeled the bier away.

Next morning in the *Daily Mail* we saw the photographs, not only of the burning caravan, but also of the great procession of gipsy chiefs from all over England who marched through the streets of Reading, ten miles or so away, to bury Plato in the corner of the cemetery where the Buckland chiefs had been laid as far back as local people could remember, always under gigantic white marble angels that drooped their wings in lamentation. None of us went to Reading, but in the afternoon we returned, fascinated, to the deserted chalkpit; the pile of ashes and embers, sparking to every lick of the wind, was still too hot for us to step on. When we went back the next morning to look for relics we found only a few nails made brittle by the heat; everything else had been cleared away, as if to keep it from profane hands.

IN THE FIFTH FORM I fell in with a new group of friends, boys who were interested in literature not merely as something to read, but as something to create. Three of them had already come together in their way up the school: a fat little Jersey boy, Le Cheminant; a tall, lanky Scot, McLoughlin, whom we called Rubberlegs because he was double-jointed and rather exhibitionist about it; and a melancholic stutterer named Mills. All aspired to be writers, though only Rubberlegs eventually made a small literary career, writing radio plays for the BBC. But the great thing at the time about being welcomed into such a circle was not what any of us would achieve afterwards, but the fact of collectively — instead of solitarily — resisting the school's imperial and athletic values. When there were four of us to civilize a cricket match by stepping deliberately aside from fast bowlers, or to run together in the mile race and reach the finish line in dignified languor far behind the pack, we were making statements that annoyed but were hard to answer. The only game we undertook with zest was fives, and there too we were making our points, for the court we so often monopolized was overshadowed by the now gigantic cedar of Lebanon under which Shelley had written a great deal of *The Revolt of Islam.*

Le Cheminant, Rubberlegs and Mills were already writing, and planned to start their year in the Fifth by publishing a literary magazine in rivalry to the school magazine. They invited me to join them as an editor and a writer. They had heard, rather vaguely, that a modernist movement was flourishing in the world outside (none of us had yet read

Eliot or Pound), and so free verse was favoured in opposition to the metrical poems printed by the snobs who ran the school magazine. Le Cheminant's father, who was in the Civil Service, got the magazine reproduced for us by an antiquated gelatine process, and we would rent out the sheaf of four or five murky purple-inked sheets for a penny a read. Surprisingly, we had a circle of customers, and each issue would bring us a profit of about two shillings to divide between us. For those first literary earnings I wrote war poems and nature poems; the only two lines that remain in my mind I remember with acute embarrassment, but at the time I rejoiced when Junk looked up from reading one of my pieces and said, sadly and censoriously, "It doesn't even scan!"

VI

DEATH AND THE FAMILY

ABOUT THE TIME I entered the Fifth Form the precarious balance of our life in Station Road began to shift. During 1926 my father showed an uncharacteristic restlessness, largely provoked, I think, by the General Strike which took place in May of that year.

Small towns with scanty industry like Marlow were little affected by the strike. My father was involved because the railway workers were the only substantial group of unionized workers in the town, and they went out almost to a man. His sympathies were divided. He had expressed concern for the coal miners who were already out before the General Strike began, but this may have been because my grandfather, as a coal merchant, had been so bitterly condemnatory of them. The General Strike was on both sides the kind of Quixotic battle that appealed to my father's sense of drama, and his sympathies went partly to the strikers and partly to Winston Churchill, who was opposing them with so much panache. But he could not go out with the railwaymen because he knew the temporary status of his employment made him vulnerable; even if the regular employees were taken back after the strike, he would stand no chance whatever of being reinstated.

So he stayed on, ashamed when he walked past the pickets, men he had worked with every day for years, and annoyed when he had to associate with the *freikorps* of ex-officers, led by a brutal former Black-and-Tan we all called Bulldog Drummond, who somehow managed to keep the Marlow Donkey running intermittently, a rather futile exercise, since there were few trains for it to connect with running on the main line.

After the strike was over, some of the railway workers understood my father's situation and bore no grudge against him, but others became hostile, and the fact that the strike had made them unpopular among the townspeople made them more aggressive. My father was much too reserved a man to talk openly of his difficulties, but from this time he showed a nagging desire to escape.

This was the time when he began to dream of returning to Canada and spent much time studying immigration literature. He must, in his heart, have known that this was impossible, and he began to think of more humdrum forms of escape. Like George Orwell, he was taken with the idea of acquiring a small tobacco and newspaper shop. It would give him lots of time for reading and a secure if modest income, since people were never likely to give up smoking or reading newspapers. Also, and I think this was more urgent in my father's mind than the rest of us realized, it would give my mother a way of living if anything happened to him.

He heard of a nice little business going for about five hundred pounds. With another few hundred he could expand it and sell books. But the bookshop side could wait until later if only he were able to scrape together the basic five hundred pounds. He had nothing near that saved from the four pounds a week he earned from the Great Western, so he asked my grandfather to give him the money now and forget him in his will. But my grandfather claimed that he was himself in difficulties because of the coal strike and refused the loan.

How much this closing of all the routes of escape affected my father's health I do not know, but during the winter of 1926 to 1927 he seemed to be losing interest in all the things that had preoccupied him before — in his stamp collections, even in his Tudor Translations — though for the first time in years he began to talk a great deal about music and to feel the need to play again. But a piano was something he could not afford, and my grandfather procrastinated about sending him the one that was standing unplayed in the drawing room at Runnymede. It was not unkindness; it was merely unimaginativeness, which I have often felt is the greater sin against humanity.

In the first days of spring in 1927, he fell seriously ill. It was his old enemy, Bright's Disease, and this time he did not escape. He was taken to the Cottage Hospital, where the nurses loved him for his fading wit and charm. But slowly, as I visited him day after day, I was aware of the growing distance between us. He seemed to be quietly and deliberately withdrawing from life. It was less a loss of the will to live than the birth of a will to escape from living. He was gentler than ever, but one felt that all his connections in this world had grown meaningless for him. Had he been a religious man, one would have attributed this to a sense that he was already hearing the trumpets sounding for him on the other side. But the name of God never passed his lips, and when the ascetic vicar of All Saints' came to see him, he received him politely but declined to discuss the future, in this world or any other.

And then, one morning just before his forty-fourth birthday, he fell asleep and died, slipping out of life so quietly that it was hard to believe he had gone. I found his departure so incredible when I was told of it that I did not react with any expression of grief until, later in the morning, the beautiful bibulous Mrs. Porter came out of her house as I was walking by and asked me how he was. When I had to say the frightful words, "He died this morning," the truth suddenly surged over me, and I burst into sobs and was swept into her house, to be held to her fragrant bosom and calmed with biscuits and a good glass of port.

I insisted on making my farewell alone. They had put my father out in the old garage that served as a mortuary for the little hospital. The sister who laid him out had crossed my father's hands across his chest, and one of the other nurses had shaved him. His face was marmoreal in its pallor, and in death it had assumed a beauty of line one was seldom aware of in life. He reminded me of the stone crusader in Bisham Church. I had never seen a dead person before, except for Plato Buckland a long way off, but I felt neither fear nor wrenching sorrow, and I am sure this was because he seemed so much at peace. Rather than any violent emotion, I experienced the strange inner silence that comes from the recognition of a loss that is irrevocable. Whatever realm he had entered, he had nothing more to do, that serene face told me, with the world I still inhabited.

Salopians in those days were rather like Chinese, in that they liked to go home when they died, and the local railwaymen, all grudges forgotten, draped the Marlow Donkey in black on the day they took him out to the main line and loaded him on to the Holyhead Express so that no unfriendly hands should disturb his coffin. But it was the funeral at Market Drayton that showed me how my father, who seemed a failure to himself and who had fulfilled none of his ambitions, had inspired an amazing amount of love in his brief life. The people of the town came out in their hundreds to receive the wanderer back and bury their own youths with him. Emmanuel Church was packed, and people crowded outside the open doors. According to Market Drayton custom, he went on an open bier through the heart of the town to the cemetery, with our archdeaconly cousin and the vicar of Emmanuel at the head in full canonicals and the surpliced choir behind them. The procession that followed him to the grave cut deep in soft red Shropshire sandstone was nearly a mile long. Cousins and friends had come from the nearby farms and afterwards there was a funeral feast of the Shropshire kind, with much food and an unaccustomed amount of drink and the release of laughter. And that was perhaps a good thing, for there was not much laughter in the months that followed.

If we had been poor before, my mother and I were now almost destitute. The family savings amounted to no more than a couple of hundred pounds. Pensions for widows and orphans had just been introduced, but on a miserly scale; my mother received ten shillings a week for herself, and five shillings for me until I was sixteen. We had to scrimp and save and ask for help without seeming to beg. Baggy Skinner persuaded the governors at Borlase to give me a special scholarship to cover school fees. Grandfather supplemented the pension with an extra ten shillings a week, still grumbling about his losses from the miners' strikes. Now my mother as well as I went to Market Drayton and lived at Runnymede over the school holidays, so that we both had three months a year free keep. But it still meant that the two of us had less than seventy pounds to pay the year's rent, to live for nine months of the year, and to clothe ourselves. I wanted to leave school at once and take whatever work I could find, but nobody in the family — least of all my mother who dreaded my falling through poverty into the proletariat — would agree; I had to stay long enough to acquire the vital certificates that would give me access to respectable white-collar work.

So we entered a period when my mother contrived and concealed and pretended and managed heroically. By great efforts of mending and making do, she contrived to keep us at the necessary level of a shabbiness that might be threadbare but was never tattered. We retained our pride, we held our heads up, but at great cost to my mother in health and to me in guilt. For I was perceptive enough to realize, no matter how much she might deny it, that my mother was still sacrificing herself, this time for my welfare as she had done previously for my father's.

But I was also aware how much my father's death had worsened my own situation. Junk Davies, to whom I became considerably closer during these critical years, took over the role of intellectual mentor, just as my father's old friend Kent Godwin would sometimes — to my mother's chagrin — act the role of manly adviser to a growing youth. But I still missed the feeling of having a covert ally in the house that I had experienced when my father was still alive and willing to advise me on how my mother should be handled. True, as I grew older and larger, my mother necessarily dropped her role of physical disciplinarian, but she still felt the need to establish an emotional ascendancy which I had to resist if I hoped to gain any degree of real independence.

Whatever she had endured through being married to him, my mother was genuinely shaken by my father's death, and in the early period of numbness and grief she found almost unbearable the task of financial management — if one can regard shillings and pence as finances — that his death had thrust upon her. She still had few friends in Marlow after a decade of residence, and she shied away from the compassion which our good-hearted working-class neighbours came to offer. Yet eventually she did widen her circle of human contacts when, from the need for company rather than for God, she began to attend All Saints' Church regularly, to mingle with other women through church activities, and finally, when she was fifty, to be received into the Anglican communion.

Here, for a brief while, my mother's inclinations and mine coincided, for the year or two after my father's death was the only time I showed even the semblance of religious inclination, at least in any orthodox way. I was impressed by the gaunt, ascetic Canon Spearing, the Vicar of All Saints', but I soon understood that I admired him for his dedication — he was one of the two really saintly men I have known in my seventy years of life — rather than sharing his faith. I had no faith; I had beliefs in the sense that I had still not really examined what I had been taught, but very soon they would dissipate because I had received no religious experience that made me proof against intellectual doubt.

Apart from my respect for Spearing, who had the thin face, enormous agonized eyes and scanty grey beard of an El Greco visionary, I was drawn to All Saints' Church by mainly aesthetic impulses. As a building it was — and is — one of the finest examples of pre-Victorian Gothic revival architecture, with soaring pointed arches, a tall spire rising high and pure-lined above the river's edge, and a splendid peal of bells.

Canon Spearing was a highly ritualist Anglo-Catholic, and during his services I enjoyed with a sense of delighted guilt the splendour that the puritans of Emmanuel Church denounced as Papist and idolotrous. I loved the processional days when Spearing in his full vestments, gold or green, red or purple, would go with crosses and banners and swinging thuribles around the church. I loved the highly theatrical Anglo-Catholic mass, so much more self-consciously and adeptly stage-managed than that of the Romans. And there were particular days to which I especially looked forward: Rogation Sunday, for example, when we would all leave the church and march in procession, crosses and gonfalons before us, through the fields overlooking the town, singing hymns to the tune of a hesitant cornet and witnessing the blessing of the crops, which a few months later would flow around the altar in the pagan foison of the Harvest Festival, Demeter's feast translated; or Good Friday, with the crosses veiled and altar lights extinguished as we waited for Easter, and Spearing — in monk's black — prostrating himself as, in a hollow sepulchral tenor, he led us in singing the litany of the Passion:

> By Thine hour of whelming fear,
> By Thine agony of prayer,
> By the cross, the nail, the thorn,
> Piercing spear, and torturing scorn;
> By the gloom that veil'd the skies
> O'er the dreadful Sacrifice;
> Listen to our humble cry;
> Hear our solemn litany.

I can hear again, clear as if it were yesterday, the strange agony that entered into Spearing's chanting voice, and the equally strange lamenting sounds that Sammy Bath drew out of his organ. On such occasions I came as near as I ever did to a religious experience. But there was much less of the spiritual in it than of dramatic empathy with the great actor who hid within our saintly vicar.

My mother obviously got a great deal more out of our religious exercises than I did, perhaps because she had a real need for consolation and I had not; she sought and found, though I am not sure what. Certainly it was not the companionship she claimed to be seeking, for the few friends she made at the church were lame ducks of one kind or another whom she could patronize and secretly despise. It was as though she had given herself to one equal relationship, with my father, and did not want — perhaps did not dare — to embark on another.

So, in the eyes of the world as well as in her own, she became a woman on her own, but since she was no more able than any of us to achieve complete self-sufficiency, she concentrated her emotional needs as far as possible on a single object. That object, inevitably, was I. I suspect that, like most English women of her class and generation, my mother had never thought in terms of a life without any attachment. She obviously married with the idea that the union she entered on that fatal day in May would last for her life as well as my father's. And when he died, and she found it impossible to contemplate another marriage, motherhood became the sacred attachment; it was the only possible escape she could see from her consuming loneliness, and it was also a cause to which she could dedicate herself.

The ambiguity of my mother's attachment to me meant that she was willing to turn an uneasily blind eye to many of the ways in which I sought to express my independence, but whenever a threat to the completeness or the permanence of our shrunken household appeared, she became alert and defensive. She detested every girl with whom I became friendly, from "Cousin" Vera onward, and under the pretence of saving me from later agonies she tried to interfere with such relationships before they reached the fatal point of marriage which, as she saw it, would have locked me into a loyalty that excluded her.

So, in the years after my father's death, a curious, partly companionable and partly hostile relationship developed, marked on my mother's side by a possessiveness disguised mainly as parental concern, and on mine by a mixture of loyalty, guilt and resentment. The guilt arose from the knowledge that my mother had physically sacrificed herself for my welfare, and persisted even though I was aware that I in turn was being sacrificed to her emotional welfare. I let my conscience convince me that because of the sacrifices she had made for me I could not abandon her to solitude, and so I accepted with somewhat bitter resignation, at the age of fifteen, the likelihood that it would be a long time before I could live independently, at least in a physical sense. What independence I hoped to attain would have to exist mainly in my mind, and so, after my father's death, I turned more than ever towards my books.

My relationship with my mother was certainly one of the most painful in my life, and even now I find difficulty in writing about it. Devotion to the father, hostility to the mother; if I fitted into Freud's oedipal patterns it was in a strange and backhanded way. And if, as I suspect, the theory that our creativity flowers from emotional wounds is correct, then there is more than coincidence to the fact that my development as a poet coincided with the most painful stages of my relationship with my mother.

VII

YEARS OF AWAKENING

M Y FATHER'S DEATH was only one of a cluster of events that began to change my life. The timeless and unchangeable world of my Salopian holidays showed its vulnerability to temporal ravages, until I began to feel an intense personal relevance in one special line of a favourite hymn: "Change and decay in all around I see." Accustomed life patterns were suddenly interrupted or transformed, and my perceptions began to change and darken and grow more intense with my emergence out of boyhood.

To begin, one of the two poles of my Market Drayton childhood vanished when my grandfather Harry Lewis decided to sell his small-holding and his sandstone cottage and become in his own way a wanderer on the face of England. After my grandmother Betsy died he had taken as his housekeeper a gaunt, melancholy widow of respectable unattractiveness. I think he felt sorry for her, since she had endured a wretched life with two bad husbands, but none of his children or grand-children saw her, despite her worthiness, as anything but an intruder to whom we had to be polite for my grandfather's sake. The arrangement worked reasonably well while he retained his job as a signalman, but when he retired to cultivate his garden and was always at home, he found the situation unendurable. He sent his housekeeper packing with a good present, and sold the property to a dairyman who quickly let the gardens run to weed, left the fruit trees unpruned and replaced the thatch on the cottage with corrugated iron which angered me when I saw it gleaming stridently whenever I went afterwards for a walk along the Shrewsbury road.

Not having read *King Lear*, Harry Lewis thought he had hit upon an excellent idea when, having sold his cottage, he decided that he would live by turns with his four daughters, paying a modest sum for his keep. His son, Uncle Harry, who had now set up as a barber in London and supplemented his income in Figaro-like ways (usually connected with racetracks) was exempt as a bachelor who, to his sisters' scandal, merely lived with a lady he had no intention of marrying, and so had no respectable household. Two of Grandfather Harry's daughters agreed because they had an eye to legacies. They were in for a long vigil, for Harry developed chronic bronchitis, and each winter, wherever he was, would take to his bed and appear to be gasping on the edge of the grave, only to recover when the crocuses bloomed and by summer to seem a man born again. Ten years running Harry Lewis fooled his daughters with these flirtations with death, and only in the eleventh of his winters of coughing and exhaustion did he finally leave the world. My mother and her sister Annie, whose husband Dafydd Jenkins had quickly followed my father into his good night, had more immediate reasons for welcoming their father. His contributions would at least supplement the meagre family budgets.

So, not long after my father's death, Harry Lewis arrived at 82 Station Road and occupied one of our bedrooms while my mother added to her discomfort and her sense of martyrdom by sleeping on a lumpy truckle bed in the boxroom. Grandfather Harry became a stimulating and at the same time disconcerting member of the household. He was inclined to be dogmatic and opinionated, at times to the point of cantankerousness. He smoked thick twist, a black compacted tobacco rather like the stick tobacco I later saw in the South Seas, which came in a coil resembling licorice; he would cut it into chunks with his pen-knife and then rub it down in his palms to the shreds he stuffed into his pipe. My mother detested the rank smell of a pipe filled with twist, and the vigorous spitting into the fire that accompanied smoking it, but I looked forward to the times when Grandfather Harry got his pipe going, for then he would start on his reminiscences and I could learn more about Shropshire history seen from the lower levels inhabited by poachers and peasants.

What disconcerted my mother even more than the smoking and spitting was Harry's entire disregard for the social evasions around which her life in Marlow had been built. He would go out, dressed in his north-country workingman's garb, with cloth cap and heavy boots, and, as he had time in plenty on his hands, he would talk to anybody willing to listen, rich or poor, gispy or gentile. We would see him on park benches, leaning his chin on his stick and discoursing with derelict figures we shuddered to recognize; or he would come home to tell of what seemed to him a highly interesting conversation with some local blackguard, Nutty Price or Nobby Clark, to which I would listen with delight and my mother with exasperation. He took to attending the police courts, and in a few weeks gained a better knowledge of the seamier side of Marlow life than my mother had accumulated in a decade. The very structure of impoverished respectability she had built up so painfully was shaken by the presence in our house of this natural proletarian, this hobnobber with rascals and "hooers" as he called them, who thought nothing of his daughter's middle-class pretensions.

After three visits of this kind, my mother refused to receive Harry Lewis again, and so did my Aunt Annie, who was trying to hold her head high in a small Welsh community given to backbiting. The inheritance watchers, who lived in larger houses and in larger, more anonymous towns, now had my grandfather to themselves, and I saw very little of him for the last few years of his life. I missed his vivid, caustic narratives, and I feel closer now to this rustic Lear than to any of my forebears except my father.

Harry Lewis, in fact, survived both my paternal grandparents. My grandmother, well into her seventies, had been greatly stricken by my father's death, and felt an obsessive guilt for the fact that she and my grandfather had not done more for him before he died and especially for their failure to buy him his tobacco shop. In the autumn after his death she went into a sudden decline. Dr. McQueen called it "old age," but that was a cause of death widely applied in those days, when diagnosis of the ills of the aging was less accurate than it is today. Since to the end she showed no sign of senility, I suspect she was suffering from one of the less painful forms of cancer or perhaps even from the lapsing of the will to survive that in late life can afflict those who have no passionate reason to continue existing.

We were summoned to Market Drayton with the news that she was seriously ill, and arrived the day before her death. My grandmother was one of the last of a generation that liked to die at home in their own beds, with clear minds and, they hoped, clear consciences. Not long after we arrived, she asked to talk to me alone, and I went to the bedroom and found her lying there, so enfeebled that she could not raise her head from the pillow. Her body seemed already half interred in the thick mattress, stuffed with the feathers of her own chickens. But when I sat down on a stool so that my face was on a level with hers, she spoke clearly in a kind of hoarse whisper, and her eyes were bright with awareness, shining out of the soft ivory creases of her exhausted face.

"You've come in time, and I'm glad," she said slowly. "We won't meet again on this earth. I'm going to die, George." She spoke with the clear finality that came from observing her own condition without illusion and without regret.

"I cannot get better." She put a finger that rested like a leaf on the hand I had rested on the bed. "Do not cry. We shall meet again. Now you must promise me you will learn hard, and do as well as you can what God calls you to do."

I promised, wondering at her lack of concern for her own condition.

"You must go now. I have not much time, and I must be ready."

I bent down, kissed her cheek, which felt like tissue paper, and as I went out the parson went in to pray with her. She died the next morning, conscious to the end, and saying sternly, "Oh, Sam!" to my grandfather as she made her quiet way out of life. We can envy such fearless deaths.

THE DEPARTURE OF HARRY LEWIS and the death of my grandmother were only the beginning of time's assault on my Salopian youth, for its best years were still to come. They were the years, beginning round about my fifteenth birthday, when I experienced a rapid and astonishing inner transformation, which not only expanded my intellectual horizons, but heightened my sensibilities so that I began to see the world in an entirely different way. I awoke to the reality of beauty and suddenly found it everywhere, so that for years I lived in a kind of manic-depressive phase of ecstatic joys and agonizing miseries.

Ever since then I have had a sympathy for those evangelical converts who describe themselves as born again, since at that time I had a knowledge that I was becoming someone else than the boy I had been. I was certainly not wiser; indeed, I was probably a great deal more foolish since I was seized with all kinds of romantic fancies that as a boy I would have mocked with a child's literal-mindedness. But I became imaginative rather than inventive, which I had been in my solitary childhood games, and I became infinitely more sensitive to the visible world around me.

It is always hard to define the reasons for changes in one's perception of existence, changes that not merely reshape one's personality but also permanently shift the compass of one's life. They come necessarily from within, from the inarticulate areas of consciousness. I am sure they are partly erotic in origin, the uprising of sexual impulses that in their direct form are repressed, yet I have never been able to swallow entirely the Freudian simplifications of such phenomena. I am sure that other facts, like my sudden experience of the reality of death at this period, and my sense of taking over my father's interrupted and frustrated life, played their parts in my awakening to the sense of a new self.

In my memory this expansion of consciousness that was my way of growing up is especially linked with Market Drayton. In Marlow I was caught up in the examination-cramming process at school and in the problems of penury and emotional self-defence at home. In Market Drayton my mother and I were absorbed into a larger household, and our conflicts became diffused in wider relationships.

But this greater ease of life would not itself have been especially productive if I had not found in Market Drayton at that time the friendships I needed. They began round about the time I started at Borlase. That Christmas my father was with us in Market Drayton, and he and Kent Godwin, who had not seen each other for years, renewed their friendship, so that one day we went to the rambling Godwin house. While Kent and my father spent the day talking about old times and playing piano and violin duets, I remade my infant friendship with Cuthbert and Lance. At first I was closest to Cuthbert, who was a year older than me. Lance, who was a year younger, still seemed very much a small boy, and on that day of reunion we ordered him around as we played our game of soldiers skirmishing through the attics and cellars of the old house. A touch of realism was given to our play by two old spiked German helmets we found in the attic, and which Cuthbert and I appropriated, playing the roles of Prussian Guards, with Lance as our enemy and eventually our prisoner.

Cuthbert had a passion for fishing, and for a time it infected me, and I bought myself a cheap cane rod to accompany him and Lance and an ever-changing tail of other boys on expeditions far into the countryside. There are no major rivers near Market Drayton, and one had to be a very clever fisherman to tempt with toasted wasp grubs the few big old wily trout that lurked in the pools of the Tern. The Shropshire Union Canal offered only its small spiny daddyruffs and an occasional perch, and to get any real fishing one had to search out the ornamental lakes at deserted manor houses or find the farm pools that had stocks of fish.

The farm pools were mostly spoilt by over-breeding in a small space. I remember one, in the middle of a cow pasture on the Cheshire border, where the water was dense with tiny rudd. Casting along the edge of the reedbeds, a gang of three or four boys could catch a hundred in two hours, but none weighed more than a couple of ounces, and seldom did we hook one of the perch, a pound or so in weight, that preyed on these slippery midgets. It was exciting to see the float bobbing down every few minutes, and to jerk up one's line with a wriggling silver mirror on the end; a kind of killing passion developed so that we found it hard to go away. But we all knew, even as we shouted and boasted and compared our catches, that this was not real angling as it had been celebrated by Isaak Walton. Our great expeditions were in search of the immense and probably mythical fish we believed lurked in the depths of pools on local estates like Cloverley and Shavington and Styche.

To get to most of these old houses meant walks of three or five or even seven miles, and on such treks my terrain rapidly expanded beyond the three fields of Runnymede and the streets of the town. We would usually get a permit from whatever estate agent was looking after a vacant mansion though no keeper ever appeared to check our credentials. And then we would set out by dusty country roads and over paths through woods and fields and snipe-drumming marshes, sometimes passing through a lost and sleepy village like Moreton Saye with the strange black sphere that surmounted its church tower or Adderley whose church was filled with tombs and brasses of the Corbets since the twelfth century. We foraged as we went, I picking unfamiliar flowers to identify in my botany books when I got home, and all of us gathering mushrooms and nuts and blackberries in season and taking pot shots at birds and rabbits with our catapults and leaping over fences to steal apples from cottage gardens.

We rarely got much more out of these expeditions than the enjoyment of the long walk and the intensity of our expectations. For though there probably were large fish in most of these pools, there were also great uncleared areas of weed in which they fed and hid. I can only remember one real triumph, when Cuthbert and I went to a small and unspectacular lake surrounded by untended woodland. It started to rain and we rigged up a kind of bivouac shelter using our raincoats, but soon the water began to seep through and soak us. We had already resigned ourselves to packing up and going home fishless when the tips of our rods both began to dip in agitation, and we rushed out, and, with more skill than we knew we had, each landed a fine red-speckled and cream-bellied trout weighing three pounds. We never caught anything so large again.

Yet they were marvellous days, many of which have left sharply clear and usually brilliantly sunlit scenes in my mind. I can still see myself standing by the sluice-gate to the big pond at Styche, looking up over the grassy slopes towards the hall whence Clive set out for Madras and casting bread on the waters which the hungry fish ate with a bubbling rush and then ignored my bait. I recall vividly another lake so silted up that one could see the bottom far out beneath the shallow pane of its water. I sat on the end of a fence that projected into the lake, and saw the fish, in their scores if not in their hundreds, moving under the clear surface: a shoal of red-finned roach actually sailing beneath my float, leaving the tasty lump of cinnamon-flavoured bread paste I had prepared for them; a barbel snuffling along like a miniature sturgeon in the mud; a young pike swirling violently out of the shelter of a bunch of sedge in pursuit of a small shoal of dace that leapt excitedly out of the water like would-be flying fish; I caught none of the fish I saw.

I went once alone to Cloverley with Lance Godwin, who was slowly taking Cuthbert's place as my chosen friend. It was the longest of our fishing tramps, eight miles each way. Cloverley had been a great house in its time, and the pond was reputed to be inhabited by enormous bream. But the weed had grown more rampantly here than anywhere else, and we soon gave up fishing and wandered in the strangely magical grounds of the old house. The mansion had vanished years ago, pulled down to avoid taxes and make a profit out of the bricks. But the terraces and the walled gardens remained, their vines and espalier trees growing wild, their rose briars surging in choking flowery masses, a few dahlias still blooming among the weeds. The woods were better tended than the gardens, for the green rides had been kept clear of saplings and we found among them clumps of giant wild campanula, six feet high and hung with bright blue blossoms as big as coffee cups. In each ride remained a little gallows where the keeper had hung the rotting bodies of hawks and crows, of jays and weasels. We caught no fish but kept the recollection.

This boyhood mania for fishing, which George Orwell has evoked so well in *Coming Up for Air*, spilled over into my Marlow life, and I would spend hours and days beside the fished-out Thames, hoping for the big catch. Although it did not happen, I still went there because I had been trapped in the ritual of angling, and loved to talk to the other addicts about their catches on other days when the fish were biting. For me they rarely bit, and finally I began to develop a revulsion from fishing. Indeed, it was perhaps a symptom of the great change in sensibility then taking place in me that I began to find incomprehensible the cruelties which a little while before I had practiced almost without thought. I would go to the backyard of a local slaughterhouse, dip a tinful of maggots out of the bristle tub, take them home and put them in bran to cleanse them, and then impale them wriggling on my hook, as I did the worms I dug out of the edge of the muck-heap. I cannot remember, when I was fifteen, feeling any fastidiousness about such acts, or any particular concern when one of the plump and greedy little Thames minnows gulped down a hook so completely that it could only be removed by eviscerating him. But by the time I was eighteen such things did begin to trouble me, as it troubled me to rob a bird's nest, which earlier I had done with boyish callousness.

Not all our expeditions into the Salopian countryside were involved with fishing. In the spring fishing was out of season, and we sought out the parklands and the tiny remnants of forest in northern Shropshire for the first flowers and to watch the birds mating and nesting. As I became more friendly with Lance, whose bookish interests resembled my own, even our summer walks tended to take us to the woods and the broken country of small hill ranges south of Market Drayton where we could relate nature as we saw it to the kind of romantic poetry which we were reading and beginning to write. We had discovered, more or less simultaneously, some of the great English books about the countryside, like *Selborne, Rural Rides, Lavengro, The Romany Rye, The Gamekeeper at Home*, and the essays on rustic southern England of W. H. Hudson and Edward Thomas. Strangely, though, we did not then discover Edward Thomas's poems, which now seem to me perhaps the best of all English rural verse.

Every fine weekday Lance and I would be tramping the roads and footpaths, and on wet days we would go into the town to the furtive backstreet tobacconists who served children, and read and talk in the Godwin house as we puffed our raw cheap cigarettes, Woodbines or Blue Lagoon, which we collectively called "coffin nails."

We were, at that time, almost perfectly in tune, striking mental sparks from each other in our search for knowledge, and our exploration of ways of self-expression. What we read paralleled what we discovered for ourselves, and even more vivid in my mind to this day than what Hudson or Jefferies wrote is the image of a splendid pair of great crested grebes we once saw swimming on the lake at Buntingsdale. Buntingsdale was an estate with a splendid mock-Palladian house, the most handsome mansion in the whole countryside. Its woods had been laid out by long-dead romantic landscapers, and we wove them into our own poetic fantasies so that, when I was fifteen or so, I could have said of Buntingsdale as the Moghuls said of the palace in the Red Fort at Delhi, "If there is a Paradise on earth, it is here, it is here, it is here!"

ON SATURDAY EVENINGS we and our friends would tramp the town, for at this time the young people showed off like amorous grouse. The streets were bright, for the shops closed late that day, and in the illumination of their windows and the street lights, groups of girls and groups of boys would parade before each other. It was, I realized years later, very much like a Mexican *paseo*, flavoured with the same strange mingling of eroticism and *pudeur*. Of course, there were other people around, the late shoppers and the drinkers wandering with increasing unsureness from pub to pub, but we had eyes — made eyes — only for those of our own age.

Our avowed aim, as boys, was to entice the girls into the alleys or gullets where one stepped off the lit main streets into sudden darkness, but I do not remember this strategy ever succeeding. Indeed, the only time I had an adventure in a dark Market Drayton alley was when a cruising garage mechanic trapped me halfway down a back lane called the Little Burgage and, fumbling me front and rear, asked me insinuatingly what kinds of naughtiness I practiced. I continued walking, pushing his questing hands away as well as I could; it is perhaps a tribute to Salopian sangfroid that we walked out of the alley into the light, a few paces apart, as if nothing had happened in that lilac-scented darkness. I sensed that I could have got the man into unpleasant difficulties if I said anything about the incident, but, as I found his behaviour strange rather than shocking, I did not tell anyone.

In fact, Market Drayton was too small a place for the Saturday night *paseos* to lead to casual pickups. If, as the evening drew on, some merging took place, it was because a boy in one group knew a girl in another group, and a kind of introduction was effected. After eight or nine, we would end our hours of tramping and chatting either by going to the pictures in the decrepit town hall, with Kent Godwin and a stumbling pianist scraping and beating out the *William Tell* overture or *Poet and Peasant* or *Tea for Two*, according to the mood of the evening's picture, or we would sit in the fish-and-chip shop on Stafford Street, eating fried dogfish (called Rock Salmon) and chips with green dollops of pease pudding and sometimes with faggots, which in Shropshire meant not catamites, but pork rissoles.

Among the girls I saw in those evening parades under the lamplight was a slim brunette with a bell of dark hair, violet-blue eyes and a heart-shaped face with a kind of dollish smoothness. She came from the Welsh edge of Shropshire, her name was Monica, and her enemies called her Babyface. I fell into an intense calf-love, and mooned away a whole summer holiday and then a winter one before I plucked up enough courage to tell my friends what I felt. By this time it was spring, time for the woods and fields; an introduction was engineered and, in the customary manner of Salopian courting, Monica and I went for a couple of tentative walks. She thought me dull as dishwater, because I talked of birds and books and did not know how to dance and was too shy to touch her. I found that my friends were right when they said she was shallow and selfish. She did not turn up for the third tryst, and I bore my small wound with pride, and elevated her to the romantic role of the *princesse lointaine*, lovely and unapproachable, and for a few months enjoyed my fantasy. Meanwhile my Aunt Ethel, who had a nose for that kind of thing, found out about my meetings with Monica, slyly congratulated me when there was nothing deserving congratulation, and achieved a small victory in her running war with my mother by telling her that I had compromised myself with a wayward Welsh girl; a fine drama of accusations and explanations followed.

Yet the violet-eyed Monica, insipid as she was, played her own role in my literary development. I was now beginning to think of writing as something more than a Fifth Form amusement. Lance and I were beginning to see it as a vocation and, pushing aside my earlier flirtation with free verse, I began the long apprenticeship of learning through imitation that would take me in a few years (recapitulating as a foetus does) through the generations of English poetry from the Elizabethans to the moderns. The conventions of courtly love, and the poetry that sprang from them, fitted perfectly my sentimental encounters with Monica and her immediate successors, and so I began by writing what I still feel are quite credible pastiches of Elizabethan love poems. One of them, a neat little derivative exercise entitled "My Lady's Eyes" which I wrote when I was sixteen, has survived the destruction of much of my juvenilia.

> The diamond shineth like a star
> When held up to the light,
> And e'en when taken in the dark
> It still doth glitter bright;
> But O, no gem of any size
> Can glitter like my lady's eyes.

> The violet demure and coy,
> The springtime's azure flower,
> Is fit to grace some wood nymph's fane,
> Or great Diana's bower,
> But Flora can no flower devize
> As pretty as my lady's eyes.

My interest in birds and flowers overflowed into my poetry as well, and here I had obviously moved beyond the sixteenth century into an intermediate stage between the Augustans and Wordsworth. Another poem written when I was sixteen, and called "The Spring," is distinctly Wordsworthian in its bathos, which I would like to claim was studied but which I fear was unconscious.

> The ice-bound streams are free once more;
> The snow has thawed away;
> The trees show buds; young plants spring up
> From out their mother clay.

> The catkins swing on hazel trees,
> The blackthorn blooms like snow,
> And down in last year's fallen leaves
> The primrose blossoms show.

> In shady nooks and woodland banks
> The azure violets bud,
> While in the marshes kingcups grow
> And beautify the mud.

Beautify the mud!

THE FIRST OF MY LETTERS that survive date from this fervent time; since they are all addressed to Lance Godwin, they refer mainly to my life in Marlow, yet they reflect the interests I shared with Lance. They also show the self-consciousness and pomposity that afflicted me at sixteen as soon as I set pen to paper.

The earliest of these letters, which I wrote in October 1928, begins with the florid statement that "the summer flowers are retreating before the mighty giant Winter, who comes in like a juggernaut and crushes all that lies in his path." Juggernaut Winter had in fact left no less than fifty-four species of flowers in bloom for me to observe on that day. "In the hedges the place of the flowers is to a great extent taken by the bright red berries of the holly, bittersweet, hawthorn and wild rose. In the woods there are large numbers of fungi, especially fly agaric and horn-of-plenty. On October 6 I saw a cirl bunting on a wire fence, and the next day I saw a green woodpecker perched upon a post." Apart from books on natural history, I had been reading More (*Utopia*), Milton (*Samson Agonistes*) and Stevenson (*Kidnapped*). "I am now in the mazes of heraldry, and am getting lost in labyrinths of garbs, gyrons, pheons, saltires, and such things, but no doubt I shall some time find my way out."

A month later, on the 14th November, 1928, I am recollecting for Lance what happened at Plato Buckland's funeral, and describing the winter beechwoods. "You walk on a dull brown carpet between numberless straight, dull grey trunks which give the woods the appearance of a vast temple with its rows of columns. Here and there the monotonous brown is relieved by the dark green of the holly . . . . The small birds, especially sparrows, finches, starlings and wagtails, are gathering together in flocks and fly from bush to bush in front of you as you pass along the hedges." Even in November I had found forty-five wild flowers in bloom. I had been reading Arnold Bennett and John Buchan and Jack London, but also *Urne-Burial* and *Anthony and Cleopatra*, the poems of Blake and Keats, and Michelet on Joan of Arc.

It was at this time, still sixteen, that I began to write prose, and already in my choices I was indicating some of the main directions of my later work. I embarked on history; in the November letter I told of completing a small history of Market Drayton ("thirty-nine pages in an exercise book") with an appendix deferring to an English obsession at that period by describing a famous local murder. Four months later, in March 1929, I told of having written "a Natural History of Market

Drayton, about twice as big as my history," and of having begun a
"Lives of the Notable Salopians," to which I had been inspired by
reading Isaak Walton's Lives. Perhaps it is fortunate that not even a page
of these juvenile works survives. What I do find interesting, and rather
surprising, about this period of early prose writing is the degree of self-
criticism I already displayed. I knew my writings were "too wordy or too
trite," and I realized that the sources I could draw on had been "rather
scanty," but I still expressed my confidence to Lance that "if we
persevere long enough, we may some day become good writers."

Nothing in these letters, except perhaps the widening scope of books I
read, quite recovers the inner excitement of the period, the sense that
for the first time I was seeing life as it should be seen and beginning to
perceive my own course within that life. A touch of the excitement
comes through the mannered descriptiveness of some of the nature
poems I was then writing, but the essence remains in the memories that
stand out with the sharpness of vignettes.

I see us walking in a clear moonlight night by the pond of one of the
many watermills that had been abandoned even before our childhood
when a big steam-operated flour mill had been built in the town: the
smooth quicksilvery water; the clearly delineated pointing of the mill's
dressed stone facade; and suddenly the water broken by triangular
heads and a family of otters beginning their play. I see a ruined sandstone cottage, the roof fallen in, great toads stirring out of hibernation
in its corners, and around it a walled garden of overgrown nut trees
whose floor is a ghostly greenish white from the opening blossoms of
wild lily-of-the-valley. I see the glades in the woods at Hawkestone, purple in April with the rhododendrons that had run wild and grown like
trees among the pinewoods after some lord's son brought them from the
Himalayas.

Such scenes, so epiphanous at the time, remain magic residue in
memory, commemorating not only the physical past but also the widening perceptions that shaped my image of it. Because my memory, in contrast to my life's craft, is strongly visual, they survive where the words of
that time have not. Yet I know that in those days when we were experiencing the natural world through our senses with a joy close to ecstasy,
we were also endlessly talking and arguing, boasting of our own
discoveries of thought, yet eager all the time to learn from others. A new
intellectual world as well as a new aesthetic world was opening out to us
in our provincial remoteness (though the themes were already old else-

where: evolution and socialism, anarchism and feminism and atheism), as we talked over the implications of Shaw's plays and prefaces and Wells's novels and Wilde's essays, as we felt the appeal of Pater and the decadents of the 1890s and became aware, by finding jazz, how a people could spontaneously create the art that reveals their genius at the same time as it exposes their predicament.

It is for such reasons that those last holidays in Market Drayton were so memorable; there I had the time and the freedom I never found in Marlow to understand how I, and the world I lived in, were changing. All through this period Market Drayton still meant earthly paradise, the place where I wanted to live out my life. The quiet beauties of its countryside, the eccentricities of its human society, seemed then to offer an inexhaustible mine of interest and pleasure. But the very awakening of perception, for which Market Drayton was the setting, carried its critical element, and the time was close when fate would take me into a more compelling world, and the life that had been wholly sufficient to me as a child and a youth would seem diminished and inadequate.

VIII

NEW FRONTIERS

I USED TO BLAME THE DEATH of my father for the life I had to accept when I left school in 1929. But I doubt if his survival would have made any difference, as we would never have lived far beyond the edge of poverty; I would have been faced with the same necessity to earn my living as soon as possible. In the short run, it involved me in a great deal of wretchedness. But seen through the patterning eyes of memory it seems to have been as good a thing in terms of experience as could have happened to me.

I had, in 1927, passed the Oxford School Certificate fairly creditably. In 1928 I went with a few of my classmates to sit for the London Matriculation examination at a college in Mile End Road. I stayed with my Aunt Jessie who was then living at Lewisham, and each day I would travel into the exotic environs of Whitechapel, an urban world of a kind I had never experienced before, with its rich combination of Cockney and Jewish cultures. I had no idea at that time that I would one day enter quite deeply into its life.

After the examination I was convinced that I had failed, since, though I knew I had done good English and History papers, I had worked out a series of mathematical problems with a splendid logic ruined by minor miscalculations along the way. However the examiners were clearly much more concerned with method than with results, for I was given the First Class status that in those days at the University of London only one candidate in thirty was granted. It was a satisfying victory, since the masters of Borlase had considered me too poorly disciplined a student to deserve any kind of prize during my Sixth Form year, and now there was great talk among them of my going on to Oxford or Cambridge.

This had little relevance to our family situation, since it was obvious that the poverty my mother endured so stoically could only be relieved if I began to earn money as quickly as possible. Junk and the other masters urged me to stay on and take the Oxford Senior Certificate; if I gained sufficient credits it would entitle me to a modest scholarship. I did in fact return to school in the autumn of 1928 to enter the Upper Sixth and follow the course of private study that was the custom at Borlase. But I had little doubt that I was merely marking time and reading for its own sake as I began to study continental European history and the lesser Elizabethans, which were on the curriculum for the Oxford Senior. I was really waiting for a job, but in the latter part of 1928, even before the Depression assumed dramatically catastrophic form, employment was getting hard to find in England, and I was not unhappy to fill my waiting time in a way I enjoyed.

The prospect of an academic career did once open out, to be closed immediately. The scholarship that went with the Oxford Senior would not be enough for all my expenses at college, and it would certainly be of no help to my mother. So my grandfather presented a proposal. He longed to have a clergyman in the Woodcock line, and he offered to supplement any scholarship I might win if I would agree to study for Anglican orders. I refused. It was partly because my faith was beginning to waver, but even more because I was still so inordinately shy that the idea of standing in a pulpit and preaching to a congregation paralysed me with terror.

So I stayed at Borlase, desultorily studying my history books and my plays, and spending just as much time on my task as School Librarian, reading more books there than I ever gave out. I went on futile searches for jobs, in banks, in insurance and accountants' offices, in libraries. Everyone admired my credentials; everyone pretended to lament they had nothing to offer so brilliant a student. In the end, when all these avenues had closed and the seasons had gone from autumn through winter into spring, my mother and I were forced to swallow the pride we shared and resort to whatever small influence we could muster. There was only one place where we had any pull at all, and that was the Great Western Railway. So we wrote to an old friend of my father, who got in touch with another old friend higher up the hierarchy, who got in touch with one of the all-powerful Potter clan (the relatives of Beatrice Webb). And sure enough, early in the summer of 1929 just after my seventeenth birthday, the summons came, and I was given a job, not as a ticket clerk, but as a glorified office boy in the head offices of the railway at Paddington Station.

Enrolled in the railway's engineering department, I occupied a variety of petty posts for eleven years, until I departed in 1940. I began in a section of the office that maintained the docks which the Great Western Railway operated in South Wales; I ended in charge of the accounts of a series of construction projects on the outskirts of London.

I have ever since thought ambivalently of this period. For most of eleven years, fifty weeks a year and five days a week, I caught the 7:58 commuters' train from Marlow and returned from Paddington on the 5:45 train; I also worked half-day on two out of every three Saturdays. My work, beginning as a stenographer and filing clerk and ending as a bookkeeper, presented no challenge or stimulation of any kind; so long as I could type without error and add and subtract accurately, nothing more was demanded of me.

I was indeed assured discreetly that, because of the benevolent presences in the hierarchy that had ensured my original appointment, I would rise eventually in the service, but that did not inspire me, and from the beginning I evolved a plan to save money and build a fund to achieve my eventual liberation. Since I started work at a salary of £65 a year in 1929 and was earning only £205 when I finally left in 1940, it was obviously going to take a great deal of time, adding shilling to shilling while I allowed myself enough to buy the books I needed and otherwise feed my cultural appetites, but I calculated that with careful spending I could by the age of forty have enough to bring me about £100 a year, and that I believed would keep me alive to pursue my chosen career. Good fortune and a touch of courage were in fact to enable me to escape twelve years ahead of my programme, when I was 28, but that I could not foresee in 1929.

At first my desire was to follow the example of H. W. Bates and Charles Darwin and to become a travelling field naturalist, but when I talked to former classmates who were taking biology at the universities, I realized that there had been a change in science since the days of the great nineteenth-century amateurs, and that what I really admired in the careers of the classic naturalists was not so much their detailed work as zoologists or botanists as the travels on which that work had led them and the clarity of mind and prose with which they understood and described their experiences. These aspects of their lives, I realized, I could combine with the poetry that was increasingly fascinating to me if

I elected to become a writer. I reached this conclusion by the time I was eighteen, so that from 1930 I had no doubt at all that eventually I would dedicate myself to writing in the complete and professional sense; I was already by that time a stubbornly dedicated amateur.

LOOKING BACK INTO THAT PERIOD, and particularly the early years from 1929 to about 1935, I often see it through what I am sure are dark and distorting lenses. One of my visions tells me that it was a time of barrenness, frustration, boredom, darkness, and there is no doubt that at times during those years I did become a victim of the most appalling accidie. I can remember months on end during which I returned home of an evening so disspirited that I would sit down after dinner with a pack of cards and play patience for hours on end because I had no urge to do anything else. Sometimes it seems to me that whole years in my early twenties were mental black holes, devoid not merely of success (which most of them certainly lacked in literary terms) but also of activity and interest. But I am sure that my mind is playing tricks similar to those it plays me on nights which I think have been sleepless when in fact I have been dreaming my insomnia.

Yet there were certain aspects of that life which I found quite appalling even at the time, for the evidence is there in poems that expressed my malcontent with the routines in which my poverty had imprisoned me. After four years of it, when I was twenty-one, I wrote a "Sonnet in the Morning Train" which expressed not only the degree of my bitterness but also the sense of being trapped in a situation of frozen employment, from which there was no evident escape except into the destitution that afflicted so many people in that bleak year of 1933.

> Draped in an acrid blue miasmic fog,
> We, the small blokes who think ourselves big beer,
> Loll in half-sleep or through the window peer
> With rabid discontent on each grey mug,
> For we, though habitude has made us smug,
> Know how mad-futile is the way we steer,
> And each has sweated in the grasp of fear
> And known himself an aimless, boneless slug . . . .

There was certainly little redeeming about my employment, at least in the six early years when I remained frustratingly trapped at my first typing desk in the office that overlooked the whores' hotels of Westbourne Terrace. There were eight other men in the room I worked in, the youngest in his thirties, and the one experience they shared was that all had taken part in the Great War. Not all had been involved in serious fighting, for railway employees had been formed into separate transportation companies, and most of my fellow clerks had worked in military railways in Egypt and Palestine, where dysentery and syphilis seemed to be the main threats to their lives. I learnt a good many bawdy songs and tales from them, and they seemed much more familiar with brothels than with any other kind of firing line. Thus their heroics had a somewhat burlesque air, since they seemed to end in encounters with cosmopolitan Alexandrian whores or in attempts to circumvent the thieving propensities of the Wogs, as they called the Egyptians. One man only varied the pattern by telling the single tale that left a vivid image in my mind; that of dysentery patients being swayed over the desert, slung one on each side of camels, with their bloody shit leaving a trail over the sand.

I was astonished, particularly as I was falling under the influence of poets like Owen and Sassoon and of realistic war novels like *All Quiet on the Western Front* that were appearing at the end of the 1920s, at the joyous nostalgia with which most of these men recollected and even regretted the days of war. Later, in Malraux's *L'Espoir*, I encountered a character who remarked that revolutions are "the holidays of life," and for these men, particularly those who had avoided trench warfare, war also had been a holiday. They forgot family cares and the drudgery of normal work and lived, within the framework of military discipline, a life that was free from both morality and responsibility; a life that above all relieved them of the onerous need to choose and justify their choices. The life they now lived was drab and anxious in comparison, even though its perils were not so starkly physical.

Like all old and patrician corporations, the Great Western Railway, which predated the Victorian age having been founded in 1835, had developed a great rambling organization in whose cracks and crevices there was room for a host of incompetent scions of old railway families who were provided with virtual sinecures, and some of them, who worked in other parts of the great old office building, were amiable and cultured eccentrics glad enough to share their enthusiasms with an enquiring youth. Soon I learnt to lengthen errands so that I could talk to these mossy enthusiasts of the theatre ("Sir Martin Harvey *begged* me to go legitimate!"), these frustrated concert pianists, these self-published pastoral poets, and gain some glimpses of the arts whose marges at least they had haunted in the same seedy and nostalgic way as the Russian gentry had done before the Revolution.

And, since like tends to meet like, I would now and then encounter, wandering in the labyrinthine corridors, some secretive rebel and, looking over the grimed glass expanses of Brunel's great arched roof, and also looking over our shoulders, we would talk quietly about the philosophic and political heresies that were beginning to stir in my mind. Yet I made no friendship that continues among all the hundreds of people with whom I worked at one time or another on the Great Western Railway, and I can think of no individual I encountered in that setting who had any decisive influence on my life unless one can count those who urged me to get out quickly before my mind fossilized, a decision I had reached without urging.

Only three individuals remain from that world as solid people in my mind, remembered warmly. One was old Fred Saunders, the resident engineer with whom I spent the last half of my time on the Great Western, working in an old house on the verge of Paddington Station, just over the road from Orsett House where Alexander Herzen had spent most of his London years and Michael Bakunin had visited him. A massive bear of a man, rather like Robert Morley in looks, with an abrupt aggressive voice and sad eyes looking through his gold-rimmed pince-nez, Saunders came of one of the dynasties of railway engineers, connected originally with Isambard Kingdom Brunel, which over a century had acquired the pretensions of gentry without land. He always wore spats; he went to Scotland each year to fish salmon; he knew Surtees from end to end and could quote him at will; and when he appeared at the office on a Friday in knickerbockers, thick woollen stockings and a ragged tweed jacket, I knew the weekend would be long, with Saunders leaving early to go on an otter hunt. It must have been in 1935 that I joined him, and he helped to mitigate my last five or six years with the railway by showing how a determined individualist can humanize any system.

He and I were agreed in treating the people in the head office as natural enemies. He ignored strict routines so long as the necessary work was done. By unspoken agreement we closed our office on Saturdays and shaved an hour off weekdays by starting at 9:30 and closing at

4:30. Saunders never worried if he found me reading when there was nothing to do, since he knew I was quite willing to take work home with me in compensation when there was a rush. Indeed, he took an astonished interest in the books which by the mid-1930s I was reading and would engage me in good-humoured discussion on world events, opposing my leftist pacifism with a kind of late Palmerstonian Whiggism. When, occasionally, he had to admit that I had out-argued him, he would give a great hooting laugh and shout, "Damn me, the fellow's going to be Prime Minister!"

Like many blustering men, Saunders had his areas of cowardice. I am sure that if he had been attacked he would have given a good account of himself with the well-rolled umbrella he always carried, but he was a hypochondriac with a typically Victorian phobia about venereal disease, which he carried so far that he would stand on the sides of the john and then squat down so that his bum was well suspended above danger when he shat. He once told me of a friend who had suffered severe injuries from standing in this way on a cracked pan that had collapsed under him. It was a phobia I shared, like many young men in that age when syphilis was still an almost incurable bogy of a disease, but I have rarely encountered anyone who manifested his fear so extremely as old Fred Saunders.

For all his oddities, Saunders was a decent and in some ways admirable man. He was a good engineer with a sharp eye for roguish contractors. He defended his staff against the head office bureaucrats and went to a great deal of trouble to get me better pay. Eventually in 1940, when I left the railway to join Middleton Murry's community at Langham, he willingly wrote a letter for me to present to the tribunal for conscientious objectors, in which he celebrated the sincerity with which he thought I held the pacifist beliefs that he himself regarded as utterly absurd and wrongheaded.

Of the other two people I remember vividly from those railway days, Michael Greening fits more clearly into the pattern of my political history. But Lily G. belongs to the happier side of the life I entered at Paddington, the life of London as a vast and wonderful reservoir of cultural and human experience. For Lily, whom I met in 1932, not only shared with me the life of the office, but also accompanied me to concerts and plays, and dinners on the way, in the cheap Soho restaurants I was beginning to discover. She was a small girl with black eyes, highly-coloured cheeks, a mane of curly black hair, a sharp wit and a bookish mind shaped in the intellectual matrix of East End immigrant life. She was quite different from any of the girls I had known in Marlow or Market Drayton, in looks, mind and emotions, for she reacted with a quite unEnglish passion to music, especially romantic music, and one strange evening the long agony of Eugene O'Neill's *Mourning Becomes Electra* stimulated her to an excitement that verged on hysteria.

But, like many East End Jews, Lily combined intellectual and artistic passions with an intense loyalty to her very orthodox family. For this reason our friendship never went beyond an intense and stimulating companionship, and even that, after a year or so, came to an end when Lily found she could not stand up to the pressure of family disapproval for going out regularly with a goy. So we ceased our expeditions, but I was sufficiently attached to Lily and disturbed by the loss of her companionship to consider, as I now remember with some surprise, converting to a religion in whose tenets I could not possibly believe. I even sought out a Scottish engineer who had become a convert and enquired discreetly about the pain of circumcision; he was discouraging. Later Lily married a young Jew, and she felt happier risking his jealousy than defying her family, for after that we met often in discreet teashops for long conversations about the political events of the 1930s which so deeply troubled us both. Like many other relationships, ours was sundered by the war; I saw her last in 1942.

Throughout my childhood London had stood on the verge of my consciousness like a looming and rarely visited continent. I doubt if I had been there more than ten times in the whole of my life in Marlow until I went to work in Paddington. Once my father had taken me to see the Egyptian collection in the British Museum, and once to stare awestruck in the South Kensington Museum at the vast skeletons of the dinosaurs of which I had been reading with an obsessive fascination in Conan Doyle's *The Lost World*. But I had never entered a single art gallery or seen a play in a London theatre or been to a concert there. And I had never walked at leisure in the cosmopolitan streets of a real city.

I was certainly ready by 1929 for what London had to offer me. The thirst for new knowledge and for artistic experience that had been developing in me for the last two or three years made me responsive and eager. But my becoming a devoted Londoner and remaining so for the next twenty years, was linked to the way the childhood pattern of my life shifted and broke apart. Going to work at Paddington not only meant an end to my Marlow schooldays; it also deprived me of the long vegetative holidays in which I had lived my Salopian life.

In the autumn of 1929 I was able to get a week or so of vacation that allowed me to go to Market Drayton. Already I found that London was making my beloved ancestral town seem provincial; I no longer was sure that I wanted to live out my life there. The next time I went was for the funeral of my grandfather. Sam Woodcock had become increasingly melancholic since my grandmother's death; then he fell sick with pernicious anaemia, still virtually an incurable sickness, and in the spring of 1930 died very quickly.

By this time I had come to resent him bitterly. I had found what a grasping employer he had always been. I blamed him for forcing me into an employment I hated by putting impossible conditions on helping me go to college. I felt aggrieved by the meanness with which he doled out money to my mother. I was in the full flow of reaction from childhood adoration and I was inclined to blame my grandfather for all my miseries. I even went to the extent of composing an elaborate rhymed curse; I destroyed it soon afterwards.

My conversion to social revolt was even a part of this process, for it came instantaneously one evening when I sat alone in a railway carriage coming home on an evening early in 1930, stewing over my bitterness towards my grandfather and his kind, and reading a volume of William Morris's socialist writings. Suddenly, with a sense of great illumination, I knew I was on the side of Morris and all who thought with him, and against my grandfather and all who acted like him. With this revelation came a sense of great relief; I was replacing my hatred of a person with my hatred of a class and its way of life; I was sinking my personal grievance in the great pool of wrong done to all the oppressed and the unfortunate. I suppose in all such conversions there is a touch of intellectual self-seeking. Realising that others share one's predicament, it seems that things may be more easily changed if one agrees with them. At first sight the process seems less noble than the conversion of the privileged to the cause of the oppressed, as in the case of the narodniki noblemen who went to the people in Russia or of Chinese patricians like Chou En-lai who deserted their own class for the sake of the workers. Yet even Kropotkin, after all, resented his father, and rebellions do not always come about through economic deprivation.

I did not feel, in my resentful mood, the kind of grief over my grandfather's death I would have done as a child. I was even contemptuous when one of his "men," Joe the drum-beating Salvationist, took me aside and said: "George, your grandfather was an angel sent from heaven!" How, I thought, could a man so exploited over so many years be in the end so servile? But perhaps he was not servile. Perhaps he had remained aware of a side of Sam Woodcock's character that I had become incapable of perceiving; perhaps the man I had loved in childhood was as real as the man I had come to despise by the day he died. I no longer find judgment so easy as I did then.

I CERTAINLY REALIZED, that day we took my grandfather in procession through the town, that with him I was burying my boyhood. My Uncle Harold inherited Runnymede and the coal business and the worthless Tsarist stocks and the worthwhile investments. A couple of thousand pounds was left in a trust, the income to go to my mother and the principal to me when she died and, unhappy as I was to accept this pittance, it did shift our financial situation a little upwards from deep poverty. But once my Aunt Ethel was in possession of Runnymede there was no question, given the hostility between her and my mother, of going there any more for our holidays. The few times I returned it was to stay either with "Aunt" Mary, the faithful retainer who had been left a little cottage in my grandfather's will, or with the Godwins. The long leisurely periods of rural life that had made Market Drayton an alternative home were ended, and more and more I drew my mental sustenance from other places, from London and also from Wales.

About 1930 my Uncle Daffyd Jenkins died of cancer, leaving a vast inheritance of theological texts that in an age of dwindling faith had to be sold by the pound. My Aunt Annie and my mother began to seek each other's company as a solace for the widowhood they shared. My aunt had a largish house at Bridgend, a Glamorgan country town not far from Cardiff, and since we had no money for seaside holidays, it was there — on my railway passes — that my mother and I now went for the five days at Easter and Christmas, and the two weeks that in those days was the customary annual vacation. We also went, very occasionally, to my mother's other sister at Colwyn Bay in North Wales.

These interludes were important to me for several reasons. They helped to break my obsession with Shropshire as a rural Eden. They brought me to close quarters with the Welsh side of my inheritance, of which up to now I had been only slightly aware. And they provided me with a number of experiences that entered quite deeply into my intellectual and literary development.

For someone who had never been abroad, Wales was like the first taste of a foreign country. There was the language, which one heard more in the mining valleys and in the villages of Snowdonia than in the towns. But even in the towns there was the lilting accent and the odd twists that the Welsh would give to English sentences, twists like "There's lovely it is!" which I always felt a lyrical improvement on "It's lovely!" There was the still small but even then stubborn manifestation of national pride; people would begin to walk out of a cinema when "God Save the King" was played, but would halt and stand when "Land of My Fathers" followed it. There were odd foods and customs, like the green lava-bread made of seaweed sold in the markets and the mask called the Mari Lwyd, of a horse's skull with a straw cape that was paraded at certain seasons. And there were the mountains.

Snowdon, a dwarf to peaks I have since seen, was vast and awe-striking to me, whose highest hill had previously been the Wrekin, barely a quarter as high. I resolutely tramped up Snowdon, and still remember the experience vividly. It was a glorious day, hot for the climb with a cool breeze at the top. Once I got there, I felt the strange sense — recollected so sharply because it was the first such experience — of commanding the world as I looked down from the little patch of rocky soil that formed the peak. I gazed over the grey rocky ridges and the August-brown slopes and the jade green lakes and the great black shadows in the dry hollows, and I had the sense that I was looking over a primaeval world that nothing man could do would ever spoil. Far off I could see the blue streak of the Menai Strait and Anglesea narrowing flatly into the distance.

I have since been on nobler mountains in the Alps and the Rockies, and have seen from the sky far wider scapes in the Andes and the Himalayas and the mountains of Greenland, but never since have I experienced quite the intensity of pleasure I knew when I had reached the top of Snowdon, a pleasure that makes me even remember with a special zest the taste of the strong beer I drank from a pint pewter tankard when I had scrambled down over the shale slopes to the Gorfywysfa Hotel in the pass below. My resolution one day to live among mountains, as I now do, was born on that day on Snowdon fifty years ago.

In Wales I was constantly aware, as I had never been in England, of the historic conflict of races that was as much a part of the British present as it had been of the past. This, after all, was the place where

English imperialism began, and it was still evident in the great and splendid Plantagenet castles I visited in the north of the principality, and also in the Norman buildings I found scattered in the Glamorgan countryside around Bridgend. A ruined castle, called Newcastle because it dated from only around 1250 A.D. overlooked the north end of the town. In spring I liked to walk out with Anne Williams, the wife of the young schoolteacher who lived across the road from my aunt, through lanes whose banks were thickly clotted with primroses and cowslips, to Ewenny Priory about two miles away, where there was a remarkably-preserved Norman church, dating from about 1100 A.D., with semi-circular dogtoothed arches and the massive columns that reflect the dour strength of the Normans. And sometimes we would walk down towards the sea, to the thatched village of Merthyrmawr, where the sea had piled the sand in high hilly dunes on whose crests stood old Norman watchtowers.

In those days the Glamorgan seacoast between the little port of Barry and the steel-making centre of Port Talbot was little inhabited except for the small and pleasant resort of Porthcawl. It was very varied in its beauty, with some fine open beaches and cliffs rising up to downland. I would often have tea in cottages overlooking the Bristol Channel which served, as a local speciality, the most succulent of blackcurrant tarts. But the dunes at Merthyrmawr, pink with great drifts of burnet rose in the summer and inhabited by many rabbits, were a place of special magic, which I tried often to catch in verse, as an artist will catch a land-scape in watercolour. Eventually I succeeded in "Merthyrmawr," which was the first poem of mine to appear in the United States, when Dwight Macdonald published it in the *Partisan Review* in 1940.

Behind Bridgend lay the mining hinterland and the two valleys of the Rhondda, Rhondda Mawr and Rhondda Vach. Here there were no Norman ruins as one advanced into the bleak bare hills through the mining towns that probed like narrow snakes of darkness up the valley floors. The hybrid, Anglicized culture of Bridgend and Cardiff, where few people continued to speak Welsh, gave way to a different kind of world. It was not traditionally Welsh in the way the pastoral hill villages of Merioneth and Brecon had remained. An occupational pattern had been imposed which made the miners and their villages seem at first sight very much like their counterparts which I remembered from a visit in boyhood to D. H. Lawrence's Nottinghamshire mining country. Chapel religion and Labour politics ran strongly in such areas, and there was a kind of community of peril among the miners everywhere that seemed to distinguish them from other workers and give them a special solidarity.

In Wales that feeling of community sometimes expressed itself in dramatic ways. One day I was walking up one of the rare stretches of road in the Rhondda where there were no houses, and heard, echoing in the hills, the sound of many voices singing. Round a bluff before me came a marching procession. It was a miner's funeral. They came on in solid ranks, chunky men with wide shoulders and coal dust bitten blue into their skin, dressed in blue serge best suits with white silk mufflers around their necks and cloth caps on their heads. Their union and fraternal society banners flapped in the wind and a single red flag glowed among them. They sang in the great rolling surges of sound that come when Welshmen sing together, and lifted the coffin from one set of shoulders to another without pausing as they marched. The hymns they sang were Welsh, for however much in material ways these valleys may resemble other mining regions, in spirit they were far more doggedly Welsh than coastal Wales.

One never heard anything but Welsh spoken among themselves by the people in the grim grey stone houses, and when they went down into towns like Bridgend and Cardiff they spoke a singsong English that was a dialect of its own, since it was often a literal rendering of Welsh forms. Bridgend people sneered at the *daios*, as they called them, but they also feared them, for the *daios* were violent when drunk and for-midable opponents in the rugby games to which the friends I made would sometimes take me. For me the most exciting moment on such occasions would come when the crowd sang "Guide me O Thou Great Redeemer" in Welsh to the formidable local tune known as "Cwm Rhondda"; I would feel all my latent Welshness rising up and know with emotion that this too was my home.

THUS, ROUND ABOUT 1930 the polar structure of my life changed. Marlow and Market Drayton were replaced by Wales and London. Marlow became more and more the place where I slept and spent my leisure hours trying to write, or playing patience or pub crawling with old schoolfellows when I was unable to write. But London was the place where I now found my Bread of Heaven, and for years I ran from end to end of the city seeking everything it had to offer.

I was so anxious to gather every scrap of experience that every morning I would take a bit of bread and cheese from home to eat at my desk so that I could spend my lunch hours roving the streets and parks. In this way I explored a great section of the city. My walking area stretched south through Bayswater and over Hyde Park and Kensington Gardens into South Kensington, west into Notting Hill and Holland Park and the purlieus of Kensington Church Street, east through Marylebone as far as Great Portland Street, and north through Paddington to the Regent's Canal and the verges of Kilburn. Within a couple of years I knew every street and lane and square in that area, had looked into the window of almost every shop and put my nose through the door of almost every pub. And in this way I rubbed shoulders with a good variety of lifestyles.

Of course, London in the 1930s was not the cosmopolitan city it became when the collapse of the Empire brought in so many people from outside the native culture. Indians and West Indians and Africans did live there, particularly in Bloomsbury near the university, but they were not numerous enough to have taken over any area, and apart from Whitechapel with its lingering flavour of Eastern Europe and the dwindling Chinese presence in Limehouse, the only area with a pronouncedly foreign flavour was Latinized Soho and its outlying colony north of Oxford Street around Charlotte and Percy streets. But there were nevertheless distinctive local London cultures. I learnt to enjoy them all, eating in the stewed eel shops and drinking rough cider among costermongers in the Edgware Road, bargaining at the stalls in Portobello Road where there were still good things to be picked up, drinking India Pale Ale in the saloon bars frequented by retired sahibs in discreet corners of Bayswater, and taking tea in the arty little places run by impoverished ladies in Kensington.

London in the 1930s was a paradise for the poor aspirant scholar and aesthete. Books were incredibly cheap by present-day standards. Series like Everyman and the World Classics cost two shillings a volume and the Reader's Library a shilling, while by the middle of the decade the first Penguins were appearing at sixpence each and Victor Gollancz was bringing out his cheap orange-covered Left Books. The secondhand bookshops were inexpensive for everything except rarities, and on the stalls in Farringdon Road one could make some extraordinary finds for a few pence. Very soon I was filling our cottage with books and building myself shelves to hold them.

Invaluable at this time were the periodicals that rapidly opened my perspectives on books, but also on the arts and on modern thinking in general. *The Listener* was perhaps the most helpful of all, not merely for its reprinted radio talks on so many unfamiliar subjects, but even more for the literary section so superbly run by Joe Ackerley, where I first encountered the younger poets of the 1930s, from Auden and Spender onward, and for the regular art reviews by Herbert Read. Even more important in a personal way, since it started me off on my literary career, was the *New English Weekly*, which A. R. Orage began to edit in 1932 and which I read from the beginning.

Through such periodicals I quickly became aware of the whole range of contemporary literature, British, European and American. Woolf and Huxley, Lawrence and Kafka, took the place of Wells and Bennett as the writers I habitually read. At eighteen I was excited by J. C. Squire's Georgian-oriented anthologies of modern poetry, but by twenty I was reading Eliot and Pound with difficulty but persistence.

Yet some of the books that most profoundly influenced me were works which are now virtually and perhaps deservedly forgotten. My Christian faith was already wavering when at eighteen I read Ernst Haeckel's *The Riddle of the Universe*, that monumental work of nineteenth-century scientism rather than science. Haeckel's hammering arguments brought my remnants of orthodox faith tumbling to the ground, and left me an agnostic. I have never tackled Haeckel again but I am sure, from extracts from *The Riddle* which have more recently caught my eye, that I would no longer be bowled over by such crude reasoning. But I was ready for the book then, it did its work, and it passed out of my life and my mind. Another almost forgotten book, Winwood Reade's pioneer world history, *The Martyrdom of Man*, completed Haeckel's task so far as I was concerned by convincing me of the role that organized religions have played in the destruction of human freedom.

Often in the evenings after work, and almost every Saturday afternoon, I would stay to extend my London wanderings. Particularly, I spent long periods in the great museums, almost obsessively studying the artifacts a great empire had attracted to its capital. I assiduously explored the great galleries of the Victoria and Albert Museum to learn the many ways in which art could enter human lives. Even before I was aware of the influence primitive art was then having on modern artists I was haunting the ethnographic galleries of the British Museum, fascinated by the African and Melanesian wood carvings, by the pre-Columbian sculptures, and by those most splendid of all the treasures that the British looted, the great bronzes of Benin; I sensed their power without needing to be instructed in it. And, having at seventeen gone through my period of adoring the acknowledged Great Masters in the National Gallery, I now began to walk down the Thames Embankment to the Tate Gallery to see the modern art about which I had read in the books of Clive Bell and the articles of Herbert Read.

Even the theatre and the concert halls in those days were within the reach of an impoverished clerk. For sixpence one could go to the opera at Sadler's Wells and for a mere fivepence one could see the great actors and actresses of the day, Laughton and Olivier and Redgrave among them, performing Shakespeare and Congreve and Chekhov at the Old Vic. It was the last great decade of Russian Ballet, when the de Basil company came year after year to Covent Garden, and even there it cost only two shillings to sit among the gods. And then there were the concerts: the Promenades at Queen's Hall, which also cost two shillings, the inexpensive London Museum concerts, and the Saturday afternoon recitals at the Victoria and Albert Museum where one heard some of the best musicians: soloists and quartets and sometimes chamber orchestras, for a few pence. Even on twenty-five shillings a week I could manage to go to a performance of some kind at least once a fortnight, and it did not take me long to give myself a basic introduction to the performing arts.

Of all those arts, the most magical and the most satisfying seemed to me the ballet, which does not mean that I was not entranced and delighted by the others. But music was, and has remained for me, an art as esoteric as higher mathematics. I can listen enrapt, and there are a few composers, notably Mozart and Handel and Vivaldi, whose music arouses in me such an intensity of feeling that I know if I had my life again I would choose to be a musician. But, I suffer from an incapacity to understand music in a technical sense similar to my incapacity to follow mathematics when it goes beyond useful arithmetic. Indeed, when I was twenty I became so overwhelmed by the music I heard that I seriously considered learning the violin, just as at the same time I did pencil drawings and watercolours and gouaches in the hope that this would make me more receptive to the visual arts. I may have profited from my slight painterly efforts, since I learnt something about the relationship between colour and form, but my ambition to become a musician, even an amateur musician, got nowhere. I remain a listener pure and simple, with a nagging feeling that I would sooner have been Mozart than Shakespeare or even Homer.

My feelings towards the theatre and the opera were and remain ambivalent. I enjoyed the theatrical ambiance, in which I always found the audience as interesting in its own way (a kind of orchestration of individualities) as the performance. But I have always had a very active mind's eye, and have tended to visualize plays as I read them, giving the characters appearances and voices that seemed to me fitting to their natures and seeing what went on in a perspective much wider than that of an actual stage. I often found it hard to reconcile my interpretation and actors' interpretations of the same characters.

Many years later, when I came to write plays for radio, I would encounter the same difficulty in another direction, for rarely, unless I had written a role with a specific actor in mind, has the performance of the play borne much resemblance to the play that has taken shape in my imagination.

Perhaps this is why I have always preferred to see plays based on wit rather than passion, since the variation of interpretation where an intellectual element is involved is always much less than when an irrational — a romantic or passionate — element dominates the play. For this reason, while I preferred to read plays by Shakespeare and Marlowe and Webster and Chekhov, it was always the sharp play of wit in comedy by Shaw and Wilde and Congreve I found myself most enjoying on the stage; wit is so much less easily betrayed than emotion.

I also found opera a difficult genre to accept. It was the verbal element in opera that disturbed me, the constant attempt to attach the plotless form, in all music its excellent absurdity, to a plot that was usually strongly romantic and often, as in some of Verdi's and Puccini's operas, had an overtone of heroic moralism. Here again I found Mozart and Rossini, whose plots were largely inconsequential (their librettists contrived to deprive even Beaumarchais of most of his political significance) more appealing than any of their successors. Wagner I found repellent from the first, and I have not changed my mind.

But ballet seemed to me quite another matter, for here, sometimes in narrative, sometimes in lyric, sometimes in comic and sometimes in elegiac terms, is the non-verbal counterpart of poetry. What is important in ballet is not the story or even the emotion that might be evoked by the sequence of action; it is the shape the body makes of it, the image it transmits to the eye, in just the same way as the heart of poetry, I believe, is the transmission of images to the mind's eye. The choreographer's task is to give a language in which the images can be transmitted, and thus it is strictly analogous to the poet's task.

Of course, I was seeing ballet at one of its high points, for the Ballets Russes in the 1930s still retained not only many of the dancers but also much of the panache and spirit of Diaghilev's original company. Massine was at the height of his powers during those years, and his performances in such roles as the miller in *The Three-Cornered Hat* and as Petrouchka would send a current of excitement that galvanized even English audiences into veritable paroxysms of enthusiasm. I remember also Eglevsky's superbly effortless dancing in *Spectre de la Rose*, Youskevich in *Swan Lake*, and Baronova, Ryabushinska and above all Danilova in a multitude of witty and romantic feminine roles.

Yet even then there were those who declared that the Russian Ballet was already in decline. I remember a long conversation with a melancholy businessman named Klein who bore a marked resemblance to Marcel Proust and used sometimes to talk to me when we went home on the 5:45 train. He was brother-in-law to the pianist Harriet Cohen, and once, at a concert at the London Museum to which we went together, he introduced me to Egon Petri, the Dutch pianist with great butcher's hands who was highly-considered by musicians between the wars. The next time we met, Klein remarked that he thought Petri was the best pianist playing in the 1930s. Then he looked at me with his sad El Greco eyes, and said, "Ah, but Petri is only the shadow of Busoni." And then, the talk turning to ballet, he agreed with me about Massine's excellence, but once again moodily remembering the past he added, "Ah, but you never saw Nijinski! Every other dancer is only his shadow." I was left with the sense of living in a degenerate age, and yet Massine, even as the shadow of Nijinsky, was the substantial man whose dancing seemed, and still seems in memory, the greatest I had seen.

Almost as important to my self-education at this time as the performances themselves was the opportunity they gave to break out of my solitude and talk to young people who were going through a similar process of awakening. Usually I would stand in a queue for an hour or more and often I would strike up a conversation with my neighbour or neighbours. There were enthusiasms to be shared, and often my new acquaintances would be more knowledgeable in ballet or the theatre than I. We would sit together on the hard benches up in the gods, discussing the performance in the intervals, shout "Bravo!" in thundering chorus during the performances, and bellow the names of our favourite dancers at the end to bring them back again and again for their bows. At the end we would go off to some cheap little Italian restaurant to eat sour spaghetti for a few pence and widen our conversation into other regions of interest, which usually meant the books we had read and the ideas they generated.

But I remember with a certain wonder how rarely such encounters at that time ever continued beyond the immediate occasion. Yet this impermanence of contact, this failure of relationships to develop and discussions to continue, was perhaps the principal reason why the kind of autodidactic effort in which we were all involved fell short of an organized programme of higher education. We read fiercely, we sought any manifestations of the arts that might widen our range of experience and understanding, we even invented and imposed disciplines of study upon ourselves, yet we found it hard to break out of the isolation of our individual enterprises and create a continuity that might offer us the advantages of continuous discussion that are part of any collegiate process. And this meant that it took us all the longer to turn our efforts to some productive end.

The nearest substitute I had for a college in those days was the Train to London, which each day in the morning and returning in the evening brought together roughly the same mixture of people. When I first began these daily journeys I was overwhelmed by shyness and found it almost impossible to strike up a conversation with the strangers with whom I was surrounded. But there were a few old schoolfellows among them, some commuting to the University of London or to the Royal College of Music, some to offices in the city, (Rubberlegs was already working with the BBC), and through them I began to make further acquaintances. In the end, I became adept at the remark about a book an interesting-looking person might be reading, or an item of news in the *Evening Standard*, or something strange seen through the window, that would break the English ice and start a conversation, which would lead to an acquaintance and sometimes a friendship. For the Train, unlike the Office, offered the variety of human types among whom it was possible to find affinities. I mingled with groups of younger people, men and women (including, grown up, some of the girls I had wandered to Bisham School with as a child). Sexual vitality held in tension, as it usually was in that unliberated period, created a field of challenge that stimulated wit and conversation.

There were also older men, like Klein, and other dilettantes, who were ready to talk about their own experiences in the arts and sometimes in politics; they included a few elderly and well-read Fabians, and one bombastic old man whose boasts of having been associated with William Morris in the Socialist League I later found to be completely justified. He was perhaps the only person in that small army of commuters who had been involved with the famous personalities of those interlocking worlds of literature and radicalism to which I increasingly felt I belonged. I pumped him for all the tales he had to tell of Morris and Hyndman and Shaw and Annie Besant and the lesser figures of English socialism in that early romantic phase. Brooks was also the first person who talked to me about anarchism as a doctrine which, while he did not share it, he thought must be considered seriously. Somewhere on the edge of the circle of ghosts that he evoked, hovered the benign, bearded figure of Kropotkin, whom he had met through Sergei Stepniak. In 1934, I think, Brooks lent me *The Memoirs of a Revolutionist*, the first anarchist book I ever read. It did not immediately convert me, but it planted a seed that survived, for, apart from anything he taught, Kropotkin's autobiography was a superb narrative, and I found his personality attractive and memorable, and understood why Wilde, whose *De Profundis* I was reading at the same time, had so admired him.

THIS CHAPTER BEGAN with an evocation of darkness, of a period that in memory sometimes seems to me like a great oubliette of negation and despair. Let it end with an evocation of light, for I also remember this, as a period of perceptions so intense that I could not hope to find a way of recording them.

A decade ago, in my book on Aldous Huxley, *Dawn and the Darkest Hour*, I wrote of these experiences when I was discussing *The Doors of Perception*. I remarked that what Huxley perceived under mescalin was:

> a transfiguration of the world outside, so that everything seemed to shine with the "Inner Light" of its own "Suchness," and through these miraculously intensified colours, these forms preternaturally significant of themselves, he gained a joyful sense of "the glory and wonder of pure existence."

I remarked that, if this were all Huxley had seen, others had been vouchsafed something very similar without the stimulation of drugs.

For a long period during my late adolescence and even into my early twenties I had the ability, almost at will, to see landscapes, buildings and natural objects with the kind of transfiguring irradiation which Huxley's description would exactly fit . . . .

Such experiences took place either when I was alone or when I had abstracted myself mentally from the company I was in. Sometimes they occurred when I was walking in the country, but more frequently when I was travelling in a train or a bus, so that the scape passed fairly quickly before my eyes, changing constantly like a scene in film. The occasions I most clearly remember took place in late summer afternoons, when the train had largely emptied at Maidenhead, its first important commuter stop, and I had a compartment almost or completely to myself as the train went on to the little branch line through little hills and orchards and chalky fields towards Cookham and Bourne End. All at once, in rather the same way as a rainbow forms, the colours of flowers, of grass, of trees, of buildings and of people's clothes would take on a preternatural vividness, even more intense than that of Arctic or Alpine flowers, for it seemed to come from a fire within. I would enter a state of great inner excitement, but at the same time be baffled by the impossibility of communicating to anyone else what I had seen; I knew these were my own privileged moments. There was never a sense that what I saw had any meaning beyond itself; as Huxley put it, I seemed to be perceiving the "Inner Light" of objects, to be seeing a "Suchness" that belonged to them only, images that were themselves in all their intensity and could not be translated. Undoubtedly my experience was visionary, since I was seeing something that was not there to many other eyes, or to my eyes at other times, but the visions were of things as they are and their inner nature, not of anything out of nature, like Blake's angels.

At first these manifestations were involuntary. Later I found that, when I was alone, I could voluntarily induce such visions merely by willing myself to see the *real* colours, the *real* light of the scene before me, and this continued until late in my twenties. Afterwards the power faded away, but still at times I would experience them involuntarily and unpredictably, particularly at times of emotional tension or physical exhaustion. For example, when I was recovering from an almost fatal heart attack in my mid-fifties, I experienced such perceptions frequently for several weeks after emerging from hospital, and it was as if I were

seeing the world anew, as indeed it seemed when I first had such perceptions in my late teens.

So I often see this period in my life as something like a painting by
Caravaggio, with strong highlights breaking the general darkness, and I
cannot dissociate my adventures in visual perception (which came at the
same time as I was developing a sense of form in painting and the other
arts) from the fact that they reached their height just about the time
when, as a poet, I began to develop a style of my own. For the first
poems I can regard as my own were strongly dominated by visual
images, and this did not come merely from the fact that now I was
reading Pound and the other Imagists. It came from my own visionary
experience, and it left a permanent mark on my writing, and especially
my verse, for I have never since been able to accept poetry that lacks a
strong visual component.

IX

LIVING IN THE THIRTIES

THROUGH THE DARK DAYS and the brilliant, I had been writing, for long periods keeping a daily journal which I foolishly destroyed, angry at its immaturities, and composing poems, so that, even after I had destroyed many, a thick folder of manuscripts still survives. I wrote because I must. Julian Symons, who knew me only a little later, once applied to me Theodore Roethke's line, "I learn by going where I have to go." And I think it certainly defines my state of mind, for I had little encouragement except an inner imperative. Editors rejected my poems; my relatives were unsympathetic, and my acquaintances did not share my passion and did not understand it, for their ambitions were quite different. For a long time Lance Godwin remained the only friend I could confide in and I continued to write to him, long letters that are the only real documentation of my state of mind at that time.

I read widely all through the Thirties, and for years my poetry was deeply affected by this. I discovered the decadent poets of the Nineties, and absorbed their mood without sharing their experiences. It was then that I first read Oscar Wilde, being first attracted by his riper and more decadent prose, and he is perhaps the one writer of that period who has remained important to me, for his profound critical insights rather than for anything original he created except perhaps *The Importance of Being Earnest* and *The Ballad of Reading Gaol*. But it was Dowson rather than Wilde whom I then imitated as a poet.

Then I fled to the country with the Georgians; even then I felt that Wilfred Owen, whom I could not imitate, and Edward Thomas, whom I could, were the best of them, and Edward Thomas has remained a source of inspiration. I paid homage to the Dark Gods with D. H.

[173]

Lawrence, falling particularly under the spell of his *Birds, Beasts and Flowers*. But I think it was my discovery, at roughly the same time (1932-3), of Ezra Pound and the Imagists that really brought me in tune with my time and at last liberated my own poetic voice.

In an article I wrote about a decade ago ("Poetry Magazines of the Thirties: A Personal Note," *Tamarack* 60), I remarked that it was through A. R. Orage that, "I was getting round to Eliot and especially to Pound." Orage in fact was the first editor to publish any of my poems. He ran a poetry section in the *New English Weekly* which he called "Pastiche," and it was indeed a mingling of poetry of various styles and schools in which I immediately recognized an opportunity. Only a few weeks after the magazine started in 1932 I picked up a copy of it in a Cardiff bookshop and immediately sent off three poems. There came back a note of typically Orageian brevity:

Dear Sir,

I would certainly publish the "Nocturne" and "Stephanie"; but perhaps you are not aware that we cannot pay for contributions.

Yrs,

A. R. Orage.

Whether or not, as I heard later, Orage paid some contributors and not others, I was too pleased with his acceptance to expect money, and I immediately agreed; in due course the poems appeared. They were pieces of good poetic craftsmanship, but impeccably traditional, almost entirely derivative, though "Nocturne," which I think the better of the two, in its sharp visuality anticipated one of the more important elements in my later work. Since I have not included it in any of my collections of verse, it seems worth reproducing as an example of the kind of poetry I was still writing when I first achieved publication:

'Tis even, day's dark requiem.
The grey gnats dance a rigadoon,
And Venus, like a pendant gem,
Hangs from the girdle of the moon.
A screaming heron homeward flaps,
Gaunt, like some demon drawn by Blake;
A laggard swallow swoops, and laps
The pallid waters of the lake.
Yon row of poplars blacklimned stands,
Screening the sun's last hectic light,

And lovers, with enclasped hands,
Worship the mystery of night.

In publishing these poems, Orage must have had an idea that I could do something different, for in the desultory correspondence that followed he encouraged me to study Eliot and especially Pound, more deeply than I had yet done. It was good advice, for it forced me to consider the ways in which I could make my observations and experiences speak directly. But it led me into a long period of rather clumsy and tentative experimentation, picking up and dropping influences: Yeats and Eliot, Pound and Edwin Muir, eventually Spender and Auden (a great though much resisted influence) and a few odd and now largely forgotten people like that modestly excellent poet, A. S. J. Tessimond.

By the end of 1932, I also started work on a novel, the first of three that I have over the years written and destroyed, largely, I think, because in my twenties and thirties I was developing so quickly that I would find I had outgrown a long piece of work by the time I had completed it. But in the process, when I threw away my third novel in 1951, I had learnt enough about the goals and pitfalls of fiction writing to make me a perceptive critic of novels. I knew by then where to look for the flaws, and where to find the triumphant solution of creative problems.

Orage's acceptance of those two poems in 1932 was followed by five years of failure and frustration, for he took no more of my pieces and died in 1934, and no other editor accepted anything I wrote until 1937. I doubt if this could have happened to me if I had been starting in the 1960s or 1970s, for in Canada certainly and doubtless in many other countries, a poet of even slight talent has in recent years been able to get his works in print with little difficulty. In England during the early 1930s there were very few magazines that published verse, though the situation improved with a small burgeoning of little magazines as the decade progressed. Even then the competition was severe and, as Orwell pointed out with some bitterness, it was harder to get published if one did not happen to belong to the Oxbridge homosexual sodality.

And so I drifted through the resentful years, destroying most of the poems I wrote, though I preserved a few, and later included them in collections. These best pieces of the mid-Thirties, though they derived much from Imagist doctrine, resulted from clear observation and spoke directly in a language that was becoming increasingly my own. "Sawmill," written about 1934, was typical.

No tenor droning of the circular saw,
snort of donkey engine,
purr of belt over slotted wheels,
clatter of new planks stacked,
crunch of tires on the gravel,
no hoarse voices of men . . . .
But black buildings stacked against the sky,
the dereliction of a rusting engine,
a tramp's fire winking behind abandoned cordwood . . . .

"Sawmill" was eventually published in 1937 in a radical magazine, *The Socialist Clarion*, which appeared briefly in High Wycombe, a furniture manufacturing town about five miles over the hills from Marlow. This was appropriate enough, for, with its evocation of idled industry, "Sawmill" was a Depression poem as well as an Imagist poem, and it showed how I, like so many of my contemporaries, was finding my voice through finding the voice of my times.

THE ONE COMPENSATION FOR MY FAILURE to be published was the discovery of at least one person involved in the London literary world who recognized that I was a poet worth encouraging. This was the famous Charles Lahr. One day in the summer of 1935 I turned into Red Lion Street, a narrow thoroughfare running between Holborn and Theobold's Road, lined with low and shabby buildings harbouring little dairies and tobacco shops and a couple of taverns mostly patronized by draymen and taxi-drivers. I immediately liked the sooty Dickensian feeling of the street, plebeian and a little raffish, but not quite squalid.

As I sauntered up Red Lion Street towards Theobold's Road, I noticed an *Evening Standard* poster beside the doorway to No. 68, the Blue Moon Bookshop. In bold red letters the poster announced: *Professor Joad's Daughter Elopes with the Pope!* It caught the eye and puzzled the fancy, and I immediately walked over, to find it had been cleverly fabricated by a fragment of one poster having been pasted over another.

This was my introduction to Charles Lahr and the irreverent wit he practiced constantly and in many different ways, usually playing — in sallies verbal or visual — on the bizarre truths that emerge from apparently incongruous juxtaposition. Charles invented such jests for his own delight, but his celebrated posters also served to attract the customers he preferred, the kind who made his bookshop one of the recognized gathering places of writers during the years between the Great Wars.

Charles Lahr had been born in the Rhineland, had become an anarchist in his youth and had fled Germany in 1905. He was interned during World War I, but afterwards contrived to stay in England. Because of his contempt for the state, he refused to be naturalized, so that in World War II he would be interned again, in spite of his long record of opposition to Nazism and to German militarism in general. He was a man of the left, but he contrived always to be his own man, undominated by the parties and their orthodoxies.

There was an almost Tartar look to Charles, with his flattish nose, his wispy chin beard, his quizzical eyes. His feet were always, summer or winter, bare in sandals; one of the astonishing sights of a London January was Charles Lahr riding his bicycle all the way from his North London home in Muswell Hill with his feet literally blue from the sharp air and no greater apparent concession made to the season than a scarf around his neck. He was one of the hardiest men I have known, but his voice was soft and quiet, the voice of an habitual ironist.

I was much interested, on that first visit, in the relics of Charles Lahr's publishing days, the piles of pamphlets by Twenties celebrities in the series he called Blue Moon Books, and of issues of the short-lived quarterly, *New Coterie*, which he brought out in the same decade. D. H. Lawrence (whom Lahr helped in distributing *Pansies*) contributed to it, and so did Aldous Huxley and other writers who became Charles's close friends, including H. E. Bates, T. F. Powys and Rhys Davies. The Blue Moon Books became for me a gateway into the world of letters, with Charles as its benign and amused gatekeeper.

I bought a set of the *New Coterie*. A week later I returned and bought some of the Blue Moon pamphlets. A week after that I asked Charles whether there was a chance that the Blue Moon Press might consider my first collection of poems, which I had put together in the spring of 1935 and sent round unsuccessfully to three or four commercial publishers. He said softly, and with a look of embarrassment, that he was publishing no more books. His ventures in the Twenties had been too dramatically unprofitable, and the Thirties was an even less promising time. But why didn't I bring my poems in? He'd be glad to read them; perhaps he could help.

I brought the poems, and Charles liked them well enough to appoint himself a kind of impresario. He got a literary agent who came to the shop interested enough to meet me. He tried to persuade the *Left Review* to publish some of them. Neither effort led to anything, and in the end I was glad, for there was a great deal in that first collection which I myself threw out two or three years afterwards. However, Charles had obviously seen something in the poems, for he kept trying to help me. Two years after I started going to his shop, in 1937, he asked if I would like to let him see a recent poem, since each year he printed a fine edition of a work by a young poet as a gesture to his lost publishing past. I wrote a special poem, "Solstice," and Charles brought it out and gave it to many of his customers.

By the end of 1938, when my work had at last begun to appear in verse magazines, he offered to publish a small group of poems as a brochure. We agreed on a selection that appeared as *Six Poems*, my first collection. Finally, in 1939, Charles published my *Ballad of an Orphan Hand* as a Blue Moon poem. I was beginning to develop a surer poetic voice, and of the eight poems which Charles first published from the Blue Moon Press, I find six still interesting enough to include in the collected poems I have just put together.

As important as the tangible help in getting published was the introduction Charles and his shop provided to a section of that London literary world which, in my provincial isolation, had been names and little more. I had already drifted into some of the famous literary pubs, like the Fitzroy, but I recognized nobody and the only acquaintances I had made were the celebrated and bedraggled Bohemian trollops like Nina Hamnett, the drunken painter who wrote *Laughing Torso*; Betty May, the former model who wrote *Tiger Woman*; and Sylvia Gough. They recognized a newcomer, and were always ready to exchange a bit of risqué literary or artistic gossip, shouted so that I could hear it above the noise of the Fitzroy's terrible pianola, for a glass of whisky. They were pathetic but tough women. Once, a few years later during the war, I heard Nina suggesting to a Free French officer that he should go home with her. He laughed. "Madame, sooner would I cut it off!" he shouted, and then, in compunction, "'ave a drink!" "Thanks! A Scotch," Nina answered with marvellous aplomb. "And make it a double!"

But in Charles's shop I encountered a special and peculiar cross section of the avant garde literary and political world of Thirties London. Charles deferred to none of his customers. He respected good writing and an honest approach to life, and nothing else, and he had an extra-ordinary way of puncturing pomposities, which I observed with amusement and edification whenever I went to his shop, which for a long time was at least once a week. James Hanley sometimes looked in, and Rhys Davies was often there. Because of the times I had spent in Wales I got on well with Davies, as I also did with Keidrych Rhys, the poet and editor of *Wales* who occasionally appeared. Oswell Blakeston, Ruthven Todd, and that belated Georgian, John Gawsworth, were among the regular customers. Sometimes I would see Mulk Raj Anand, the Indian novelist who became my lifelong friend, and George Padmore, the West Indian who became Nkrumah's grey eminence, and Peter Abrahams, the black novelist from South Africa. Always there was Charles's close friend, the maverick socialist historian Frank Ridley, pale and haggard as Marat, lifting his feet alternately in a kind of static walk as the words tumbled through the barriers of his large protruding teeth, recounting scandals of imperial Rome, scabrous tales of the Jesuits, fascinating fragments about the original Assassins, and facts about the Stalinist repression in Russia and the Communist betrayal of the Left in Spain that shocked my innocent mid-Thirties leftism, though eventually they convinced me.

Ridley's counterpart and perpetual foil was a bizarre figure with hair flowing over his shoulders, dressed in a purple mediaeval gown and a flat velvet hat like those worn by LL.D's. He styled himself King of Poland and Waldace of Moldavia, with a dozen other even more exotic titles which in nearly forty years I have forgotten. He went by the name of Count Geoffrey Potocki, though some of his enemies cast doubts on the authenticity of even that title and maintained he was really the son of a New Zealand sheep farmer. Potocki edited the *Right Review*, a periodical of ultra-ultra-conservative views which he printed on a hand press in his Lamb's Conduit Street attic. He offered to make up for the poor judgment of his rivals, the editors of *Left Review*, by publishing my poems. Anxious though I was to appear in print, I was too dominated by the political sectarianism of the time to offer him any. Nothing delighted Charles Lahr more than to provoke Ridley and Potocki into long arguments in which the opposing extravagances and absurdities of left and right could be exhibited.

By the time Charles Lahr published my *Six Poems* at the end of 1938, I had already begun to publish my work in periodicals. "Sawmill" and "Winter Wheat," another partly-imagist partly-radical poem, had appeared in *The Socialist Clarion*. In the same year, at Manchester University, Lance Godwin had begun to edit, with Anthony Burgess and others, a student magazine called *The Serpent*. In 1937 and 1938 he published seven of my poems and two short stories, somewhat con-gested and poetic little exercises in a genre I soon abandoned. These poems, written in 1937, mostly represented a brief and odd deviation in my poetic progress. I had belatedly discovered Swinburne, and been fascinated enough by his good poems to try and develop a roughly equi-valent contemporary verse style. The best of these, called "Scythemen," balanced romantic nostalgia with the real harshness of past lives, but I think, as the first two verses will be enough to show, "Scythemen" owed what virtue it attained to my discovery of Hardy as a poet at the same time as I discovered Swinburne.

Aged men skilful in the deft swung thrust
　　Of flat-snake scythe steel through the tumbling grass,
Leave, as Death's scythe fells their ripe heads to earth,
　　No skilled apprentice hands to whom the craft may pass.
And tempered azure blade that undermined
　　In tottering swaths of fragrance grey-gold hay
Clammy cobweb cloaked hangs in the harness room,
　　Forgets the keening stone where, blunt, it lies away . . . .

BUT PUBLICATION IN STUDENT MAGAZINES and small-town radical magazines, temporarily soothing though it might be to a frustrated ego, was not what I really wanted. I had been following Geoffrey Grigson's prestigious *New Verse* since its first appearance in 1933, and I had recognized its importance as the representative organ of the dominant Thirties movement in poetry — that associated with Auden and Spender. So, when I had written "Memorandum from Arcadia" and "Panegyric," which seemed to me as good as most of the poems *New Verse* was then printing, I sent them to Grigson. I heard nothing at all from him, and I did not know he intended to publish them until they appeared in his Summer 1938 issue.

I was staying with Aunt Jessie at Lewisham, where my mother was recovering from a nervous breakdown, and I went to nearby Blackheath to see Charles Madge, one of the *New Verse* poets, and his current wife, the very much better poet Kathleen Raine. I had been corresponding with Madge over *Mass Observation,* for which I had done a little amateur reporting as some of the younger poets did, but I had met neither of them. Madge was one of the public-school poets (Winchester and Cambridge) and I remember how uncomfortable I felt with him and Kathleen, for all their bright Marxist chatter, in their big patrician home with its enormous garden, and how awkwardly I behaved. I always felt uneasy with Madge, who I am sure found me a young bore. I got to know Kathleen somewhat better after they parted, and found that she too remembered the awkwardness of our first meeting as an example of how, in the Thirties, class tensions still existed even amongst those who were trying to lose them. There was a kind of crevasse, concealed with light snow through which one's foot went very easily, between the mental attitudes of the public school writers and those of the lower-middle-class graduates of the grammar schools — without university education — who were then becoming a significant element in the English literary scene.

At that first meeting, Kathleen Raine showed me a copy of *New Verse* with my poems in it. This was the first I knew of their acceptance, and Grigson never sent me a copy; of course no one expected payment from little magazines in those days. All I ever heard from Grigson was that he wanted to print "Memorandum from Arcadia" in *This Year's Poetry* for 1938, which he did.

New Verse was run in a very autocratic way; outside the inner circle there was little personal contact between the editor and his contributors, or between the contributors themselves. I never met some of the *New Verse* poets, like Kenneth Allott and Bernard Spencer, and my contacts with Stephen Spender began long after the Thirties had ended.

In any case, I had already found a much more congenial milieu and a circle of friends in a rival magazine of the late Thirties, *Twentieth Century Verse,* edited by Julian Symons. I submitted my poem, "The Island," to Symons just after the other poems had appeared in *New Verse;* he not only accepted it, but sent me a very cordial letter, and forty years later, in *Critical Observations* (1981), Julian still talked of "The Island" as "one of the finest and most typical poems of the period."

We met almost immediately afterwards at the York Tavern near Victoria Station. Julian was then working as secretary to a firm of electrical engineers in Victoria Street, and I was surprised to learn that he already knew I was working for the Great Western Railway. But that was an example of the way gossip immediately began to spread about anyone whose work as a neophyte in those days appeared in a London literary magazine. Madge had told Ruthven Todd about my visit to him, and Todd was the go-between of literary London in those days, keeping one well informed on what everyone was doing and on how to earn modest pickings from book reviewing, reading for publishers or other hack jobs.

From that time I began to meet regularly with Symons and with the half-dozen poets most closely associated with *Twentieth Century Verse*: Roy Fuller, Todd, Herbert Mallalieu, Keidrych Rhys, Gavin Ewart and, somewhat on the periphery, Philip O'Connor, Lynnette Roberts and Celia Buckmaster. We would meet in the York and in the Salisbury in St. Martin's Lane, and sometimes we would go and eat enormous meals at Poggioli's in Charlotte Street, where in those pre-war days one could get a spaghetti for sevenpence, a large dish of ravioli for tenpence, and for half-a-crown a gigantic Chateaubriand garni which two people had difficulty eating. We also went to Bertorelli's, farther up Charlotte Street, and to the Café Bleu in Old Compton Street run by the fiercely-moustachioed anarchist Taborelli, but Poggioli's was the most reasonable good restaurant we knew. It vanished when Poggioli himself was whisked off in the great roundup of enemy aliens at the beginning of the war, and we were all greatly saddened to know that this friend of poor poets had been drowned when the *Arandora Star* was torpedoed taking a cargo of Italians to internment in Australia.

I developed a special friendship with Roy Fuller and his wife Kate, and began to visit them in their flat on the opposite side of Blackheath from Madge and Raine, and this, like my friendship with Symons and some of the other poets of the time, survived the years; he and Symons will appear often again in these pages.

Most of the *Twentieth Century Verse* poets had published an item or two (and Todd and Fuller quite a number of poems) in *New Verse*, but there was, nevertheless, quite a difference between the two magazines. *New Verse* was really early Thirties, a continuation in occasional periodical form of the classic Thirties anthologies, *New Signatures* and *New Country*, and the same people — Auden, Spender, MacNeice, etc. — contributed to all three, with the addition in *New Verse* of a few younger writers and of that mentally-youthful figure from the Twenties, Herbert Read. But *Twentieth Century Verse* was essentially late Thirties, and one recovers in its files a sense of the extreme variety of English poetry in those last three or four years before World War II, a flowering of excellent minor verse rather like that of the Nineties just before the Wilde débâcle. Much good poetry from the later Thirties now goes unappreciated because no adequate anthology of the end of the decade has yet been collected.

Unlike the *New Verse* group, the poets who clustered around *Twentieth Century Verse* were all lower middle class in origin, coming from the London suburbs and the small towns. Fuller, Symons, Todd, Mallalieu, Rhys, myself — all of us were autodidacts from the moment we left grammar school (Symons did not even go to grammar school and ended his formal education at fourteen), as were other contributors like Dylan Thomas and George Barker who did not belong to the inner group. We shared the experience of coming to literature in a different and harder way from the early Thirties poets, and this, possibly, made us more conscious of poetry as a difficult and patient craft and less inclined to see it as the diversion of a scholar who, for all his professed political radicalism, retained the speech and behaviour patterns of a gentleman.

Politically, there was probably a great deal more openness and variety in the attitudes prevalent around *Twentieth Century Verse* than in those around *New Verse* (though in Herbert Read the latter magazine could boast one lone anarchist), and this was in keeping with the less doctrinaire kind of leftism that appeared in the later Thirties with the disillusionment caused by the Moscow trials and Russia's equivocal role in Spain. Symons himself was a Trotskyist, but much nearer to American intellectuals of that persuasion such as Dwight Macdonald and the *Partisan Review* group than to the London working-class Trotskyists who, by a further twist of the British class complex, distrusted Symons for his literary pretensions. Roy Fuller was a kind of free Leninist, Derek Savage a Christian personalist, Keidrych Rhys a Welsh nationalist, and I eventually became a pacifist anarchist. Yet one whole issue of *Twentieth Century Verse* was devoted to that very occasional writer of verse and noted gadfly of Thirties leftist orthodoxies, Wyndham Lewis.

Coming out of my semi-rural isolation, I found this an exciting and congenial milieu. I feel that I owe my relatively rapid literary development from then on largely to its stimulus. Yet there was not much talk about writing, and very little about verse, when we met; we spent more time on politics and on the gossip of the floating world of literary Bohemia, and when we did discuss books it was more likely to be novels (particularly crime novels in which all of us were then greatly interested and which Symons and Fuller were beginning to write) than current books of verse. We would exchange poems with each other, but the habit of reading them aloud in small circles did not exist among us, and I found it disconcerting when I first encountered it in Canada. I remember Symons, when I handed him one of the poems he did *not* publish, stuffing it in his pocket and saying: "I never read anything when the writer is looking at me." Except among the proletarian literature enthusiasts who gathered around the *Left Review* and would occasionally spout their verses in Hampstead pubs, the fashion of public readings, which Dylan Thomas later did so much to establish, hardly existed. We wrote with the sense that verse must stand on the page and satisfy a rigorous inner ear. Our disinclination to discuss poems in great detail perhaps arose from the feeling, which I think all the regular *Twentieth Century Verse* contributors shared, that poetry should strive for the greatest possible intellectual clarity; a poem that did not explain itself to a sensitive reader seemed to us a failed poem. We acknowledged the talent of the better of the irrationalist poets who appeared in the later Thirties, such as Dylan Thomas, George Barker, and Philip O'Connor, all of whom were published in *Twentieth Century Verse*. But we rejected, and I think time has proved us right, the pretentious nonsense of those who followed Thomas without either his talent or his rigorous craftsmanship, particularly the work of the now almost forgotten New Apocalyptics who, for a while in the 1940s, dominated the poetic scene.

New Verse and *Twentieth Century Verse* died as the war began, late in 1939. Their editors abandoned them because, I think, both Symons and Grigson felt that the period the two magazines in different ways represented had ended, and that a new climate for which new organs were needed had come into being. Certainly a different literary ambiance began to take shape from 1940 onwards, and new magazines offered it their fresh voices.

The effect of my association with *Twentieth Century Verse* lasted some time after the journal ended, for in 1940 my first book, *The White Island*, appeared in a series called "The Fortune Poets," which consisted mainly of writers associated with Julian Symons and his magazine. The publisher was a certain Caton, one of the strangest of London publishers and a true successor to the disreputable Leonard Smithers who had published Wilde and others of the decadents in the Nineties. Caton lurked — there is no other word that properly describes his way of existence — in a basement in the Buckingham Palace Road. One would go down the iron-railed stairs from the pavement and knock on a door which, after two or three minutes, would open a crack to reveal a long cadaverous face topping a tall and stooping figure. Recognizing his visitor, Caton would open the door enough to let him slip in, and then quickly shut and bolt it behind him. He would lead the way into an office whose walls were piled high with parcels and stacks of books. The desk, behind which Caton would mournfully seat himself, was always chaotically piled with files of letters, overflowing ashtrays — Caton was a compulsive smoker — and bottles of Damaroids, a potency pill much favoured at the time.

Any conversation with Caton was a matter of stealthy fencing, for he hated to commit himself, and never gave more than an oral agreement. He was a man wholly without humour; I never once heard him laugh, and he was in a state of perpetual nervousness. Any knock on the door, he believed, might herald the police.

For Caton carried on a strange double business. He made his money on marginally pornographic books. Highlights in an old Caton list I have beside me include *Bachelor's Hall* by Miles Underwood, *Boy Sailors* by Gundry Grenville-Hearne and *True Yokefellow* by Humphrey Lancaster, but his best selling-items were a series of five, starting with *Fourteen, A Diary of the Teens* by "a Boy," and ending with *Seventeen, A Diary of the Teens* by the same "Boy." Rarely sold in ordinary bookshops, these works were most often to be seen among the trusses, douches and French letters in the "rubber shops," as they were then called, of Praed Street and Charing Cross Road.

But Caton always hankered to be considered a publisher of real literature, so he leavened his list in two ways. He published a few spicy classics, like John Cleland's *Memoirs of a Coxcomb* and *The Twilight of the Nymphs* by Pierre Louys; I remember his asking my views, on the first occasion we met, about the riskiness of publishing *Don Leon*, the pornographic parody of *Don Juan* which Caton firmly believed was also written by Byron. Caton's second claim to respectability lay in his willingness to risk some of the profits of smut on the work of young and little-known poets. His record in this direction showed a good deal of insight, or perhaps of luck, for Caton never said anything to me which suggested he actually understood the poems he was publishing or had even read them very thoroughly. But certainly he had an odd flair for picking winners, since he published the first books of writers as varied and eventually as celebrated as Cecil Day Lewis, Dylan Thomas, Kingsley Amis and Philip Larkin, as well as Julian Symons, Roy Fuller and Ruthven Todd. He also brought out in 1940 the first manifesto-anthology of the leading Forties movement, *The New Apocalypse*.

So far as I know, nobody ever got a signature out of Caton. He insisted that each of his poets buy fifty copies of his own book, and those who were wise sent these out for review on their own, since Caton spent almost nothing on publicity, for he carried all the furtiveness of a smut merchant into the other side of his publishing business. Though he would make vague remarks about sending royalties some day in the future, I do not know any poet who actually extracted payment from Caton. Not that, at least to start with, he can have done anything but lose money on the books of verse he published. But he always hoped, and for this reason he never dated a book, calculating that if its author did become famous, he could then announce his work as if it were a new publication in one of the little one-inch advertisements he placed in the *Times Literary Supplement*. He did not, of course, have to advertise his less respectable books; they found their own word-of-mouth market. But for all Caton's devious and obscure methods, he gave first publication to many younger writers who were not acceptable to T. S. Eliot at Fabers or to Leonard Woolf at Hogarth Press, in those days the only established publishers actively involved in publishing new poetry; grudgingly, I acknowledge my debt to the old pornographer.

THE DEVELOPMENT OF A SENSE of my own way of speaking in verse, and the acquisition of the kind of experience that gave poems their content, emerged from the opening out of my life in many directions during the years from 1935 onwards. It was in 1935 that I began, very tentatively, to get involved in left-wing politics. It was in that year I first went to France, repeating my visits every summer until the war began, and that I first experienced, in my expeditions to the mining valleys and metal-working areas of South Wales, the full meaning of the Depression and of the callous way in which capitalism exploited the workers. And this was the period when I began to develop friendships that took me completely outside the earthly territory and the mental realm of my childhood and youth.

I have already told of the emotional conversion to a misty concept of socialism which I had experienced when I was eighteen. For a long time it remained little more than a matter of reading Marx with difficulty and underlying distaste, and William Morris and Bernard Shaw with a great deal more pleasure. Shaw's *Intelligent Woman's Guide to Socialism* gave me the basic concepts of socialism, and Morris's *News from Nowhere* provided me with the vision of a libertarian socialist society that would later make it easier for me to slip into anarchism. I read some of G. D. H. Cole's writings on Guild Socialism, and through the *New English Weekly* I encountered Social Credit and tried without much success to puzzle out the strange economics of Major C. H. Douglas. I read John Reed's *Ten Days that Shook the World* with great excitement, seeing the October Revolution it described as the prelude to a new world order of justice and freedom, and for a while I kept a photograph of Lenin on the mantelpiece of my bedroom. I had as yet no real comprehension of the nature of the regime that the revolution had initiated, and at the same time as I applauded the Bolsheviks I was developing a repugnance for war, under the influence of such books as Erich Maria Remarque's *All Quiet on the Western Front*, Richard Aldington's *Death of a Hero*, and Robert Graves's *Good-Bye to All That*, which led me towards the pacifist position adopted by such predecessors of the Peace Pledge Union as the No More War Movement.

I think I resembled many other young people at that period who felt a general disillusionment with the social and political order they had been brought up to respect, but who were unable to decide which of the new movements appearing in the world were good and which were bad, so that they tended to accept everything that was new. Communism, pacifism, the avant garde movements in painting and music and writing, sexual liberation, monetary reform, the Russian ballet, they seemed to come in one glorious package, to be accepted without discrimination, and only the grim events of the later 1930s taught some at least of us that everything new was not necessarily good. The most curious thing about that period of indiscriminate acceptance, so far as it affected me, was that I did not then include anarchism in my spectrum of acceptable beliefs. I was to come to that somewhat later, largely through my interest in Spain, which began when the abdication of Alphonso XIII in 1931 encouraged me to believe that peaceful overthrow of authority was possible, that pacifism and revolution might be reconciled.

I read and thought and talked with the few people who then shared my interests, but it was not until 1935 that I did anything to give practical shape to my left-wing inclinations. In the general election of that year I voted — the first and only time in my life — for the Labour Party, and in the same year I moved obliquely through the trade union movement towards political involvement. Union membership was not encouraged in the head offices of the Great Western Railway, but a tiny minority of mavericks did belong to the Railway Clerks' Association. When one of them approached me, I joined the union, largely because of warnings from other colleagues that I might be endangering the career from which I wanted to escape. Towards the end of 1935 I decided that I must become more active than a mere dues-payer, so I began to attend the meetings of the union branch in the Paddington Borough Hall.

I learnt immediately one of the prime lessons of labour union activity; that far from involving the mass of the membership, it is operated always by small active groups. The membership of the RCA's Paddington local was 500, yet I never attended a meeting at which more than twenty-five members were present, and usually the attendance was between fifteen and twenty. They divided into two groups: a cluster of older militants of conservative disposition who held onto the branch offices; and a clique of mostly younger men who were more militant and anxious to attach the union to left-wing causes. This group immediately made overtures to me, and before long I was meeting its members once a week for sausages and mash in a dim little workingmen's eating house near Paddington Green where the discussions usually began with arguments about how to wrest power in the branch from the old guard (which we stood no chance of doing since they could always mobilize more of the inactive members for a vote than we could) and went on to wider political issues. The brightest and most influential member of this group was Michael Greening, a dark young man with long effeminate eyelashes and dirty chewed fingernails, a soft voice and a compulsive way of talking. Greening spent most of his spare time working in various front organizations linked with the Communist Party. Though he would never admit it, I was sure he carried a Party card.

I liked Greening. There was a sensitivity and an inclination to open laughter that seemed alien to the Stalinist cant he would often spout; he was to be one of those who suffered early disillusionment with the Party, for later on in 1944, he wrote to tell me of his departure from the Communist ranks. At the time, however, he was the true believer, and he tried hard to convert me. We would spend whole lunch hours tramping the streets and talking, or sitting in some dingy cafe where Greening nervously poured out the salt on the dirty tablecloth and made abstract patterns with it — rather like the rice patterns one sees on floors in South India — as he talked away about Five Year Plans and Soviet democracy.

Perhaps his eagerness, and the sense it gave me of a warm-hearted person trapped in a mould of dogma, was one of the reasons why I continued to fight shy, and never at any time actually committed myself to communism, as so many of the Thirties writers did. Greening would press on me all manner of Party pamphlets, and he gave me every issue of *Inprecor*, the international communist magazine. This continuous immersion in the turgid, slogan-ridden prose of Stalinism, with its doctrines as absolute and absurd as those of Catholicism, bred in me the sense that these people were the enemies and not the friends of literature and art, and that I should treat them with caution. Long before I heard such sentiments elaborated by George Orwell, I had developed the rule of thumb in considering political pundits: By their prose ye shall know them!

Nevertheless, I did not yet entirely reject the communists, for much of their negative criticism of English society in the 1930s accorded with my experience. I read the books published by the Left Book Club; except for Orwell's *The Road to Wigan Pier*, which the Club published with manifest regret, they were virtually all works by fellow travellers if not convinced Party members. I read the *Left Review*, and in the 1937 May Day demonstrations, not wishing to identify myself directly with the Party, I marched under the *Review*'s banner with people like Jack Lindsey and Randall Swingler, who I felt had at least more respect for the life of the arts than the human gramophones who ran *Inprecor*.

Finally, I was impressed by the movement towards a Popular Front, which swept in a great many people who were far from being communists. I never had a great deal of use for that secular puritan, Stafford Cripps, and his Socialist League, but I did respect the Independent Labour Party, or ILP as we generally called it, largely because of the great charisma of leaders like James Maxton and the patent honesty of others, like Fenner Brockway. Many of the constituency groups within the Labour Party were also working to bring about an alliance with the Left, a Popular Front resembling that which had recently been formed in France. It seemed to many of us at that time a logical move for all left-wing parties to take. Fascism appeared to be gaining momentum, particularly after the beginning of the Spanish Civil War, and one feared that, unless it were stopped, it would become an irresistible force.

In Britain the National Government was coming increasingly under Conservative control and showing itself willing to make compromises with fascist governments abroad, while in London itself the followers of Oswald Mosley were marching in their black shirts. If the Left were only united, it could perhaps reverse the trend in Britain and hence, in alliance with a united Left in France and Spain, change the direction of European events.

The Labour Party leaders and the powerful and then rather conservative trade unions were opposed, though I am not sure whether they were fully aware of the reasons why they were in fact right. For nobody completely recognized the destructive effects of communist infiltration and manipulation until writers like Franz Borkenau and George Orwell in 1938 began to publish the truth of what was happening beyond the Loyalist lines in Spain, and at first the news of the Moscow trials and the Stalinist purge seemed so bizarre that, on the patriotic principle of *credo quia absurdum,* people were inclined to think the accusations against the Old Bolsheviks might have something in them.

Somewhere early in 1937 I joined the tiny group that in Tory Marlow passed as a Labour Party. I was led into it by a young London office worker named Jack David who had migrated to the country, built himself a bungalow among the chalkhills at Marlow Bottom, and used to cycle in to the station every morning. Jack was a good example of the idealistic healthfood leftist of the period. He could not endure, any more than I could, the jargon of the Communists, or the Party discipline which we knew existed, but he was himself honest enough to trust them, and for the time being I followed his example, particularly as the same trust was shared by the other friend I made in the local Labour Party, a former colonial civil servant, A. K. Jameson, who had served his term of office in West Africa.

Jameson was a man of wide reading and liberal sympathies whose career had left him with a profound distrust of governments and armies. I used to visit him occasionally in the pleasant old cottage where he lived, with his wife and his two step-children, in Little Marlow. As we drank tea on the lawn with his step-daughter Pamela Oaten, a bright, forthright girl who is still my friend, he gave me the first direct accounts I had heard of colonial rule, as well as vivid impressions of native life on the Gold Coast and in Sierra Leone. His experience had left him with a rooted hatred of imperialism, and this had led him to join the Labour Party and to become a determined pacifist.

Jameson took a quasi-paternal interest in me. He would arrive at our cottage on a Sunday morning, with his blackthorn stick and his old spaniel, and we would walk down along the river to Temple and cross over the ferry to return through the Berkshire beechwoods, or go up into the chalk hills towards Frieth and Fingest. As we went we talked with a kind of freedom that spanned age and background, and largely, I think, because neither of us — the old man or the young man — had a dogma in his head, or anything else except the search for free truths. He had only recently come to terms with his experience and liberated himself from the conservative attitudes that had sent him out as a colonial officer in the beginning.

In the meantime, still feeling that political salvation would come through political parties, I had gone to the head offices of the ILP and been welcomed by John McNair into that party of honest if sentimental revolutionists. The ILP was in the process of reassessing its adherence to the concept of the Popular Front, since McNair had just returned from Barcelona where he had witnessed, during the May Days of 1937, the attempt by the Communists, described in Orwell's *Homage to Catalonia*, to destroy not only the Anarchists, but also the independent socialist Partido Obrero de Unificacion Marxista (POUM) groups with whom the ILP had allied itself. McNair had helped Orwell and others to flee from Spain, and when I talked to him I had no doubt of the truth of what he had to tell.

At the same time I had learnt so much through Charles Lahr of the real facts behind the Stalinist purges, and of the tradition of Bolshevik terror going back to Lenin, that by the end of 1937 I had become entirely opposed to the communists and was moving in quite other directions. My reaction to the prospect of oncoming war was one of complete emotional and moral revulsion. I could not accept the communist notion of creating a military alliance that, even if it came about (as eventually it did) would merely multiply the destruction of World War I. I had begun to recognize that even the violent resistance by the Left in Spain had been largely counter-productive, in the sense that it had not defeated Franco; every month of war consolidated, behind Loyalist lines, an authoritarian government which masked a communist political terror imitating that of post-revolutionary Russia.

Meanwhile, my growing knowledge of what was happening in Spain had drawn my attention to the anarchists. After the Russian Revolution, when the success of the Marxists eclipsed the record of their historic rivals, anarchism had withdrawn into an obscurity that continued through the 1920s, though it remained strong in Spain, where the anarchists in 1936 emerged into a degree of world celebrity, partly for their successful opposition to the generals in Barcelona, which frustrated the Francoist coup there, and partly because the communists advertized them by denouncing them. When I became disillusioned with the communists because of their denial of freedom and their pursuit of power, it was natural that I should be attracted towards the anarchists, who exposed the psychoses of the power-hungry and who rejected government at the same time as they affirmed freedom.

Yet I reached my anarchist views independently of the anarchists themselves. Facts about the anarchists in Spain were very hard to find at the time of the Civil War, since even the liberal press was dominated mainly by fellow travellers like the arch-hypocrite Kingsley Martin, and my impressions of the libertarian trend in Spain were derived almost entirely from Franz Borkenau's fair-minded book, *The Spanish Cockpit*, which appeared in 1937. The classics of anarchist theory were almost all out of print, and the only one I read before 1940 was Kropotkin's *Mutual Aid*, one of the early Penguin reprints. I came to anarchism through my pacifism, and through the decision I had made to refuse to serve militarily if a war came about. I felt a deep repugnance towards the idea of taking a human life for any political cause, and I felt equally angry at the thought of fighting to defend the British Empire and the system that produced the conditions which during the later Thirties had so appalled me when I visited the industrial areas of Wales.

MY TRIPS TO THE COAL MINING VALLEYS of the Rhondda and to the metalworking areas nearer to Swansea made an impression that entered deeply into my poetry, producing in the last years of the Thirties a whole cycle of "Welsh" poems dominated by what I had seen. Time has not greatly diminished the vividness of my impressions, and I remember almost as if it were yesterday the first visit I made to Rhondda. I took the bus from Bridgend to the lower end of Rhondda Mawr, the Big Rhondda valley, and began to walk. In all these mining valleys there was a continuous ribbon town, one narrow street of small terrace houses and little shops and pubs running up to the head of the valley, with the pitshafts and their great wheels on either side and two railway tracks, one to serve the pits on each slope.

In 1935 I felt a curious blind lifelessness in this continuous community. More than half the shops were boarded over with stained and weathered planks, and as I walked past these dead places and past the little grey stone houses, grimed with the soot that in prosperous years had drifted from the tall brick chimneys of the mines, I sometimes passed vacant lots. On each of them there would be a few miners squatting on their heels, idle because the mines were idle and they had no money for the pubs. They played pitch-and-toss, a game in which coins are normally used and the players win or lose according to the way they fall. But nobody now had any coins to win or lose, so they played with small flat pebbles. And then, walking down the road towards me, came a man alone. His dark pit clothes had been worn to rags. He slouched along, shoulders hunched and hands in pockets, and as he did so he whistled the "Red Flag." The "Red Flag" is usually sung in a rhythm of jaunty defiance, but this man whistled it slowly and mournfully, so that it sounded like a dirge. In that dead valley the song of rebellious labour had become a lament.

There was no road linking Rhondda Mawr, or at least its upper end, with Rhondda Fach, the Little Rhondda, so when I recognized the big valley had nothing to offer me except a continuous repetition of dead buildings and idle silent men, I decided to tramp over the mountain to the smaller valley. It was really a range of high bare hills that I had to cross, running up to about 500 metres. Beyond the mines and the houses there were some stunted copses, but I soon climbed above them on to the bare grassy hillsides, where centuries of turf growing layer upon layer had formed great accumulations resembling peat. On the upper slopes the rain had scored deep gulleys into this deposit, and I had to watch my steps to avoid falling into them. The hilltop actually formed a flattish moorland, broken by patches of heather and little bogs with tiny marsh flowers, and on a fine day it would have been pleasant walking. But all at once a great storm blew up, with a high wind dashing the rain across the completely open ground. There was not even a bush to give me shelter, and the gullies were racing with water, so that I feared to climb down into them. So there was nothing to do but to put my head down into the wind and accept my drenching; I had not thought to bring a raincoat, since it had been sunny in Bridgend. Eventually I found my way across the hilltops and scrambled down the grassy slope into Rhondda Fach, drenched to the skin.

I came down beside a great pyramid of a slag heap belonging to one of the idle mines, and overtook a man who was walking away from it. He was even more ragged than the whistler in the big valley, and he was pushing a bicycle that had no seat and no tires on its wheels. On the bar he had perched a sack, and he told me it was full of walnut-sized pieces of coal he had picked from the slagheap. "There's about fifty pounds," he said, "and it took me all afternoon to pick it." He shrugged his shoulders. "There's nothing else to do. And they let us pick. There's some mines as doesn't."

He spoke in a low, resigned voice. I sensed that he had no particular resentment of me as a stranger, so I asked him how long he had been out of work. "Not a day's work, man, for nine years!" Nine years took us right back to the General Strike of 1926. For nearly a decade, as the miner emphasized, almost nobody had been working in his village. "*Ach y fi*, we're all in the same boat, man. And there's no consolation it is."

Yet, for all his own misery, he was concerned about my condition, and kept telling me I'd get a chill if I didn't dry my clothes. But nobody in the village lit a fire except to cook the mid-day meal. Then he had an idea. "Go to the Bracchi shop, man. They'll have a stove on, indeed." In the South Wales villages of the Thirties the Bracchi shops were grocery stores with little bars where they sold coffee and tea and sandwiches. The first Italian to start up in the Rhondda had been called Bracchi, and though he was long dead the miners still named these little shops after him. So I found the local Bracchi shop, with its grimy windows almost empty of stock, and went in. There was a dark, dejected girl behind the counter. She looked Italian but spoke with a strong Rhondda accent. I ordered a cup of tea, which seemed to be all one could get there, and then I asked if there was a fire. She looked at me gloomily. "We only light a fire for cooking," she said, "and a gas ring to heat the kettle to make a cup of tea." So I had to let my clothes dry on me as I went home on the bus, but I caught no chill. I had seen a life stripped down to the barest and greyest of elementals.

Later I went farther west to Landore and Pentre. These were small tinplate and copper towns. When the mills were in operation the hills around used to be bare because of the fumes the tall chimneys emitted, and many of the children were sick from the same cause, but at least men worked and there was enough for a meagre living. Now the mills had been idle for years, and I described the strange result in "Landore," one of the best of the poems my visits to Wales inspired.

Now the down of grass sprouts, fire galvanic
bursts the yellow flowers, harsh green
new moss veins the stone brows,
birds nest on the mountains,
the air is pure and hunger is in the valley,
dereliction
of sag-roof factory and smokeless stack,
young men squatting for talk in the lee of walls,
the slow round of mountain and stone-grey street . . . .

THE LATER THIRTIES were doom-obsessed years. Living, as we now have done, through thirty-five years of suspended terror, it is hard to remember the immediacy of the threat we envisaged at that time. Any politically-aware person believed that war was inevitable, and though even the most extreme anti-fascist was secretly relieved when Chamberlain came back from Munich in 1938 with his year's reprieve, none of us believed his fatuous prophesies of peace in our time. We all expected war by the end of the decade, and we thought it would be devastating, with great fleets of bombers immediately destroying the cities of Britain and the Germans probably using poison gas from the beginning. There was no way out, and we realized that we had to make up our minds where we would stand and declare ourselves.

This meant that even before the war began one was aware of one's acquaintances sorting themselves out into friends and enemies and agonized neutrals. As soon as I declared my intention of becoming a conscientious objector, some people became very hostile and my mother, fearing the appalling shame of having a conshy son, begged me to change my mind. I refused, and that was one among several disputes that further soured our relationship at the end of her life. If I had been merely concerned to save my skin, I could quite easily have registered for service, played on my poor eyesight, and wangled some cushy job in information or army education, as many of the writers I knew succeeded in doing. But I preferred the clear stance and, less worthily, enjoyed the drama of it. Uncle Harry, who remembered his own last war with bitter cynicism, clapped me on the back and took me to the pub near his barber's shop to drink a couple of Scotches to my good fortune. I had become very close to this amiable gambler and music-hall frequenter since we got drunk together at grandfather Harry Lewis's funeral the year before.

Having decided that I would resist the dictates of the state, if necessary to the extent of going to prison, I realized that war resistance led naturally and logically to anarchism, since one was necessarily putting one's own conscience above the law, and therefore denying the presumptions of the state and of legality. Reason forced me to pursue this course, and at the meetings of pacifist groups which I now began to attend — a little circle that met in a private house in Marlow and a larger one that met in the Friend's Meeting House in Maidenhead — I began to expound my conclusions, and found to my surprise that I had few sympathisers. The Quakers themselves divorced their pacifism from any intent to transform a society in which so many of them had prospered, and the movement still carried a good many other people who had signed the Peace Pledge in 1935 or 1936 on an emotional impulse but had not thought out their reasons; many of them, once war came, would shift directions radically.

But I did meet two people who shared my views and became very close friends. One was Elizabeth, a Bermudan, a small, dark, attractive creole. She travelled to some job in the city; we began to talk to each other on the train about books, and soon to look out for each other mornings and evenings so that we could travel together and continue our conversations. Her lover Tom, who later became her husband, was a Welshman from the Pontypridd Valley, a school teacher with a preacher's aquiline face who developed into a good poet. He and I immediately became friends because of our shared love for music and literature, even though he adored Beethoven and Lawrence while my preferences ran towards Mozart and Joyce. The three of us developed an excellent companionship, yet Elizabeth and I had a relationship of our own which Tom amiably accepted. We would go together to the great French films of the time, like *Quai des Brumes* and *Hotel du Nord* and *La Femme du Boulanger*, and anything else with Louis Jouvet or Raimu, Michel Simon or Arletty, all of whom we admired greatly, and would eat in the Soho restaurants, sometimes on our own and sometimes with Julian Symons and the other poets with whom I had become friendly.

I was going about with other girls as well at this time, for I was earning more money and had got through the uneasy period when, like Orwell's Gordon Comstock in *Keep the Aspidistra Flying*, I believed that girls despised me for my poverty and my general shabbiness. Perhaps some of them did, and undoubtedly several promising flirtations got no further either because I suspected the girl's contempt or she grew exasperated with my surly shyness. Among those young women to whom I now became close, Giselle was the *belle laide* wife of one of the younger masters at Borlase, perhaps seven years older than I, and Ilse was a startlingly Nordic-looking Jewish refugee recently arrived from Germany, a Valkyrie of a girl with blonde hair and bright blue eyes. Like Elizabeth, they helped notably to civilize me.

FRANCE GAVE A DEEPER PERSPECTIVE to all I was learning in England at this period. In Wales I had already sensed something of the flavour of a foreign country: a place where a language other than my own was spoken, where the loyalties I had been taught were not all accepted. Indeed, at Cardiff I had my first real sense of being in contact with France, for down at the docks I would come across the little blue-painted wooden sailing boats that the Bretons would bring up the Bristol Channel with their cargos of cauliflowers and onions. From these ships the men would fan out over the Welsh countryside in their corduroy jackets and trousers, carrying strings of onions hung on their shoulders. Their Breton language was near enough to Welsh for them to be easily understood, and the Welsh welcomed them and called them collectively Shoni Onion, which they adopted and would use to announce themselves when a door was opened. They did not understand very well my school French, yet when I talked to them I felt I was touching the edge of a realm that, through its paintings and poetry, through the tragic stories of its artists, had already aroused in me something resembling nostalgia, as if this were the country I had somehow lost and must recover.

It was not until 1935 that I had saved enough money to go to Paris. Knowing nothing about travel, I went with an old school friend on a Cook's tour and stayed in a tourist hotel on the Right Bank near the Madeleine. Even on that first trip, when we spent our time seeing all the famous monuments including one of the legendary Edwardian brothels off the rue Montmartre, I got the flavour of a way of life that was far freer and more life-accepting than that in which I had been brought up. Even though, on that first visit, I was highly conscious of walking as a stranger, seeing new things and aware of my ignorance and my bad

French, I felt drawn towards the world I saw, and had no doubt I would be returning.

Indeed, I returned every year until 1939, when the war turned France into my personal lost Eden. I quickly concluded that this was my spiritual second home, my final destination, and though in recent years I have gone much less frequently to France than I did in the Thirties and again in the later Forties and the Fifties, when scarcely a year went by without part of it being spent on French soil, I still have a sense that in the end I shall go home there.

My second visit I made on my own, having read thoroughly in the annals of French poetry and painting. This time, as I continued to do in later years, I made for the Left Bank and stayed in the Hotel de Fleurus in the Rue de Fleurus, though I never saw the most famous inhabitant of that legendary street, Gertrude Stein. I spent a good deal of time on this visit in the old streets of the Latin Quarter and in the galleries and bookshops, familiarizing myself with the latest trends in the arts and flirting temporarily with surrealism, though in reality the writers and artists who impressed me most deeply even then were the Symbolists and their successors like Gide and Proust, and the late Impressionists like Pissaro, Seurat, Cézanne and Van Gogh. I still find in them the most satisfying exemplars of the French creative vein. I was impressed not merely by the work of these men, but almost as greatly by the dedication with which they lived the life of the artist, which was my goal.

I remember with a poignant intensity many of the lost sights and sounds of 1930s Paris. The sound of the milk cart clattering just after dawn in the Rue de Fleurus; the freshness of the early morning streets when the water channels were opened, and the streetmen swept the rubbish away with their long *besoms*; the strange violet light of evening over the Seine; the colour and smell of the markets in the Place Maubert and the Rue de Buci; and that strange apparition as one sat drinking after midnight in the Boul' Mich' and a steam train chugged down the middle of the street towards the Gare d'Orsay.

I usually ate in cheap student restaurants around the Rue de l'Ecole de Médicine where one could get a meal for six or seven francs (somewhat less than a shilling) though I would sometimes treat myself to an excellent six-course meal with wine for fifteen or twenty francs (two shillings or a little more) at one of the more pretentious restaurants in Montparnasse. France was then so cheap that one lived very well indeed for a fortnight on a couple of five-pound-notes. Later in the evening, if I felt disinclined to go to the Opéra or to one of the music-halls that specialized in feminine nudity, I would visit either the student bistros of the Boul' Mich' or the big cafés in the Boulevard Montparnasse, La Coupole or La Rotonde or — my favourite — Le Dôme.

I preferred the Montparnasse cafés, since it was much easier to strike up acquaintances in them, though these friendships of an evening or at most a few days were never with French people. I soon became aware of the rather contemptuous distance Parisians maintain towards strangers, and I never found myself talking to anyone in the places which the French mainly patronized. In the Dôme, on the other hand, there were always lonely foreigners, and if one stood in the bar instead of sitting at the tables, it was the easiest thing in the world to become involved in intoxicated and interminable conversations with wandering Danes or Swedes, Germans or Americans, and this was all grist to my mill, since I had gone to France to find a life different from my own, and anyone who came from some other background helped to create that alternative vision.

But sometimes I would go deliberately to a place less frequented by foreigners and sit quietly drinking Pernod, whose peculiar virtues intrigued me. I found that after a few glasses I had the physical sensation of walking on air cushions, and two or three times I had hallucinations of beds of flowers blooming brightly on the pavement before the table where I sat. I wrote some splendid poems while solitarily drunk on Pernod and in the clear sobriety of morning found them rubbish.

In 1937 I went yet again to Paris, and this time, through an exchange arranged by Morley College, where I was trying to learn German in night classes, I stayed for a fortnight in the Cité Universitaire. I lived in the Maison Franco-Britannique, where the rooms were larger and more pleasant than in any hotel that I could afford, and I ate regularly at the big student cafeteria where the food was good and varied and where I came into contact with people whose variety of origins — Dutch, Czech, Egyptian, Syrian, American — showed me what a cosmopolitan society existed in France beside the closed world of the Parisians.

At the same time, on this third visit I began to feel much more at home with the French. On the 14th July I went to the great demonstration that converged on the Place de la Bastille, which reflected the enthusiasms of that period when the Front Populaire was still in the ascendant and the workers, after their great sit-in strikes, were conscious of their power. I was caught up in the euphoria of the occasion and the mystique of the French Revolution, and felt I had friends all around me.

Indeed the most memorable of the friendships I struck up at that time was with a young Frenchwoman, Simone Saint Sabin. She was a schoolteacher, two or three years older than I, with the face of a Clouet madonna. Simone spoke an amusing English, full of literally-translated witticisms. She knew Marie Laurençin, whom she adored, and she also had a great admiration for the poetry of Anna de Noailles, who had died only two or three years before. Simone combined, in a way I had never encountered in England, a radical kind of socialism with a very devout Catholicism and an intense patriotism. She introduced me to the writings and the legend of Charles Péguy. We spent afternoons wandering around Paris, searching out places evocative of Baudelaire and Verlaine and Villon. I remember especially one occasion when we had been in Montmartre following the track of Toulouse Lautrec and were standing up on the Butte near Sacre Coeur, looking out over Paris. We were talking about war, and Simone's patriotism suddenly came out as fiercely as Péguy's when she hotly repudiated my pacifism and shouted, "I would stand behind a mitrailleuse for France!" After I left we wrote to each other, and I saw her again in October, 1938, when I went over after the Munich crisis with the feeling that time was running out and I must see as much of France as I could. This time the differences in our attitudes seemed more obvious than the similarities, perhaps because we were both conscious of the doom that hung over Europe and were reacting in different ways, and afterwards our correspondence lapsed. But I have often wondered what happened to Simone in the collapse of Europe. I never heard of her again.

I went to France once more before the decade ended, in July 1939. The war was less than two months away and fear hung thickly over Europe, for we all knew there would be no second Munich Pact. Already people in England were beginning to choose their roles. Some of the fairweather pacifists began to move away, particularly if they were in situations that would prevent their being called up. The rest of us knew that, one way or another, the war would radically change our lives and we half-welcomed, half-dreaded it. On the 4th June, a month before I left for France, I wrote to Lance Godwin:

It is obvious that conscription is aimed far more at you and me than at Hitler. This war fever sickens and astounds me! Even the Labour

Party and the Communists seem taken in by it, and most of the fools seem ready to throw away their freedom in the name of freedom. What a bloody fantastic paradox! Conscription to preserve the liberties of England! .... The only people who seem to retain sanity in this whirlwind of hysteria are the uncompromising pacifists. They at least realize that in the last resort the individual is above the state. So I'm lining up with them, to strive for Man against the Country, State, Race, or whatever old fusty mumbo-jumbo is going to be dragged out as fancy dress for the vested interests of the Tory moneybags, to the accompaniment of applause from comrades Attlee, Pollitt and all! What apes men are! What less than apes!

In such an atmosphere, going to Europe was a demonstration of one's refusal to be cowed by the possibility of war breaking out at any moment. But it also meant taking the last opportunity to see France for a long time, so I decided to go beyond Paris, down to Provence, which my imagination peopled not only with the great Post-Impressionist painters like Cézanne and Van Gogh, but also with a rich, romantic past that included the Greeks and Romans, the troubadours and Cathars, the gipsies of the Camargue and, emerging in memory from my naturalist childhood, the gardens and vineyards where Henri Fabre had made his fascinating observations of cicadas and dung beetles and praying mantises.

I picked Arles for my destination, crossing the Channel on the night boat, and reaching Paris in time to catch the Italian express at the Gare de Lyon. There were no tourists on board, for the Americans, who were beginning to return to Europe in the late 1930s as the Depression eased, had all vanished when the voices of the politicians grew more bellicose. I travelled in a compartment full of French people. I had bought myself one of the excellent lunch baskets which the French railways put up in those days, so that I was able to enter into the convivial and conversational atmosphere of intermittent sipping and chewing that began in mid-morning as my fellow passengers opened their own well-stocked baskets. Now I can remember only two of them: a grocer from Marseilles who was returning from a merry weekend in Paris; and a tired and pretty nightclub dancer who was going for a restful week to Avignon. The high point of the day came when the grocer jumped out at Dijon and rushed back waving a newspaper. *"Messieurs, mesdames,"* he announced with ebullient pompousness, "I have won five thousand francs in the lottery!" In those happy days five thousand francs was a handsome windfall, and we congratulated him and smoked his cigars and drank his wine with gusto. For the rest, we talked war, which everyone dreaded and nobody wanted to admit was possible. None of the French in that carriage talked as Simone had done and when France surrendered with hardly a fight less than two years later, I remembered those worried and unbelligerent people on the train to Arles.

So the long day passed, going through the rich landscapes of the Côte d'Or and eventually, somewhere near Lyon, entering the narrowing valley of the Rhône. The river was a milky jade colour, and the hillsides above it were patterned into terraces on which the vines shone with the rich blue of the copper sulphate that had been sprayed upon them to kill the phylloxera. Soon we were in Provence itself, passing through its ancient towns, Orange and Avignon and Tarascon, old towers and walls and the ringing bells of history. At Tarascon it was twilight, but the moon came up and in the last few miles to Arles the leaves on the olive trees shone silver in its light.

I was in the new world of an ancient land, my first encounter with Mediterranean Europe, and life as well as the landscape seemed entirely different to me when I got out of the train at the station outside the city, and my taxi drove through the town gates into a maze of interlacing streets so narrow that the people on the sidewalks seemed only a few inches away as I looked at them through the car windows. We emerged from this labyrinth into a tiny tree-shaded square and there, built into the eroded walls of the old Roman forum, was my hotel, the Nord Pinus.

I spent a strange hectic week in Arles, weakened by mild dysentery, often half-drunk on Banyuls and on the heady Chateauneuf du Pape which one bought so cheaply. I always managed to keep in motion as I took buses into the hills to Les Baux and St. Rémy and into the marshes of the Camargue to Les Saintes Maries de la Mer and Aigues Mortes, and trains to Tarascon and Beaucaire, Orange and Nîmes and Avignon. I experienced the warmth and colour of life in the Midi, but also my first overwhelming physical sense of the classical heritage. I was intrigued by the red-shirted cowboys herding the black fighting bulls of the Camargue; by the gaily-painted fishing boats of Les Saintes Maries drawn up on the wide yellow beaches under the cloudy pink thickets of tamarisk trees, long boats pointed at both ends and coloured in rich yellows and blues and reds, with eyes painted on their prows to protect them from the hidden dangers of the sea; by the strange haunted solitudes of the empty walls of Aigues Mortes looking out over the salt marshes, and the ruined mansions of Les Baux high over a valley from which the song of the cicadas rose in a great eruption of sound.

But this is not a travel book, and more germane is the fact that the experience stimulated me to write a good many poems, inspired by the melancholy sense of tragic history permeating a brilliant landscape. On my way back, when I stayed a few days in Paris, I found my impressions counterpointed by the feeling of a doomed era nearing its end as I talked to people I met when I mooned around the Montparnasse cafés and stocked up with French books for what I anticipated would be a long siege. Also in Paris — another portent — I went with an introduction from F. A. Ridley to search out the French left-wing socialist Marceau Pivert at the offices of the small dissident party to which he belonged. I found the premises padlocked, Pivert vanished, and a plain-clothes man from the Sûreté lurking in a doorway. I put on a show of gormless sincerity, and the detective politely walked me to the entrance of the courtyard and, laying a paternal hand on my arm, told me to go home quickly to England. *"Pour nous, le futur n'existe pas."* He did not appear to relish his task.

Yet I also gained a sense of something more than the impermanence of human institutions from my first trip to Provence. I was deeply impressed by the mysterious resonances between art and the physical world which I found exemplified there, and some months after my return I wrote some observations which may well represent my first stumbling into art criticism.

The difference between the flat plains of the Camargue and the barren hills to the east of Arles is striking. But despite their bareness, these Provencal hills are the reverse of desolate. It was only when I travelled through the gnarled grey olive groves into their arid solitudes that I realized how faithfully the painters like Cézanne and Van Gogh interpreted the intensity of their atmosphere. Cézanne caught their peculiar angularity of formation, which often makes them look like piles of enormous weathered crystals. But while Cézanne painted the elemental structure of Provence, Van Gogh caught the motion that gave it life, like the rippling tension of the flesh under the solidity of bone. The twisted and wind-dwarfed shapes of the cypresses, the sudden violent scarlet of blossoming pomegranate trees, the mauve-grey drifts of wild lavender running over the yellow rocks — all these were pure Van Gogh, and in the shimmering heat of the summer days among the stones I would often notice that vibrancy of tone which is characteristic of his work.

It was this vision I took back to England with me, when I crossed the Channel back to the summer-bleached downs and the green fields; it helped sustain me in the long years of absence, and led me back to Provence when the frontiers finally opened again.

X

THE ENDING OF PEACE

THERE IS AN OLD ENGLISH saying about the month of March; if it comes in like a lamb, it goes out like a lion, and, of course, vice versa. World War II came in like a lamb. Our expectations of immediate destruction were proven wrong as the Luftwaffe, month after month, neglected to bomb the cities of Britain, while the small British army across the channel, like the large French conscript army, rotted inactively behind that strange phantasm in material form, the Maginot Line. In my own life, as in the life of the great British millions, there was little perceptible change, except that we had to use ration cards. The politicians, conscious of the recruiting chaos of the Great War, had evolved a National Service system which for more than a year left most young men in the illusion that they might never be called up, or alternatively, face a tribunal to test the sincerity of their opposition to war. We called that period, which lasted a full year into the autumn of 1940, the Phony War, and its prolongation, I am sure, reflected the reluctance of the British ruling caste and the Junkers who were still powerful in the Reichswehr and in the German foreign service to admit that their aims might be divergent and that destiny had not meant them to unite in a crusade against the detested French and Russians.

Be that as it may, the Phony War created a strange sense of euphoria mingled with the dread that lingered from the pre-war months. We felt rather like condemned men who had received, if not a reprieve, at least a stay of execution. When I remember my own situation, still travelling backwards and forwards from Marlow to London (the only difference from a few months before being that I shamefacedly tucked into my briefcase a gasmask I was convinced would be useless), desperately hoping, as I had hoped at Munich, that the ultimate struggle would somehow be avoided, and knowing that almost everyone travelling still to their familiar jobs shared that hope, I recognized that by the late 1930s there had been a profound shift in human consciousness. Whatever aberrant bellicosity might temporarily be flourishing in Germany, the glory had gone out of war; the *Iliad* had become at long last an antiquarian text. They waited patiently to be called, but few attempted to hasten that day by volunteering; at most they accepted the war as necessary, but I encountered nobody who gloried in conflict even so mildly as Rupert Brooke had done. The shift in the general European consciousness had indeed been so radical that, despite the explicit warnings of *Mein Kampf*, despite the cumulative series of Nazi provocations, few people outside Germany really wanted to believe they would lead to war; I am sure many people in Germany shared the mental condition of those who lived west of the Rhine.

Yet our lives were beginning to speed up even during the period of the Phony War. Any war is a great loosener of manners, and World War II, even in its tentative stage, was no exception. It did not matter what stance we might take; our lives would never be the same again; they had been thrown into an arena of emergent possibilities and decaying securities in which one knew only that the adaptable would survive and prosper.

So, for the first year of the war, I went about my life almost as if nothing had changed, but at the same time I was aware of new opportunities and new threats. So far as the threats were concerned, a letter I wrote to Godwin in October, 1939, shows how I was then thinking of them.

Of course, it will be some months, probably nearly a year, before our classes are called. So we have plenty of time for thought. But, for myself, I've decided the main lines of my conduct. That is, I'm definitely not going to fight. However, I'm still a little undecided how far I'm willing to go in the way of a compromise with the authorities. As a good individualist, anarchist and pacifist, I ought to stand out as an "Absolute" — but I'm not sure yet if I have the enormous moral courage needed for that. Still, you may be getting a letter from me from behind prison walls one of these fine days. At any rate, I won't kill or be a party to it. And I shall do my best throughout to keep the neutrality, spiritual and intellectual, which the poet should maintain in the conflicts of ordinary people. The imperialist squabbles of England and Germany aren't our quarrels. Nor are the dog fights of ideologies. Our world is without boundaries and creeds. As Barker says: "It is not a shape on the map; it is the image of the imagination with the littoral of the intellect."

OPPORTUNITY PRESENTED ITSELF first of all by the fact that, for reasons I still do not fully understand, Geoffrey Grigson and Julian Symons both decided to close down the magazines that had done so much to encourage poetry writing in the later 1930s, *New Verse* and *Twentieth Century Verse*. T. S. Eliot had already ended the *Criterion*. At the end of 1939 Cyril Connolly and Stephen Spender had started *Horizon*, but that great eclectic magazine was too much of a mandarin journal to continue the avant garde role of such little mags of the late 1930s as *Twentieth Century Verse* and *Contemporary Poetry and Prose*, which I think vanished at the same time.

Faced with this sudden silencing of voices I decided to start a magazine for young and disaffected writers. I talked to my poet friends and my pacifist friends and my radical socialist friends (for still I knew no other professing anarchists). Jack David, and Mike Pitts, a pacifist who worked in publishing, were the people who collaborated with me most closely in the practical matters of publication. Julian Symons offered editorial advice until he vanished into the army. I found that my credit among other young writers was higher than I had expected, and when the first issue of my new magazine *NOW* appeared, its contributors' list showed the patchwork of friendships I had been making in the last few years. Charles Madge and Kathleen Raine were there, representing my *New Verse* and *Mass Observation* links, Roy Fuller and Keidrych Rhys and Derek Savage as fellow contributors to *Twentieth Century Verse*, F. A. Ridley and Oswell Blakeston among my friends from Charles Lahr's bookshop (Charles figured on the masthead as London distributor) and, from the far past, Lance Godwin, who gave a story and also an anonymous statement that contained the superbly Nietzschean sentences: "Now only the naked, unarmed adventurer may live . . . . What do I think of the war? I scorn it. I tremble for clear thinking."

That first issue was mimeographed, the stencils typed by Jack David and run off on the Gestetner in Mike Pitts' publishing house; the total cost was around three guineas, which is somewhat less than the price of a single unblemished surviving copy today. Mike Pitts, one of those big Chestertonian laughers who counterpointed the long-faced Quakers in the pacifist movement, became the business manager, operating distribution from his cottage in Grubwood Lane among the cherry orchards of Cookham Dean. As for *NOW*'s contents, in those early issues it attempted a fusion of avant garde writing and militant pacifism. Later on, when anarchism was inevitably added to the mixture, *NOW* became a literary organ for the wartime dissident literary left, with George Orwell, Henry Miller, Herbert Read, Dwight Macdonald, Alex Comfort, John Middleton Murry, James Hanley, Lawrence Durrell, George Barker, E. E. Cummings, Victor Serge, Kenneth Rexroth, Paul Goodman, André Breton, Denise Levertov, Lynette Roberts and Ruthven Todd all appearing in its pages. Forty years later, in his *Critical Observations*, Julian Symons remembered *NOW* as being "much the best periodical of a radical kind in England during those years. The general editorial attitude combined radicalism with the utmost freedom for contributors." And he added that "for anybody wanting to know what non-communist literary radicals thought and hoped during those years *NOW* must be an indispensable document, as *Horizon*, for example, was not." *NOW* in fact represented the neo-romantic, personalist and regionalist strains that began to appear in the late 1930s; the more typical 1930s manner continued to find a place in magazines like *Horizon* and John Lehmann's *Penguin New Writing*.

NOW lasted from 1940 to 1947 and much of its history will be woven into the pages that follow. Its early history was broken by an event that entirely turned the course of my life. For the second issue, which appeared in July, 1940, showed me as a nomad using Mike's cottage in Grubwood Lane as a mail pickup while I found a new base for my existence. My mother had died early in May, and the household at 82 Station Road was no more.

I came home one evening and found Percy the milkman waiting outside the station. Percy was a gentle birdlike man I had known since early childhood, and he understood our neighbourhood and its inhabitants with empathy, so that if something was wrong, Percy knew. He had noticed that my mother looked ill when she took in the milk at ten o'clock. A little later one of the neighbours had seen her hanging out washing and then abruptly going indoors; later Percy had knocked, got no answer and found the door locked. As Percy walked beside me, going on with his narration, I realized with a sick certainty what had happened, since over the past few months my mother had been going to her doctor with heart murmurs, and though she reported improvement I had been particularly disturbed one evening when we went for a walk, and on the way home an owl flew over our path. "That means a death in the family," my mother said sombrely, and I knew that her superstitious reaction was strengthened by a personal anxiety, perhaps even a premonition.

So I asked Percy if he had a jackknife, and managed to jemmy open the kitchen window at the back of the house. I called out as I climbed in through the window, and the house was silent. We ran upstairs, and my mother was lying in her bed, fully clothed, with the sheets drawn over her.

I never slept again in the house that had been my home for well over twenty years. Hearing of my trouble, Giselle sent her husband to help me with what had to be done, and insisted on my living in her house until the funeral was over and I had decided what I should do with my life. I remember with gratitude those days when we talked for long hours about life and death as we waited for the undertakers to make their dismal arrangements and the lawyers and doctors to perform their formalities, and for the relatives to gather for the cremation at Reading and then the drive north to bury my mother's ashes, as she had wished, in Salopian soil.

Giselle helped me find my way through the maze of mingled feelings that assailed me at that time: shock and sorrow and guilt and relief entangled in a strangling bewilderment. By the end it was only loyalty I felt towards my mother; I had never loved her as I did my father, and in the years after her death I felt gratitude and guilt for the sacrifices she had made for my sake during the years of poverty, accompanied by a resentment at my own sense of obligation that prevented me from breaking free. Yet it was the sense of relief I felt that this was all over, the sense of liberation into my own life, that appalled me most in the days after her death; Giselle helped me to accept such feelings as natural and inevitable.

AFTER I RETURNED from Shropshire, Elizabeth, who was going to join Tom as an evacuee teacher in Sussex, offered me the flat they had just acquired in Muswell Hill, and I lived there until the end of the year. It was a time of immediately heightened experience. Charles Lahr was my neighbour, and I soon made contact with the local pacifists. But most of my spare time, particularly over weekends, was spent in the centre of London, where I began to frequent the pubs and clubs favoured by the avant-garde writers and artists.

The drinking round in those days was ritualized in terms of locales, so that it was always possible to find a friend if one made the circuit of the pubs. But one could always have a quiet drink or a confidential chat, even in Soho, merely by stepping into one of the pubs which were not accepted Bohemian haunts. The taverns most favoured by Bohemians in central London were the Swiss, the Helvetia and the York Minster (known as the French House from its splendidly moustached proprietor, Victor Berlemont), all in Soho; the Fitzroy in Charlotte Street, the Wheatsheaf in Rathbone Place, and sometimes the Marquis of Granby round the corner, though that was already a gay haunt. Then in Chelsea there were the Six Bells and the Admiral Nelson where I could always find Mervyn Peake and sometimes Vernon Watkins and Narayana Menon, and the Salisbury in St. Martin's Lane.

The Café Royal, with its old red plush benches and marble tables from the 1890s, was still a place to go when one was flush. There was also a variety of shabby afternoon drinking clubs where we weathered closing time. Perhaps the most popular was Pedro's, run by an enigmatic Spaniard who wore great solitaire diamond rings on his fingers. There one could usually find Dylan Thomas and Roy Campbell and Malcolm Lowry's friend Tom Pocock; Lowry himself was already in Canada. There were also equally shabby night clubs, and a few coffee houses to which we would resort when every fountain of alcohol had dried up, such as Fama's in Soho, where old Italian anarchists played cards until dawn, and an underground den on the edge of Seven Dials called the Coffee An', where poets, painters and Indian student revolutionaries mingled with a range of half-world figures.

About half way through the war the police closed down the Coffee An', ostensibly because it harboured deserters and black marketeers. One did encounter fugitives there and towards the end of 1941, when I had a room in Hampstead, I gave hiding to a lesbian girl I had met in the Coffee An' (Olive or to her friends Oliver) who had deserted from the ATS and whom for a while I found an amusing companion. And the place certainly had its contingent of people who lived on the knife-edge that divided artistic Bohemia from the half-world of petty crime. One could order black market goods there with as much ease as one could talk of poetry or sculpture, though few of us had enough money to benefit greatly from this kind of trade.

The most intellectual of the Bohemian crooks were the book thieves, young men often dedicated to some kind of literary or artistic occupation who felt that stealing was a fair way to subsidize themselves. They would work the large bookstores of Charing Cross Road or Piccadilly and then sell the books to smaller dealers in obscure streets. I knew several of the book thieves, who were usually intellectual and innocent-looking young men. The greatest virtuoso among them, a dancer named José, boasted that he could lift any named book from any shop without detection, and he would take orders which he scrupulously fulfilled. His greatest feat was providing a client with a complete set of Freud. He once gave me, as a gesture of admiration for my poetry, a handsome Shakespeare which I accepted without asking questions. After a distinguished career in pilfering, in which he was never caught, José fulfilled his ambition, and once he was enrolled in the corps of the Ballets Kurt Jooss, he never stole again. Another of these frequenters of the Coffee An' who waged his small private war against society was Old Dick, a snuff-stained printer with a passion for fine typography. He kept himself by printing false identity cards which he would peddle around Soho — cheap at a fiver — and, when he had enough to buy food and hand-made paper, he would return to his workshop and continue the beautiful printing he loved.

Every now and again, in the Coffee An', a hurried whisper of "Bogey" would run from table to table, and a few people would slide to the back entrance as a silence fell over the room and a batch of gloomy detectives padded through, looking into every face and making honest men of letters feel they were living dangerously. But most nights we were undisturbed, and in the summer would emerge from Fama's or the Coffee An' into a misty dawn, and see the night-club musicians trailing home through the Soho streets, with their fiddles under their arms and double-basses slung on their backs, and the helmeted policemen enjoying quiet smokes in doorways, and the newsvans driving at breakneck speed towards the railway termini. The hardy would head for Covent Garden, where the pubs opened with daylight for the market porters, and then perhaps go on to Billingsgate, where the fish porters' taverns opened an hour or so later. Since the underground stopped running at one o'clock in the morning, the rest of us would trudge home, if we had not the offer of a Bloomsbury floor to doss down on for the rest of the night, and often, on the way, catch the first of the morning buses. While it was novel, it was exhilarating; for those to whom it became permanent it was a sad life, as much a habit as the 8:00 o'clock train for the commuter.

It was mostly in the pubs and clubs that avant-garde writers and editors met each other, and many manuscripts were exchanged over the tables of Soho taverns or in the cheap restaurants of Charlotte Street where we ate together. Only Cyril Connolly at *Horizon* could afford to maintain a real office; it was in an old Bloomsbury house where he and his assistant editor, the coldly beautiful Sonia Brownell (later Sonia Orwell) would sometimes invite favoured writers to tea. The rest of us were to be encountered on the regular pub circuit. There was the flamboyant Tambimuttu, a Ceylonese Tamil who ran *Poetry London* with a subsidy from an artistic margarine manufacturer; Wrey Gardiner, a bit older than most of the young poets he published and as grey as his Grey Walls Press, who brought out *Poetry Quarterly*; the gentle Russian exile, Stefan Schimanski, who began with *Kingdom Come* (which we all called Condom King) and finally edited the excellent *World Review*. At least half-a-dozen other editors ran little magazines that flourished in the new market for literature created by the long periods of empty leisure so many people in military and other service endured in wartime.

Some of my pleasantest and most poignant memories are of people who never made on history the mark for which they strove. I remember, in that Bohemian chorus, a vast number of medical students and art students and apprentice ballerinas, of commercial artists and advertisement copywriters and charming but untalented hangers-on of the arts (names often forgotten but faces usually remembered) with whom I talked and shared meals and drinks and — much less often — beds. They were often vain and trivial, but a great many of them had nimble minds that shamed my own slow sureness, and my acquaintance with them confirmed for me the truth of Oscar Wilde's observation that it is the second-rate artist, or even the failure, who has the most interesting personality. Most of them have vanished. A face, a voice, an incident, is all that remains of those fleeting contacts of such youthful intensity.

There were others on whom fame has shone its flickering light. Some, like the bizarre and eccentric MacLaren Ross and the erudite and surprisingly modest Philip Toynbee, were better writers than their later reputations suggest. William Empson, at times hiding behind a great spade beard, was often to be seen drinking Cordial Medoc in the York Minster, and Randall Swingler, the only good poet who remained a long-run devotee of the Communist Party, was also a habitué of Victor Berlemont's saloon bar; with what we all regarded as great appropriateness, he eventually dropped dead on the pavement outside the York Minster. Sometimes the old greybeard Augustus John would wander into one of the pubs, his basilisk eye still searching for likely young girls, and once I remember E. M. Forster leading a covey of grand Bloomsbury queens on a slumming jaunt into the Wheatsheaf. Of course, there were many writers who kept away from the Bohemian pubs, though at some time or other one would see most of them in the Café Royal, which still retained its reputation as the prime literary meeting place where writers often made their deals with agents or publishers. A perpetual juvenility was needed to maintain the Bohemian habit, and this was an attribute of the two major poets I came to know well in the Soho pubs and clubs, Dylan Thomas and Roy Campbell.

Dylan Thomas, probably the best lyric poet of his time, was a man of unpredictable temper and impulse. At times when he was writing poetry he would maintain a rigorous sobriety; indeed, it is hard to imagine how poetry of such technical complexity could have been produced in any other condition. His drunken bouts were the holidays of a highly serious artist, and the fact that they grew more frequent and obsessive towards the end of his life was linked to the comparatively early failure of his inspiration. London was the place where he earned money; there was a period when he had some success as a broadcaster, and he became at times insufferably pompous as a result of it, particularly if one encountered him in the vicinity of Broadcasting House with the briefcase and homburg hat he then affected.

But London was also his place of relaxing debauchery, and though at mid-afternoon in Pedro's club it was possible to discuss poetry very seriously with him, as the day wore on he was much more prone to aggressions and extravagances. One night he and I went arm in arm, barking like dogs, through the blacked out streets of Soho, and were nabbed by the police in Golden Square for committing a nuisance. We were let go by a fatherly sergeant who seemed to recognize the errant boy that survived in Dylan alongside the maturing inner vision that enabled him to write his score of great poems. That perpetual boy, greedy for sensation, emerged in Thomas's fine stories of childhood, but also helped to ruin his body and his life. His failure to reconcile the two sides of his character produced the sense of doom and failure which, in the last years, undermined his success as a peripatetic bard and let him allow the American flatterers to kill him with drink.

The same kind of Peter Pan syndrome was evident, rather differently manifest, in Roy Campbell, who lived mentally in a world of romance, so that it was always difficult to tell which of the adventures he narrated with such gusto were true and which were fictitious. Campbell had certainly been a soldier and a fine horseman and even when he had become a permanent resident in the London literary world, after he left Spain, he could not forget his active past. His conversation was full of bullrings and battles — he was the one British poet who fought on Franco's side — and secret-agent adventures, when he hunted down German spies in Spain after 1938 on behalf of the British.

We got on surprisingly well, considering our vast differences of outlook. Campbell was not as his enemies suggested, a fascist; his support for Franco came from his strong right-wing Catholicism. Though he had a hatred of communism in its own way as bitter as Orwell's, he found in anarchism the opposite to Catholicism. He would say that the last great struggle would be between those two creeds and that until such time anarchists and Catholics should respect each other as honourable foes and perhaps enjoy good friendships. Campbell liked me, which was perhaps why he rationalized so amiably. But there was a ferocious strain in him which emerged in the company of people he disliked or despised. One day when I was drinking with him in the Fitzroy, Nina Hamnett came in with the necromancer Aleister Crowley, by now aged and decrepit. Campbell poured down his bitter contempt on this man who had once set himself up with pride as the personification of evil. There was not much left of the Great Beast 666,the anti-Christ he had once claimed to be, in the pathetic creature who began to weep into his beer under Campbell's insults. A more pleasant recollection is of an evening when we left the Café Royal at midnight; Campbell, drunk and merry, danced in the middle of Piccadilly Circus, making veronicas with his trenchcoat at the taxis as if they were bulls and he a matador in one of the corridas of his youth.

I DID NOT REMAIN in London all that sunny first summer of the war. France of course was cut off; I found my way instead into unfamiliar corners of England and Wales. I went down to Brighton to see Elizabeth, and in that time of few visitors I was able to enjoy the graceful Regency town that in 1940 still survived. I went to Cambridgeshire to stay in the poet Derek Savage's mediaeval daub-and-wattle cottage in the village of Dry Drayton. Derek was and is a devout and unchurchly Christian who then called himself a personalist and was much under the influence of Berdyaev; we shared our pacifism, but disagreed on matters of action. Derek regarded the anarchism I was then developing as too chiliastic, too directly aimed at creating an ideal social order; he believed that the Kingdom of God could be achieved only by spiritual changes that in turn would affect social forms. But it is the other visit I made that summer that haunts my memory with the image of a lost idyllic world.

Keidrych Rhys, the editor of *Wales*, had left London and moved down to Carmarthenshire with his wife, the poet Lynette Roberts. He had invited me to his village of Llanybri, before he was called up into the army, but Lynette wrote to tell me the invitation held, and I went down, taking the overnight train to Carmarthen and then a bus over the bounding country road to the seacoast and the little stone town of Llanstephan, with its tiny esplanade and its multitude of seabirds.

Lynette was awaiting me there, for Llanstephan was the end of the regular transport system, and we would have to walk into the hills. She was a tall young woman with a soft intelligent face, not beautiful, but very striking in the long scarlet Welsh cloak she wore. Lynette came from Argentina, from one of the Welsh settlements of the pampas, and the English she spoke combined a Welsh lilt with an exotic Spanish plumminess. I liked her at sight, and she seemed to reciprocate the feeling; as we took the long climb, we talked with something like the ease of old friends reunited. Every now and again we would pause to observe a further extension of the view over the glittering sea and the coast, and soon, over to the west and a good way beneath us, we saw the silvery slate roofs of Dylan Thomas's village of Laugharne, nestling in its cluster of hills and headlands. Then we topped the last ridge, and Llanybri lay below us, built in a depression in the hills like a gigantic lark's nest. Down we went through fern-hung lanes into this sheltering saucer of rock beyond which the hills ran north in green waves into the lilac distance where the faint grey mountains of central Wales reared their bulky forms.

In one of her poems, Lynette has described Llanybri as "the village of lace and stone," and the phrase gives a sense of the charm and solidity that formed my first impression. Its cottages were indeed of solid grey stone quarried out of the Carmarthen hills, but they were all bright with white or pink wash, and the stone walls that divided the gardens from the road were robbed of their severity by hedges of purple fuschia or by trailing garlands of arabis and saxifrage and stonecrop.

Lynette lived in one of the cottages, and as a concession to village ideas of propriety she had arranged for me to sleep in one of the two inns, kept by Mrs. Price who, to identify her among all the other Prices of the village, was generally called Mrs. Price Red Dragon. It was to the great beamed kitchen of the Red Dragon that we would go every evening after a day spent talking in Lynette's cottage or roaming the hills with their lush west Welsh vegetation and their abundance of birds and butterflies. There we would meet Jenkins the Grocer and Jones Blacksmith and Bevan Carpenter and all the other village worthies.

Llanybri was a Welsh-speaking village, and the first time we entered together the drinkers were speaking their own language, of which, through my own Welsh links, I had picked up no more than a few phrases. It was an extraordinary sign of the natural courtesy of these people that, as soon as we entered, they switched, by an unspoken consent, to English. And never, during the rest of my week in Llanybri, did anyone speak Welsh when it might look as though I were being excluded from the conversation. Their English was very musical and took the graceful liberties that help explain why so many Welsh poets writing in English — notably Dylan Thomas and Vernon Watkins and R. S. Thomas — have used our language in such a freshly unorthodox manner.

Many of the Llanybri people were themselves poets, and my own poetic role, as well as my friendship with Keidrych and Lynette, helped to explain why I was so well received. They wrote in Welsh, following the elaborate traditional forms, and some among them, Bevan Carpenter and a farmer everyone called Evans Llyn Fach (Evans of the Small Lake), had competed in local *eisteddfodau*, the bardic gathering of the Celtic poets. To be a poet in Llanybri was a matter of serious import; it was, in fact, the next best thing to being a preacher.

Llanybri, as a community of amateur poets, inspired my imagination in much the same way as Les Baux the town of troubadours must have inspired the poets who wandered through the Languedoc seven hundred years before. It reminded me that just about a year before I had myself been in Berengaria's Provence. But it also interested me as the nearest thing to a genuine peasant community I ever encountered in Britain. There was no lord of the manor, though there was an almost deserted Anglican church, and as far as I could trace, the pattern of life in the village since mediaeval times had always been that of every man as a small independent landowner. There were no large farmers, but there were many moderate farmers and even more smallholders, who combined agriculture or grazing with some other occupation. The grocer, the baker, the blacksmith, the roadmender, the postmaster, all of them had their bits of land and their few cattle, and every morning as I ate breakfast in the inn I would see Price Red Dragon driving his cows in for the morning milking. The Anglican vicar might face almost empty pews, but he had his glebe to cultivate.

So far as I could tell, the only men who had no land at all were the schoolmaster and the policeman, both outsiders, and I encountered only one fulltime agricultural labourer, Roberts Cwm Goch (Roberts of the Red Hill). Far from being relegated to a lower class all his own, Roberts Cwm Goch was one of the most respected men in the village for the dignity with which he bore the misfortune of having to toil every day for somebody else, though even he had his handkerchief of land which he spaded on a Saturday afternoon. Many of the smallholders, in fact, had hardly larger pieces of land, and they worked them by primitive methods; Llanybri was the last place in Britain where I saw a field of barley being cut with sickles. But all these people seemed to get along well and if there were no rich men in Llanybri, there were also no paupers.

An independence of mind had sprung from this economic simplicity. While almost all the people of Llanybri attended one or other of the little whitewashed chapels on a Sunday evening, they had scanty moral smugness and, whatever their conventicle, were determined to defend their right to drink beer when they wished. In those days, owing to the disastrous influence of the temperance movements, it was the general rule in Wales for public houses to be closed on a Sunday. The people of Llanybri regarded this as an unnatural law, to be resisted, though without undue ostentation. So on a Sunday the front door of the Red Dragon was locked and bolted, and drinkers went round to the back lane and climbed the garden wall at a spot where two stones had been knocked out for footholds. They picked their way through the raspberry canes and slipped discreetly into the kitchen where the assembled village worthies would be found taking their illicit ale to the tune of sober conversation. No rowdiness, man, on the Sabbath!

Since everybody knew of this custom, its safe continuance depended on the reasonableness of the local policeman, and the Sunday I stayed in Llanybri was a critical one. Amiable, bumbling Constable Morgan had taken his glass with the rest on a Sunday morning, but he was being replaced by a daio from the Rhondda Mawr, and nobody knew how he would act. The kitchen of the Red Dragon was fuller than ever that Sunday morning. All the farmers had turned up, the tradesmen, the schoolmaster, Lynette and I, and even Dylan Thomas had walked up from Laugharne; he had a special interest in the liberties of Llanybri, since his mother had been born there. The door to the garden had been left open, and at last we heard the scuffle over the wall, the steps on the flagstones outside, and then the new policeman entering, dressed in mufti, the blue serge suit and white silk muffler of the man from the valleys. There was a tense instant as he looked around. Then Jenkins the Grocer spoke up. "There's a fine *Saturday* morning it is, Constable." The policeman laughed and accepted the drink Price Red Dragon was holding out to him. It was afterwards, talking of politics, that Dylan expressed in an emphatic aphorism his own nihilist individualism. "I would like to see a Britain," he said, "of forty-five million little Hitlers each screaming at the rest, 'You dirty Jew!'"

I am sure the generosity I encountered in Llanybri was the natural product of the economic and general independence that flourished there. In every way, the people did their best to make me, as a visiting poet, feel comfortable. Each morning there would be some gift on Lynette's doorstep to help her entertain me properly: a rabbit, or a pair of wild pigeons, or an apple pie. One day, when we were out walking, some farmer dumped a load of logs beside the back door. The crowning act of generosity came at the end of my week, when I went after breakfast to Mrs. Price Red Dragon and asked for my bill. "Bill?" she said. Nothing of the kind! I was a friend of Mr. Rhys and a poet and they had been honoured to have me. She obstinately refused to take a penny.

It was market day in Carmarthen when I was leaving Llanybri, and in the spirit of mutual aid prevailing there, Jenkins the Grocer offered space in his van for anybody who wanted to go to the county town. So I embraced Lynette, who used my lost Welsh name of Meredith when she said goodbye and whenever we met afterwards, and climbed in over the two pigs belonging to the Methodist preacher that were lying in the bottom of the van, and took my place among the women who had spread their baskets and sacks of market produce on every side of them. The van started, and as it rode over the lip of the giant saucer of rock I saw the last white gleam of Llanybri lying below me, and, a moment later, the glittering waters of Carmarthen Bay which represented the outer world.

XI

A WORLD AT WAR

LANYBRI'S NATURAL BARRIERS and its traditional life did not save it from the storms of the outside world. A few weeks after I left, it was scarred by the bombs of the Luftwaffe and for more than one of its people there were no more genial evenings at the Red Dragon. For my visit there was followed quickly by the turning of the Phony War into the real war. While I was with Derek Savage in Dry Drayton we had heard of the invasion of the Low Countries and the crumbling of the myth of the Maginot Line as the German armies surged into France. We had talked of the possibility of Britain being invaded, and had discussed how passive resistance could be organized if we were left alive to organize it, since the example of Nazi actions in Germany suggested that pacifists would be among the first people rounded up into concentration camps. We also talked of going underground, but there was still a vagueness to all this.

It became an immediate reality when the Germans began the campaign of air-raids — we borrowed a word from them to call it the "Blitz." One afternoon in August I stood on Muswell Hill looking east at the smoke rising high from the great fires at the London docks. This was the prelude, for very soon the Germans were flying almost every night over London and the other cities of Britain, and the heavy drone of their loaded planes, the whistle of bombs, the crash of explosions, the barking of anti-aircraft guns and the clatter of shrapnel on roads and roofs became the familiar sounds of one's life.

Inevitably one's pattern of living changed. The Bohemian round defiantly continued until the centre of London became a bombing target and the days shortened. As I wrote in October to Lance Godwin:

The extreme difficulty of getting about after dark, and the gradually earlier coming of nightfall, make it very hard to keep contact with people in other parts of London, and the centre is dead after seven.

Not only the cities were affected. There was the surprise raid by a solitary plane on Llanybri which I have mentioned, and I was myself involved in a similar incident. Jack David had invited me for a few days to his cottage in Marlow Bottom, where he promised me peaceful sleep. The first night there I spent lying under the bed as the bombs whistled down on the chalkhills and the beechwoods; the Luftwaffe had received false reports of a military installation being built there. I returned next day to the predictable dangers of London.

There one lived a curious alternating existence, travelling each morning to work or wandering into Soho and the West End at weekends, returning by dark, and then, just after nightfall retreating from external activity, going off to the shelter or, as I did, staying above ground with a pride that acknowledged fear. One never knew which of one's colleagues might be missing from work in the morning, or which of one's friends might not turn up for a rendezvous.

I HAVE ALREADY DECIDED that the time had come to end my connection with the Great Western Railway. After my mother's death I had received the money left in trust to me. I was still uneasy about the way in which my grandfather had accumulated his modest wealth, so I decided not to keep it and live miserably on the interest, but to spend the principal as fast as I felt inclined in the hope that by the time this dubious money was spent I might be able to live by my writing. In any case, I was now free to leave the railway, and I had to decide what to do upon my liberation from employment. I felt confident that I would be exempt from military service and, having observed how the London tribunal was operating, I thought the condition of agricultural work would probably be imposed. I had no real objection to this. So far as I could see, people had to be fed, war or no war, and it was killing that I rejected. Besides, my ancestors had all been farmers, and the thought of trying their way of life for a while did not displease me. The only problem was to find a way of farming on my own terms and not on those of the authorities, which would have offended my nascent anarchist ideas.

The solution came quite easily. I had become interested in the communitarian movement emerging among the pacifists. John Middleton Murry had been preaching in the Adelphi and elsewhere the need to create, "in the interstices of the totalitarian order," communities of like-minded people who would form the nuclei of a future libertarian society based on voluntary sharing rather than imposed equality. Pacifists, Murry and many others argued, need not be merely negative refusers; in withdrawing from the war society they could lay the foundations of a peaceable order. I found these ideas attractive, and had discussed them extensively with Derek Savage.

Now something more definite presented itself. A young poet, Peter Wells, had sent me some verse I accepted for NOW. He was working with the pigs in the community of Langham in Essex which Middleton Murry had founded. Langham was now guided by Max Plowman, the Great War poet and Blake critic and editor of the Adelphi, which he had also taken over from the community. Wells put me in touch with Plowman, and Max, his wife Dorothy and I met in London to discuss my going. There was a three months' probation rule, he explained. It was arranged I should go there early in December, so I immediately gave my month's notice to the Great Western Railway.

The next day the summons to my tribunal hearing came and I went down to Fulham to bandy arguments with a lean, dour County Court judge, a pedantic Oxford historian and a stocky north-country trade union boss. I had taken the precaution of gathering an impressive battery of letters and my brief, which spoke up for the freedom of the artist as well as against the practice of war, was sufficiently out of the ordinary to provoke a discussion which the members of the tribunal seemed to enjoy as a change from the routine submissions of the religious objectors. They granted me what I was willing to accept, exemption conditional on doing farm work. Part of my application survives because I printed it in NOW, and the sentences I quote show not only the influence of Gandhi but also the somewhat individualist anarchism into which I had already advanced, partly under Wilde's influence.

. . . I cannot believe it is right to use violence against other violence. What is intrinsically wrong is always wrong, and to counter one evil by another only produces greater eventual evil. We can defeat evil only by good. I believe that to be practical as well as wise. War has been tried as a means of ridding the world of evil, and has failed miserably. It is time peace and love were given their chance . . . .

I can admit only my own conscience as controller of my actions, and cannot place myself in a position where I might be called to perform any act against my beliefs. To me, as a pacifist and a poet, the individual is the supreme unit. Society exists for the individual, and it is in the individual personality that man must reach fulfilment. I therefore believe the rights of the individual to be governed by his conscience are paramount. Anything other than this freedom is a slavery, and of all slaveries I believe military life the most terrible, because the soldier's whole life is governed by the compulsion of destroying his fellows. I find such a life incompatible with my whole conception of morality and service to mankind and entirely opposed to the function of the artist. As a man and a poet I will face anything rather than what seems to me such an evil servitude.

So, when I took the train to Colchester, and then a bus into the Essex marshes, I knew that I would not have to become a martyr for the cause and though I was prepared to accept prison if I had to, I was content to witness my opposition in a less dramatic way, since I have always felt that martyrs, like heroes, dominate people by shaming them.

I was happy to be leaving Muswell Hill for another reason. My affair with a pacifist school teacher had just foundered, mainly because she wanted us to set up a household and I was not yet prepared, as I would be a little while afterwards, to commit myself to a stable relationship.

"THE OAKS," AS THE COMMUNITY building at Langham was called, was a decayed late Victorian mansion built by a general who had been a friend of Edward VII, and strange tales circulated in nearby villages about the goings-on there before Edward assumed the crown. The only physical evidence was offered by the baths, each long enough for an eight-foot giant — or a pair of normal-sized people end to end. The gardens were still well kept and elegant, but most of the estate had been sold off long ago to the former tenant farmers. A home farm of about a hundred acres remained, and there was also a small wood. The land was flat for miles, the hills distant, and the damp, by December, universal and penetrating.

When I went to Langham, I thought I might enter wholly into the community pattern of living and stay for a long time, perhaps for the duration of the war, as a kind of lay monk in a model of the ideal society.

I stayed only a few months; it was a period of hope and disillusionment, of joy mingled with frustration, of intense new friendships which did not last and of bewildering hostilities with people whose ideals and aims I shared. I lived through that period both as an involved and, at times, agonized participant and as a detached observer, as a novelist or a Mass Observer might have done. Perhaps the only reason why I did not attempt to make a novel out of the experience was that, having abandoned my eleven-year routine of office work, I had gone to the other extreme of living without much thought from day to day. During the whole time I was at Langham I wrote hardly any letters and made no notes of my experiences; even *NOW* I let lie fallow, and did not bring out another issue until I had left. The only urge that plagued me was to write poetry, but in the conditions of community living I found it almost impossible.

Langham has its interest as a minor footnote to both the literary history of England and the history of alternative life style movements in that country. I found myself in a group of thirty people, of whom six were women. Apart from the Plowmans, who occupied the old farm building, we all lived in the big house, sleeping in the bedrooms which were turned into small dormitories. I shared a room with a laconic youth of eighteen named Peterkin, who told almost nothing of his background, and an Anglo-Catholic ex-librarian, Jonathan Edwards, who eventually became a Benedictine monk in the Society of the Sacred Mission. Peterkin loved fresh air and Jonathan and I liked to sleep in dense tobacco fogs, so that an immediate conflict of slamming windows occurred and lasted until we stank Peterkin out and he laid down his sleeping bag in the corridor outside. We ate at common tables, and went out each weekday to work in the fields for the benefit of the community.

Sharing did not go beyond that; everyone kept his personal belongings, and though some of us paid a few shillings each week for our food, such contributions were entirely voluntary, and those who had no funds at all were given pocket money. Each day at breakfast, A., the community member who acted as farm manager, would announce the tasks that needed doing and those of us who did not have assigned roles like caring for the cattle or pigs would decide more or less freely among ourselves what we should do. There was no actual compulsion, but, as in all such groups, a good deal of moral pressure was unobtrusively exerted on the idle ones, so that in the end they conformed or departed.

It seemed a workable system, but its success was hindered by a number of circumstances. One was the sheer variety of people who had come together into this community. Under the same roof were anarchists, left-wing socialists and secular-minded pacifists; there were Quakers, Plymouth Brethren, Catholics and one mild-mannered man who professed himself a Satanist; there were vegetarians, bicycle-club enthusiasts, esperantists and nudists. Such a mixture was inevitably volatile, and cyclones were inclined to blow up over small but deeply-felt issues. Cooking was shared by vegetarians and non-vegetarians, and food was provided for both. A dispute that rumbled and flared for weeks began when a red-headed herbivorous giant rose in Viking fury at the dining table wielding a rabbit bone he had found in his vegetarian soup.

All this showed us that our alternative society was just as divided ideologically and temperamentally as the world outside. Not that the variety was without its own compensations. By no means all of us were intellectuals, though there were three practicing poets and a couple of painters as well as a superabundance of teachers. We also had mechanics, a good carpenter, a nurse, and several people with some experience of farming. Jonathan Edwards played excellent Bach on the drawing room piano and an epicene young man named Francis was a fine recorder player. There were certainly enough talents and skills to make the community viable in a material way, and I believe that even the divergences of approach might have been reconciled, if the community had not suffered from the curse of prestigious initiators.

To begin, the property did not belong to the community as such. The Oaks had been acquired by a trust set up in connection with *Adelphi* magazine to promote the Christian communism that Murry was propagating in the 1930s, and had originally been used for summer schools and other gatherings. Murry had already started gathering a community when he was living there, but had departed with some of his disciples to found another community in Norfolk. The *Adelphi*, which Murry and Richard Rees had formerly edited, was handed over to Max Plowman, as I have mentioned earlier.

Plowman found his relationship with the community uneasy; he was a gentle man who, as an officer in the First World War, had been converted to pacifism and poetry and had suffered a great deal in consequence. By now he was really much more interested in the study of Blake than in the practical details of running a farm with a gaggle of quarreling ideologues. He therefore encouraged the community to act as an autonomous and democratic group, and to discuss practical matters at full meetings. Even so, the relationship between the community and the trust that owned the Oaks remained ill-defined.

A., the manager, had not been elected by the community; he was the appointee of the trust, and was consistently supported by Frank Lea, Murry's Langham confidant and later his biographer. A., supported by Lea, tended to act arbitrarily, sacking the experienced old farm bailiff without consulting anyone else. When he was challenged by the other members of the community, he would appeal to Murry or Rees, who sometimes appeared to mediate differences — an intervention that was deeply resented by those members of the community who wished to detach it from all external influences. The Murry I met on these occasions seemed a strangely devitalized and cadaverous individual compared with the passionate participant in the D. H. Lawrence legend; at Langham and in later years he was friendly enough to me, yet in memory he always seems cold-blooded, lizard-like. The situation at Langham was further complicated by the fact that Mary Gamble, Murry's current lover, was living at Dedham, Constable's village a few miles from the Oaks; she also played her part in the community intrigues, and not always in a way Murry might have wished.

I did not remain at Langham long; in fact I was there less than three months. But I could not avoid becoming involved rather passionately in the arguments over the direction the community should take, and inevitably I lined myself with those who wished to see the group making its own decisions independently of Murry and Rees and Gamble and all the other outsiders.

At the same time I was trying to find my own directions. I found an unexpected pleasure in the manual work I did, even though it was not always comfortable in the damp and penetrating winter cold of the Essex marshes. I became adept in trimming tall hedges with a billhook, and I learnt how to fell trees with axe and handsaw, and a few other chores of field and farmyard; my satisfaction may have come largely from a feeling that I was resuming the life of the land my ancestors on both sides had followed. In the evenings we would sit around the big fire in the main room of the mansion, playing poker for matches and taking turns reading Rabelais aloud, and in the late late nights we sneaked down to the kitchen to make ourselves *croques-monsieur* on the Aga stove. Saturdays we went into Colchester to eat charcoal-broiled steaks in the local hotel to make up for the week's dull food.

In the end, life at Langham was made impossible for me by the lack of privacy to carry on my writing. There was really nowhere in the great house where I could settle down, free from interruption; I was grateful to Dorothy Plowman for letting me hide at times in her cottage, and to Mary Gamble for giving me occasional evenings of refuge at Dedham, but these were mere fragments of time, and in February, 1941, I was writing to Lance Godwin:

> I sit down . . . on the eve of a further change of place and life. Nowadays I certainly roll and roll, and gather very little moss. In fact, I lose the moss, the metal moss of money that I gathered in the static dull days that, God be praised, are over at last. How pleasant it is to be relieved of the burden of security, to be freed of the manacles of permanence and responsibility!
>
> I've lived in this community now some nine weeks, and in another fortnight — or less, I shall be moving on to Dry Drayton, near Cambridge, to satisfy the tribunal with a little market gardening, in collaboration with D. S. Savage, the poet. Life here at Langham has been, in many ways, not unpleasant . . . . But the lack of privacy is the one thing that has decided me to go away. It is quite impossible to write when one lives right on top of a great many people, when one even sleeps in a communal bedroom. And the fact of writing being impossible has forced me to realize more vividly than before how much it is my raison d'être. So I must get back to privacy, to a "room of one's own."

TOWARDS THE END OF FEBRUARY, 1941, I wandered north into Cambridgeshire and stayed with Derek Savage, whose plans for a community had foundered because the two other Dry Drayton pacifists had gone their ways. He suggested that we should start market gardening in an old orchard he had a chance to rent, building up an economic basis for a community before other people arrived to join us. Derek had already arranged for me to rent an enormous room in the rambling local rectory, built for a vast Victorian family and now inhabited only by an ageing parson and his wife.

I had time to think over this scheme as I humped pails of water from the village well to Derek's house, which had no water supply, and assisted in his daily ritual of spreading the excrement from the outhouse buckets over the garden beds, a process that involved extracting the paper and burning it separately. I soon saw more flaws than virtues in his plan for our future. Derek began to complain of a bad leg which meant that I would have to do all the digging and rough work. The room at the rectory was intimidatingly vast, with not a stick of furniture, and the paper hung from the damp walls in limp seaweed-like shreds. After a week I went to Cambridge; Jonathan Edwards and Jack Brent, another novice in the community, had also left Langham, and together we got work with the local War Agricultural Committee round about the beginning of March.

War Agricultural Committees had been set up in 1939 with the aim of increasing food production and thus diminishing Britain's vulnerability to a maritime blockade. I do not know what the Committees in the other counties did, but the WAC in Cambridge was mainly concerned with bringing back into production the many farms that during the 1920s and 1930s had been allowed to fall into decay. It employed conscientious objectors, out-of-work farm labourers and, indeed, anyone who had not been called up for the army and was willing to labour for 48 shillings a week.

Jonathan, Jack and I found a set of rooms in a house on Huntingdon Road that was too raffish to be approved for student habitation; it suited us well, for the landlady was usually half-drunk and quite uninterested in our behaviour so long as she got her rent. Every morning we walked to the bus stop where the WAC trucks picked up the workers, and went jolting out over the country roads to the farm on the edge of the fens where the gangs were working on that day. On a large farm we would work together, but more often we worked in groups of thirty or forty.

Because it was centred in Cambridge, and thus offered a reasonably civilized existence in what leisure time one enjoyed, the Cambridge WAC attracted a high proportion of intellectuals and artists. I was in a gang of twenty, supervised by a ferrety little man named Dave who owned a pub in one of the villages which his wife looked after while he worked for the Committee. Apart from two village half-wits and a couple of arthritic labourers whom no farmer would any longer employ, my fellow labourers included the poet Nicholas Moore; the painter Patrick Heron, who later became a notable art critic; a young publisher named Peter Quick; an Orientalist from the British Museum; a Jewish Vedantist, Yehudi Amias, a convert to Marxism; and an East End barber, Jack Braverman, who had served in the International Brigade in

Spain and as a result had become as bitter an anti-Stalinist as George Orwell. There were always interesting companions and good conversation as we toiled in the ditches. There was also much controversy, since some of the workers were political objectors who veered towards communism, and as the weeks went on we tended to polarise into two more or less opposing groups: a loose ILP, anarchist and pacifist confederation, and the party-liners who, as Russia became more deeply involved in the war, grew more inclined to co-operate with the authorities.

At one time Jonathan Edwards and I found ourselves thrust forward as the leaders of a movement of discontent over working conditions. We agitated for a strike, only to be frustrated by an alliance of communist fellow travellers with the officials of the farm workers' union. Only then did I begin to realize that anarchism is a matter of positive action as well as of passive resistance, and this would soon lead me to seek out the small active anarchist movement which existed in England during the 1940s.

But it took me several months. In the meantime I enjoyed the work I was doing and was delighted to find myself far more capable of manual tasks than I had ever believed possible. We were not involved in the ordinary routines of farming; more expert gangs would follow us to sow and cultivate the fields we had prepared. We cut back hedges that had gone wild, cleared acres of thorn bush from the neglected lands, and dug herringbone networks of ditches to drain the soggy soil. I especially liked the ditching, and gained an expertise in that minor craft which I have never lost. I found I had an eye for falls so exact that, after a ditch was dug, I could finish it with a special tool to give an even fall of a small fraction of an inch per yard — very desirable in the flat country of East Anglia. Very soon I was always picked for this delicate task, which relieved me of a great deal of the heavier digging work.

Our gangs were seldom on the same farm for more than two or three weeks at a time and this gave me a good knowledge of the Cambridgeshire countryside and its old villages. I remember especially one day of heavy rain in a village whose name I have forgotten. We refused to work when there was even light rainfall and this day, while most of the gang sheltered in a barn to play cards, Patrick Heron and I wandered into a church and found on its walls a series of remarkably preserved mediaeval murals. I cannot remember the paintings in detail, but I do retain an impression of their faded luminosity, their clear paled blues and greens, and the strange jointless-looking human beings in fourteenth-century garb who moved across the space.

Another week we went into the deep fens, where the weeding of the abundant potato crop that grew in the black alluvial soil had become urgent. Normally most of the labouring work in this marshy area was done by gangs of women known as the Fen Tigers, and much feared by visiting officials. We ourselves were apprehensive of the attitude of these redoubtable people towards conscientious objectors, for we had become accustomed to the children in some of the villages running out of the cottages when our trucks drove through and shouting "Yellowbellies!" We need not have worried, for a set of women more cynical about the pretensions of authority I have rarely encountered; the very fact that we were "agin the government" was enough for them. The only remarks I heard from their side of the field, as we worked in the mutual segregation our foremen were anxious to maintain, consisted of speculations about our physical endowments which were not entirely flattering.

Scattered through the whole period of my work in the Cambridgeshire countryside I remember noontimes when we would settle down under a pale blue East Anglian sky, around a great blazing fire of the brushwood we had just cut, and eat our lunches of potatoes baked in the hot embers, and cheese, and the mild-flavoured wild onions we gathered in the field verges, washed down by the weak cold tea in whisky bottles which was the standard mid-day drink of English farm labourers.

WE LIVED A STRANGE and exhilarating double life: ditch diggers during the day and, at other times, members of an intellectual community changed by the incursions of war workers and military personnel and by the increased proportion of women to men in the student population. I arrived late in February, and I must have left by the end of August in the same year of 1941, but I used every day to the utmost, and in memory it is a time dense with relationships, luminous with epiphanies, perhaps best remembered in one of my poems of that year, "Behind Trinity."

Behind Trinity the liquid green slides down
Under Venetian bridges, lapping the solid green
Of old lawns funnelled by golden crocus, swept
By the long, fingery brooms of willow boughs.
This moment the mask of an evil time has slipped.
It is the orders and the tramping feet are false.

It is an illusory evil present that passes
As falling beauty breaks the reflected faces
That gibber from ponds and mirrors the speech of death.
Here and for an instant I am eternal,
Swept out of time as dustmotes swept in breath,
Until the hours ring and here and present fall.

NOW had receded from my mind at Langham. But in Cambridge I decided to start again, and whether it was that the people I met encouraged me or that I met them because I had a magazine I wanted to edit again I cannot remember. The fact is that at Easter 1941, NOW appeared again, this time from Cambridge, and the editorial board included Alex Comfort, then at Trinity, Anthony Huxley, Julian's son, and two Newnham poetesses, Anne Richmond and Anne Romanis.

I would often climb the stone stairs to Alex Comfort's rooms in one of the Trinity turrets, admire his collections of cacti, and listen with large pinches of salt to the tall tales he would tell of the faroff voyages to Africa and South America he claimed to have undertaken as a teenager. In more serious moments we talked of the new kind of poetry, more romantic and less political, that in the 1940s was succeeding the socially conscious verse of the 1930s, and we also elaborated an anarchist-pacifist strategy of victory by evasion and survival.

Anthony Huxley, who eventually followed his father's scientific example by becoming an excellent botanist, was then imitating his uncle Aldous, for whom he expressed little respect, by writing stilted intellectual poems. I once greatly embarrassed Anthony by rejecting a sadly bumbling piece of prose fiction which he had persuaded his father's friend, H. G. Wells, to submit to NOW.

And the Newnham poetesses; the two Annes. Romanis was dark, perhaps the better poet, but tense as a racehorse and unnerving company. Richmond was blond and easy, visually aware and rather impressionistic as a poet, and extraordinarily good company, as I found when we explored together the makeshift restaurants of wartime Cambridge.

We sold that first Cambridge issue, for which Middleton Murry and my ditch companion Nicholas Moore wrote, on the sidewalks; quite a few were bought in Petty Cury and along King's Parade. The editorial board rebelled over the clearly anti-war flavour I had given the issue and resigned, but they continued to submit their work, which I felt demonstrated a typically Cambridgean inclination to have and have not. They were all there again in the Whitsun issue, together with Herbert Read and Julian Huxley. The issue after that was an even stranger mixture, for Anne Romanis wrote a stirring introduction condemning the limitation of points of view, and we published, alongside known leftists like Julian Symons, Roy Fuller and Alex Comfort, a couple of very controversial figures because we felt every kind of anti-war opinion should be represented: the Duke of Bedford and Hugh Ross Williamson.

It was through publishing Williamson and Bedford that, in a roundabout way which I shall later describe, my friendship with George Orwell began. I never encountered the Duke of Bedford, except for our correspondence about the innocuous article on the responsibilities of the press that he sent to *NOW*. He was one of those English noblemen who become involved in fringe causes from a sense of duty to the traditional eccentricity of their class. He had associated with A. R. Orage and, as the Marquis of Tavistock, had contributed regularly to the *New English Weekly* in support of the Social Credit Movement. He was also a pacifist, and one of a singularly naive kind, since he believed that Hitler had an underlying goodness to which nobody had yet appealed, so that he discredited himself by wandering off to Dublin in the early months of World War II in the hope of negotiating single-handedly an honourable peace between England and Germany. For his pains he got himself unfairly dubbed a fascist sympathizer. He differed notably from the more radical pacifists with whom I associated; we had no illusions about Nazism, but, following Gandhi's example, we believed that passive resistance would in the long run be just as effective as violent resistance and much less costly in human terms.

Hugh Ross Williamson was living in Cambridge during 1941, and I met him at one of the teas which Canon Raven would give to the local conscientious objectors in his chambers at King's College. Hugh was a big, laughing man, with pointed eyebrows in the Mephistophelian manner, a prodigious knowledge of English history and literature, and a power of writing that now makes me think he may be one of the forgotten prose masters of that time. It was his political wanderings that were responsible for his loss of celebrity. Just before the beginning of the war he became involved in a curious group called the People's Party, a naive gathering of radical socialists disillusioned with the Labour Party, of pacifists seeking some kind of political vehicle, and of imperceptive idealists who for a time had really imagined that Oswald Mosley aimed at a revolutionary reconstruction of society and left him when they realized he was cast in the same mental mould as Mussolini. Started in the desperate and already doomed hope of creating before it was too late a popular movement opposed to Britain's involvement in war, the People's Party failed from the beginning because it lacked any basis for unity between the various groups. It gathered no popular support and quickly collapsed, one of the casualties being Hugh Ross Williamson's literary career, for he found editors and publishers unwilling to accept his work, and his name faded away without any later recognition of the spirited vigour of his writing or the wayward aristocracy of mind that led him into his scrapes with the party-lining intellectual orthodoxy of the time.

Hugh was really an exile from the 1920s, and in his company one was translated into a state of mind rather like that Norman Douglas evoked in *South Wind* and his disciple Aldous Huxley in *Crome Yellow*. He could discuss abstruse philosophical and even theological issues with so much wit and light that any occasion with him seemed a kind of intellectual entertainment. He had a vast zest for living, whether it was the life of the spirit or the senses, and everything he did he endowed with an air of grand theatre. He would discover the last good bottle of Chablis in wartime Cambridge and make it the occasion for a proper homage to civilized drinking. He and I had a shared interest in Wilde and the Restoration playwrights; when I left Cambridge he searched the bookshops for a rare and suitable keepsake, and presented me on the day I departed with a copy of Montague Summers' *Restoration Theatre* which I still possess.

Perhaps more than any of the people I met in Cambridge, Hugh personified the peculiar character of that interlude, its extravagences, its intensities, its ambiguities.

XII

ANARCHISTS AND OTHERS

D URING MY TIME IN CAMBRIDGE I often hitch hiked to London and dossed down for a weekend on the floor of Elizabeth's flat in Muswell Hill. By the early summer of 1941 the air raids had diminished, at least for the time being, and literary London had returned to its customary ways, so that all my friends were to be found again in the familiar eating houses and drinking places. But now I ventured beyond the floating world of artistic Bohemia into the old meeting halls, smelling of generations of dirty clothes and black tobacco, where the anarchists and the other small political sects of the time held their public meetings. I was impressed by the combination of austerity and enthusiasm that I sensed among these rebels against a belligerent society as I listened to their speeches on the war, and on the proper organization of society, which agreed in almost every respect with the ideas I had been evolving; I had all the pliant impressionability of a neophyte.

The only point on which I silently disagreed with many of the speakers was in their romantic cult of revolutionary violence, yet there were some among them who were almost completely Gandhian in their approach. The more radical pacifists in the Peace Pledge Union had formed themselves into a Forward Movement which taught that without radical changes in political and economic relationships, brought about by direct action, the attainment of any sustained peace would be impossible. In revolt against the centrist Quaker elements in the PPU, whose links with the powerful Fry and Cadbury families made it difficult for them to accept radical social doctrines, the Forward Movement direct actionists had moved towards the anarchists. They, along with the ILP and a few tiny Troyskyist fractions, represented the anti-militarist left in Britain at the time. Their presence assured me that the antidogmatic traditions of anarchism still allowed a wide range of views once one had accepted the basic principle of opposition to government. But for the time being I was content to listen and observe the people who attended the meetings, whom I found personally congenial; I did not make any move towards them until after I had met Herbert Read, who was then the best-known anarchist in Britain.

I had written to Read asking him for a contribution to *NOW*, and he had sent a short piece on Paul Klee who had died the year before. Not long afterwards, early in the summer, Read came to Cambridge to do some research for *Education through Art* at the Fitzwilliam Library. He sent me a postcard giving me his telephone number, and we met for tea at the Copper Kettle on King's Parade.

Read was then almost fifty, but he looked younger. He had in fact the kind of features that gave little hint of his age, rather like the faces of some Tibetans I have since known, though there was nothing oriental about the cast of his features, but rather an elfin quality, so that I have often thought that in Read the genes of some ancient and wise race of the Yorkshire fells were manifesting themselves. He wore that day the black pork pie hat and bow tie that had become almost a uniform for him, and his expression had a defensiveness that created a curious impression of anonymity. From that first meeting, sipping Earl Grey tea and eating scones and Tiptree's Little Scarlet among the academic wives of long ago, I remember, as I do from many later occasions, the silences, the tentative approaches, the warmth in the eyes.

Though I knew Read until he died more than a quarter of a century later, and during certain periods saw him often, I never really made up my mind whether he was an excessively shy man, or whether, as he would assert, it was his Yorkshire phlegm and taciturnity that made the silences so long and yet so living. He seemed to deploy them as a kind of strategy in conversation, and I cannot remember that they ever impeded the free interflow of ideas. Read was not a natural monologist, as I later found George Orwell to be, and though he would recite anecdotes that portrayed some other person with concise accuracy (I remember from that first meeting a description of Henry Miller that has coloured my impressions of him ever since), he said surprisingly little about himself, and particularly about his past, which was unusual in a writer, and surprising in a man whose autobiographical essays are among his best work. In later years, when he travelled often, he came back with little to tell that had a personal flavour. On his return from his first visit to the United States after World War II, for example, he came to see me and talked mostly about supermarkets, which he had seen for the first time, and which interested him because people took what they wanted from the shelves. It seemed to him that, if only the cash desks at the entrances could be removed, the supermarket would be the perfect model for free anarchist communist distribution as envisaged by Peter Kropotkin, whom he greatly admired, in *The Conquest of Bread*.

I remember that first encounter in Cambridge with such vividness because the directions of our conversation — little magazines, poetry, and anarchism — tended to chart out the areas of interest we shared in later years, for I did not become an active art critic until after Read was dead. From Read's reputation in the literary world I had imagined him to be an active anarchist militant, committed in the same way as some of my literary acquaintances like Randall Swingler and Charles Madge were then committed to the Communist Party. I thought he would be working actively with the best-known anarchist group, which had inherited Freedom Press (Kropotkin's foundation) and published a fortnightly called *War Commentary*. I was bewildered when he answered my questions vaguely. I assumed he must be an initiate following a politic line with an untested stranger. In fact, as I later discovered, Read's vagueness in talking about the anarchist movement arose not from a desire to conceal, but rather from a deliberate ignorance. He chose to stand apart, with a poet's freedom, from a group of middle-class intellectuals whose proletarian aspirations he distrusted. He believed that anarchism was a doctrine which each man must relate to his own experience, and his experience was that of the artist; his political beliefs were linked inextricably with his view of the relationship between art and society.

But Read did tell me that one of the most important members of the Freedom group was the tall, dark girl whom I had admired at the anarchist meetings. She was Marie Louise Berneri, daughter of the Italian anarchist Camillo Berneri whom the communists had murdered in 1937 in the streets of Barcelona.

I MET MARIE LOUISE when I returned to London two months after my meeting with Read. By this time I had come to realize that I could edit

NOW, which was beginning to gain a reputation among the younger writers, much more effectively from London than from Cambridge. At the same time I was getting tired of working for the War Agricultural Committee, where the bureaucrats were trying to curb our inclination to take days off whenever we felt inclined and to stop working at the first sign of rain. When they made threats of dismissal, we began to talk again about striking. This alarmed the bureaucrats, who immediately showed their ignorance of the real situation among their gangs by sacking a dozen of the communist-liners, who were indeed active in the farm workers' union, but whose influence had recently been directed towards avoiding a strike. The real malcontents — the anarchists and radical pacifists — were delighted at the turn of events. Our communist rivals were turned into unwilling martyrs whose situation we could exploit, and the War Agricultural Committee had dismissed the very people who were most eager to co-operate with it. We immediately proclaimed a go-slow campaign, and for the week until the sacked men went, hardly a shovel of earth was lifted out of the ditches.

Then, when the communists had gone and we had no challengers, we advised our sympathizers to give in their notices and cripple the operations of the Committee. We declared a day's holiday, on which the trucks went out almost empty from Cambridge to the farms and forty men followed Jonathan and me to hand in our notices at the Committee's office. Its operations were crippled for months ahead, for not only were more than a third of the workers lost in one sweep through the bureaucratic mishandling of the situation, but a word-of-mouth campaign among conscientious objectors resulted in a virtual blacklisting of the Cambridge Committee.

Back in London I found a lofty room in a Hampstead crescent to use as a *pied à terre*, and then set about seeking congenial land work in some place not too far from the city, to which I continued to return each weekend. I worked through September as gardener at a progressive school run by a small urban community in Epsom, and in October went into partnership with another conshy who was finding the market garden he had started at Ashford in Middlesex too large to run single-handed.

Jack Humphrey was an unusual conscientious objector, fitting into none of the customary patterns. He had no religion of any kind. He did not claim to be a pacifist, and declared himself quite willing to fight to the death anyone who attacked him or his family. Nor was he a political radical, since he believed even the most idealistic leader became corrupt the moment he smelt power, and he disagreed with the anarchists by contending that revolution was impossible without the taking of power. He had registered as a conscientious objector because he felt no one had the right to expose him to the risk of death and he had put on a good enough show to persuade the tribunal to exempt him. I found his entirely Schweikian amorality refreshing after the varieties of pacifist smugness I had endured at Langham and in Cambridge, and we got on well, largely because we both despised paraded virtues. We worked together for about a year and a half, arguing furiously on all manner of subjects, for Jack had a stimulating way of going accurately for the weak joint of any theory I propounded. He was not very well educated or well read, but he had a kind of plain man's sagacity, and whenever I read Orwell's *Coming Up for Air* and consider the character of George Bowling, I remember Jack, who also had been an insurance agent.

The garden we rented was four acres of good alluvial land. There were large old fruit trees, apples and pears, which bore well and earned us a fair amount of money as food shortages increased during 1942. The land itself had been left fallow for a year or so, and we spent the autumn and winter digging it by hand whenever the weather allowed. As the spring came on we broke it down by dragging over the surface a kind of harrow we had made of a wooden frame with the biggest iron spikes we could find driven through it to serve as teeth and stones to weight it down. Once we had broken the soil and used it for a first crop, we cultivated it shallowly with a small plough share attached to a hand cultivator. There was no machinery available, even if we had been able to afford it, and all the other market gardens around us were cultivated in the same primitive way. Next door to us there worked an old man bent almost double with arthritis; he could hardly raise his head high enough to turn his face towards one, but in his habitual stooped position he was the fastest digger I have ever seen.

We made most of our money out of cabbage and cauliflower plants, which were in great demand now that people were going in for Victory Gardens, and cut flowers, which it was illegal under wartime regulations to cultivate on land that might be used for food, but which we nevertheless grew in all the unobtrusive corners of our plot. The flowers followed the plants as spring gave way to summer, so that we had a good basic income until the autumn, which we supplemented by growing cabbages and root crops, more to fulfil the requirement that we rear food than for the money they earned us. The war had given us a contempt for looking towards the future in financial terms, and every week we would pay our immediate expenses and divide the surplus, so that often I went up to London at a week end with more than twenty pounds in my pocket, which in 1942 was still a respectable sum of money and many times as much as I had been paid in Cambridge.

Ashford was a dismal place, a flat river plain that had ceased to be farming country and not yet become suburban. It was certainly no place to live. My room in Hampstead, however, was too far away for commuting, and I fixed on Richmond as the nearest acceptable habitation during the working week. It was a pleasant riverside town, and had what I most needed, some good evening walks, and a variety of pubs and eating houses, including one of the best Indian restaurants in the London area. Through the pacifist information network I found a top floor on Richmond Hill in the house of a lady of multiple radical sympathies. Elsie Jones had been imprisoned as a suffragette, she was now a war resister and a near anarchist, and though she was loosely married to a pharmacist who lived a long way off in Bethnal Green, she was still, in her late fifties, carrying on an affair with a white-haired Welsh Labour M.P. who had the look and the manner of a good Methodist preacher. Elsie was a bright, nimble-witted woman, and delighted to have someone in the house who could talk about books and social problems. The attic room she gave me, with a fine view over the Thames towards London, was large enough to hold my books and a good kitchen table for work, and for many months it was the base for the triple life I then lived.

I KEPT MY HAMPSTEAD ROOM, and every Friday I went to spend the weekend in London. Before going to Richmond I had already visited the bookshop the anarchists then ran in one of the little streets off Red Lion Square, and had found Marie Louise Berneri looking after it. I bought a few pamphlets and then we started to talk, and though we disagreed, as we would continue to do, on the question of violence, we discovered already that day a kind of mental affinity that as the months went on grew into a close friendship.

The development of that friendship was tangled with my growing involvement in anarchist activism. In those days between 1941 and

1944, the Freedom Press had its offices in the top part of a house in Hampstead, near to the Finchley Road tube station. Every Friday night I would hurry from my garden by bus to Richmond, catch the train to London, change in my Hampstead room, snatch a quick dinner, and be among my anarchist friends in time for the regular weekly lecture, which would vary in quality from brilliant (if it happened to be someone like Comfort or Read or the surrealist E. L. T. Mesens) to excruciatingly boring (if it happened to be one of the rare proletarians who had been enticed into the movement). A Trotskyist wit at this period remarked that the anarchists consisted only of children and old men, and in fact these gatherings were distinguished on the one hand by a large number of people on the young side of twenty-five (Marie Louise herself was then only twenty-two) and on the other by a handful of veterans from earlier struggles, like Matt Kavanagh, a leprechaun of a man with a glowing red cyst at the end of a long pointed nose, who had fought at Easter 1916 in the Irish Citizen Army, and Lilian Wolfe, who had worked with Kropotkin in the original Freedom Group before the First World War.

There were very few people from the intervening age groups, but the young people were enthusiastic and demonstrated the way in which anarchism at that period was cross-fertilizing with the lively literary and artistic movements of the time. New Apocalyptic poets and Belgian and French surrealists in wartime exile were often present at the Finchley Road meetings and took part in the passionate discussions that followed the lectures. By a tacit understanding that was rarely broken, the proceedings ended in time for the lecturer and the whole audience to hasten for an hour's drinking before closing time in the big public house at the crossroads near the Finchley Road tube station. This pattern, by which the gathering did not immediately dissolve but broke down into smaller conversational groups, was very anarchist, and it enabled a multiplicity of interlocking personal relationships to be established.

Apart from Marie Louise, the leading members of the Freedom Press group were her engineer husband Vernon Richards, the physician John Hewetson and his companion Peta Edsall, Tom Brown the syndicalist factory worker, and a pompous young man of undefined education, Albert Meltzer, who gained credit from having been patronized by Emma Goldman. Two others who appeared on the scene at about the same time as I did, and who soon became closely involved in the group, were the painter Philip Sansom and the architect Colin Ward, who later developed into one of the most interesting recent writers on anarchism.

Richards, whom Marie Louise had married to escape from the wandering expatriate existence of a political refugee, was the son — his name Anglicized — of an old anarchist friend of Errico Malatesta, who had long operated a celebrated wine and pasta store on Old Compton Street, named King Bomba in memory of the notorious tyrant of Naples, King Ferdinand II.

One member of this group, Albert Meltzer, was hostile to me from the beginning, since he posed with little justification as an authority on anarchist history and quickly recognized that my interest in that field made me a potential rival. Tom Brown merely harboured towards me the kind of proletarian suspicion that made the Trotskyist factions refuse the collaboration of Julian Symons, who was devoted to the Old Man's cause but was suspect as a middle-class poet. But the other members of the group were interested from the beginning in recruiting me, since they recognized the need for writers who would put their case to the potentially sympathetic literary and artistic communities.

I was invited to write for *War Commentary* and I did, beginning with some pieces on land workers and agricultural problems in general, which I later tied in to a reconsideration of Kropotkin's ideas of intensive farming, and expanded into a pamphlet, *New Life to the Land*, which demonstrated how Britain could feed herself; it was my first prose publication outside the pages of periodicals. Looking back at it in an age of acute environmental anxieties, I realize how naively we then accepted the developments of applied science. I, for example, then advocated the widespread use of chemical fertilizers with no real understanding of their perils to the vital ecological balances. All of us in those days, anarchist or socialist, still sustained the illusion that the earth had endless productive capacities. We despised Malthus, and did not foresee how events would vindicate his argument of population ever pressing on resources, so that now we seem to be approaching the collective disaster he prophesied.

BY 1942 I HAD BECOME a regular contributor to *War Commentary*, moving quickly out of agriculture to write about imperialism and education, about French-Canadian politics (I even then approved of those who worked for Quebec's autonomy) and American radical traditions, and especially about libertarian history, including pieces on Gerrard

Winstanley and William Morris and a four-part reconsideration of the libertarian implications of the Paris Commune. It was an excellent apprenticeship to journalism, for the editors of *War Commentary* were sharply critical of loose thinking and flabby writing. Soon they invited me to join the board, and for the next six years I was closely involved (with brief interruptions) in producing *War Commentary* and its successor, *Freedom.*

Marie Louise and the other more intellectually inclined members of the Freedom group were greatly interested in *NOW*, even though they disagreed with a great deal I had printed. For my part, I was tired of bringing *NOW* out independently, for the distribution arrangements had broken down since my departure from Cambridge. Jonathan Edwards, in whose hands I had left them, was much more interested in his impending novitiate in the Society of the Sacred Mission than in a magazine that for him was already a part of the secular past, and though the recent issues were the best to date, I lost money heavily on them. I was now more willing than in the past to make *NOW* an anarchist-oriented journal, as long as there was no attempt to impose an ideological strait jacket on the literary content, and after a great deal of negotiation Freedom Press agreed to take over publication with me as editor.

The first issue of the new series appeared early in 1943. In the editorial I remarked that by the end of the previous series: "I had come to realize the justice of a criticism made by Julian Symons, in which he attacked the 'free expression' policy, which had united in one review so many incompatible opinions, and contended that a small magazine was only justified if it represented a defined attitude." Therefore, in future, *NOW* would be edited "from an anarchist point of view" so far as its "social content" was concerned, but for literary contributions "the quality of writing would be the only criterion." "Nor do we intend to exclude poets, essayists, story writers, because their political views do not coincide with our own. Indeed, we are grateful for their willing co-operation."

In fact, the only "social content" of the only issue of *NOW* published by Freedom Press consisted of a piece by Read on the "Cult of Leadership" and a translation by Marie Louise and me of part of H. E. Kaminski's *Bakounine,* which had never been published in England. This was not enough to satisfy those on the editorial board, notably Meltzer and Brown, who saw the function of the Press as propagandist in the most

simple way. What relevance, they asked (and with a great deal of reason
from their own narrow viewpoint) did a Ceylonese short story by Alagu
Subramaniam, or Julian Symons' reflections on Stephen Spender, or
my own observations on libertarian elements in the culture of Restoration England have to do with the problems of workers in London or
Glasgow in the middle of World War II?

Anarchist opinions, I began to learn, are no guarantee of broad-
mindedness. And since I had no intention of letting *NOW* be crippled
by partisan disciplines, as had happened to *Left Review* at the hands of
the communists, I resumed the responsibility for publication as well as
editing. However, the more intelligent members of the Freedom Group,
notably Marie Louise and John Hewetson, were anxious to sustain the
link between *NOW* and the anarchist movement, and we worked out
an arrangement by which the magazine would be printed by the press
(Express Printers in Whitechapel) which the anarchists had recently
acquired and distributed, along with its own publications, by Freedom
Press. Eight issues of *NOW* appeared under this arrangement, spanning
the period from late 1943 to early 1947.

As time went on the political flavour of the journal grew weaker, and
it changed into a predominantly literary journal, though its contributors were drawn mainly from writers of the non-communist left.
Herbert Read wrote regularly for it, as did such old friends as Julian
Symons, Roy Fuller and Derek Savage, who contributed some excellent
pieces on twentieth-century novelists. Other British contributors to
these later issues included George Orwell with a devastating essay called
"How the Poor Die," Laurence Durrell with his magnificent "Elegy on
the Closing of the French Brothels," Alex Comfort, Philip O'Connor,
Louis Adeane, Emanuel Litvinov, Keidrych Rhys, George Barker, W. S.
Graham, Jack Lindsay, Derek Stanford and Denise Levertov, in her
years as an English poet before she made her second American career.

NOW also brought me into contact with American and European
writers. Victor Serge sent me two fine essays from his exile in Mexico,
and André Breton from his exile in the United States contributed a
fiery surrealist-anarchist manifesto entitled "The Colours of Liberty";
the Polish painter, Jankel Adler, exiled in London, contributed some
excellent drawings and the Belgian surrealist, E. L. T. Mesens, who ran
the London Gallery and was an anarchist sympathizer, got me drawings
by André Masson and Picasso. Edouard Mesens was a gourmet driven
to extremities by the wartime food regulations; these put a five shilling

limit (with varying extra cover charges) on a meal, which meant effectively that one could obtain only a single decent course in any one
restaurant. So lunches with Mesens became lengthy and marvellous
pilgrimages. We would often start off eating one of the excellent hors
d'oeuvres which the Alsatian Mrs. Maurer prepared in her little restaurant in Greek Street. Then we would cross Charing Cross Road for a
fish course of sole or lobster at Wheeler's. Then up to Vaiani's on
Charlotte Street for a picata of the most expensive kind or perhaps
down to the Spanish restaurant kept by the anarchist Pepe Pradas on
Old Compton Street for his superb *calamares in su tinto*. And finally
back to Mrs. Maurer for one of her succulent torten or to Bertaux's, the
Belgian patisserie in Holborn, for a plateful of cakes.

I also published work by such varied American writers as Henry
Miller, who hailed *NOW* as one of the best magazines of its time and me
as "a Pharos in the English night," Paul Goodman, E. E. Cummings,
Harry Roskolenko, Philip Lamantia and Richard Eberhardt. Some of
my contacts with American writers in fact led me much farther than the
pages of *NOW*. Dwight Macdonald, when he founded *Politics* in 1944,
invited me to write regularly on English books and English life, and this
I did as long as the journal lasted. My favourite among the articles I
wrote for Dwight was the essay on Orwell which appeared in 1946.
Holley Cantine invited me to write a regular London letter for the anarchist magazine *Retort* which he edited from Woodstock, then in the
hinterland of New York State; I continued it from 1945 to 1948. The
poet William Everson wrote to me from a conscientious objector's camp
in Oregon where he and other poets were keeping their art alive by
publishing a magazine, *Compass*, and running a little publishing house,
Untide Press. I contributed poems to *Compass* and eventually, in 1947,
Untide Press published in Pasadena my third book of poetry, *Imagine the
South*. My second book was *The Centre Cannot Hold* which Herbert
Read persuaded Routledge and Kegan Paul to publish in 1943. Finally, I
owe to *NOW* my long friendship with that fine poet, Kenneth Rexroth,
who had started a literary anarchist group in San Francisco.

BUT ALL THIS IS RUNNING ahead of those days in 1942 when I was working at Ashford. Every evening, when I got back from the market garden,
I would sit writing away in my attic room, forming the work disciplines

that have guided me ever since. I had not yet acquired the ability to compose directly on the typewriter and wrote laboriously in longhand before revising and transcribing. As well as my articles and pamphlets (for *New Life to the Land* was followed, dipping into my transportational past, by *Railways and Society*), I embarked at Richmond on a partly historical and partly polemical book on anarchism. I learnt as I wrote, for my research led me to read extensively for the first time the writings of the anarchist masters: the verbose and violent Bakunin; the gently persuasive Kropotkin whose *Memoirs of a Revolutionist* remains one of my favourite books; the brilliantly irascible Proudhon and the grandiosely rational Godwin.

Every night I would sit writing in a big yellow-covered manuscript book that I had bought to enshrine what I regarded as my first major prose work. Each evening after dinner, before I went upstairs to write, I would read what I had completed the previous day to the always approving Elsie Jones and her usually critical daughter Jean, who had recently come home because her husband had gone to the wars and whom I came to esteem for her acerbic honesty.

Out of these strange domestic exercises emerged *Anarchy or Chaos*, my first published book in prose, which Freedom Press published in 1944. Read liked the book, and it sold well among the literary left of the period, but I see it now as no more than a passable apprentice work, its ideas half-digested, its history distorted, and the desire to please my new comrades — especially Marie Louise — painfully evident. But it was not wasted work. My interest in the anarchist theoreticians led in later years to much more tempered and critical books, such as my lives of Godwin, Kropotkin and Proudhon and my critical history, *Anarchism*.

Meanwhile, in addition to my anarchist journalism, I was writing poetry; I boasted to Lance Godwin at the end of 1941 that I had written fifteen poems in the first ten weeks of working in the garden at Ashford, and some of them at least found print, not only in *NOW*, but also in Schimanski's *Kingdom Come*, Wrey Gardiner's *Poetry Quarterly*, Tambimuttu's *Poetry (London)*, John Bayliss's *New Roads*, Alex Comfort's *Poetry Folios* and in the *Poetry Magazine*.

The *Poetry Magazine* was the organ of the Poetry Society, which we had all dismissed as the last refuge of the remnants of Georgian poetry, and when Tambimuttu told me I must meet the editor, who was interested in my work, I was almost reluctant to accompany him. I soon changed my mind, for the magazine had just acquired a new editor, a charming young woman of pink-and-white prettiness and astringent wit, Muriel Spark. Muriel was still in her early twenties, and it was long before she became a celebrated novelist, but she was trying very hard to open the *Poetry Magazine* to the younger poets. I found her pleasant and amusing company, and often went to her office to pick up books for review and talk over coffee with her and the young critics, like G. S. Fraser and Derek Stanford, who were often in attendance. Muriel persuaded me to give a lecture on Restoration literature to the Poetry Society, which I did with great nervousness, for it was the first time I had ever spoken publicly. And it was she who first aroused my interest in modern Canadian poetry by giving me a volume of Earle Birney's *Strait of Anian* and saying to me, "You're a Canadian, aren't you, George? Isn't it time you read what your own people are doing?"

The older members of the Poetry Society resented this intrusion of younger and less conventional writers into their midst, and the conflict, in which the traditionalists were led by a pompous poetaster called Chevalier Kyle, came to a climax at a meeting in which Kyle lost his case morally by slapping Muriel Spark on the cheek. Everyone took the part of the witty delicate-looking young woman against the blustering Papal Knight, though in fact — as her novels have since demonstrated — Muriel was by far the tougher personality. She and I remained good friends until I left England for Canada in 1949.

NOT LONG AFTERWARDS, in a very strange manner, I gained the friendship of George Orwell. Orwell was writing regular London Letters for the *Partisan Review*, in which he enjoyed himself greatly by lashing out at anyone who did not support his own very ill-defined kind of socialism and who had not followed his example of switching abruptly in 1939 from anti-war to pro-war. In the March, 1942 issue of the *Partisan*, in a general attack on pacifism which he tried to prove was "objectively" allied to fascism, he naturally picked on the "little anti-war paper *NOW*" and attacked it for the pieces I had printed by the Duke of Bedford and Hugh Ross Williamson, and also, less explicably, for pieces by Alex Comfort and Julian Symons which were as left-inclined as anything he himself wrote. Alex Comfort, Derek Savage and I replied rather ferociously, and our pieces (my own dated 19th May) were printed in the October issue of the *Partisan Review*. While the others mounted a theoretical defence of the pacifist position, I became personal in a somewhat Orwellian way, pointing to George's own antecedents: that he was an imperial police officer now opposing the empire; that he was a turncoat war-resister; that he was now attacking the anarchists beside whom he had fought in Spain.

Thus I was surprised a week or so later when Mulk Raj Anand approached me in the Swiss tavern with a message from Orwell, who was then working at the BBC arranging broadcasts to India. Among other things, Orwell and Mulk ran a series of literary discussions. Orwell knew that the audience for such broadcasts must be minute, but he always gathered the best people he could persuade to take part in his programmes. Out of curiosity, and to show that there was no rancour, I accepted his invitation, and when I got to the BBC I found that the other writers with whom I would be talking were — apart from Orwell and Mulk — Herbert Read and William Empson, whom I knew, and Edmund Blunden, whom I did not know.

Orwell I saw as a thin angular man, with worn Gothic features accentuated by the deep vertical furrows that ran down the cheeks and across the corners of the mouth. The thinness of his lips was accentuated by a narrow line of dark moustache; it seemed a hard, almost cruel mouth until he smiled, and then an expression of unexpected kindliness would irradiate his face. In contrast to the fragile, worn-down look of the rest of him, his hair grew upward in a vigorous brown crest. He was wearing that day his rarely-changing uniform of an old tweed sports coat, leather-patched at the elbows, and baggy corduroys. I was impressed by the size of his hands and feet; the latter were enormous — size twelve — which made it difficult for him to get shoes during the austere war years. Orwell greeted me in his flat-toned voice, with a reserved but not unfriendly smile. He questioned me about the market garden; he seemed to approve that I was engaged in manual work and that my hands were chapped and ingrained with soil.

The radio programme turned out to be a made-up discussion which Orwell had prepared quite skilfully beforehand, and which the rest of the participants were given a chance to amend before it went on the air. All of us objected to small points as a matter of principle, but the only real change came when Orwell himself produced a volume of Byron, and smiling around at the rest of us, suggested that we should read "The Isles of Greece" to show that English poets had a tradition of friendship for the aspirations of subject peoples. At that time the British government was opposed to the Indian independence movement (Gandhi and Nehru were still in prison), but all of the participants in the broadcast supported it in sentiment at least, and as Herbert Read spoke the ringing verses of revolt, the programme assumed a mild flavour of defiance which we all enjoyed. Orwell, I noticed, had a very rudimentary idea of radio production and his own voice was too thin to make him an effective broadcaster.

After the broadcast was completed, we went to a pub in Great Portland Street frequented by BBC staff, and I sat in a corner talking to Blunden, that gentle and still surprisingly youthful man who astonished me by his detailed knowledge of what the younger poets — myself among them — were writing. Orwell discoursed rather cynically about the futility of our having taken so much trouble over a programme to which he doubted if more than two hundred Anglophile Indians would bother to listen. He was already experiencing the frustration of a job that involved him mainly in the dissemination of official propaganda.

I learned about his feelings on this point shortly afterwards when we began to write to each other over our various points of disagreement. Orwell's first letter, in December 1942, began on a characteristic note. "I am afraid I answered rather roughly in the *Partisan Review* controversy. I always do when I am attacked — however, no malice either side, I hope." Orwell liked to start friendships by clearing up any resentments his sometimes intemperate way of expressing himself may have caused. Julian Symons, whom he had accused of fascist thinking, received an apology on their first meeting, and to Stephen Spender, whom he had attacked before they actually became acquainted, Orwell remarked that he found it very difficult to continue a feud with any writer after actually encountering him, "Because when you meet anyone in the flesh you realize immediately that he is a human being and not a sort of caricature embodying certain ideas."

Later in this early letter to me Orwell discussed his connection with the BBC. "I doubt whether I shall stay in this job much longer," he said, "but while here I consider I have kept our propaganda slightly less disgusting than it might otherwise have been . . . . To appreciate this you have to be as I am in constant touch with propaganda Axis and Allied. Till then you don't realise what muck and filth is normally flowing through the air. I consider that I have left our little corner of it fairly clean."

He was so obviously unhappy in broadcasting that I was not surprised to hear in 1943 that he had managed to get himself released from the BBC, and had joined as literary editor the staff of the *Tribune*, the left-wing socialist paper then being run by Aneurin Bevan and Michael Foot. The *Tribune* suited him because it was critical of the Churchill government from a pro-war standpoint, yet did not share the communist adulation of Stalinist Russia. In practice *Tribune* served as a meeting place for both pro-war and anti-war positions within the dissident left and, especially in its literary pages, gave space to anarchists, Trotskyists and pacifists as well as to supporters of the Labour Party. Moreover, when the authorities went too far in their use of restrictive wartime regulations, the *Tribune* would usually stand in defense of the fundamental human rights for which the war was theoretically being fought. In this way it gained the distrust of officialdom and the goodwill of the avant-garde writers, who would willingly contribute articles to its pages for token payment. It was the kind of paper in which there was room for an unhappily independent spirit like Orwell, and I think on the whole he enjoyed the two or three years he spent there.

It was at this time that I saw Orwell again. I had now moved my London *pied à terre* to Parliament Hill Fields, and I would often take the bus from South End Green into the centre of London. One morning, when I climbed on to the upper deck, I caught sight of Orwell's crest of hair and his familiar grimy trenchcoat towards the front of the bus. He had evidently seen me crossing the road, for as I came up the stairs he turned round and waved to me. I sat beside him. He immediately began to talk, with the urgency of a man who has to get something off his mind, about our disagreement in the *Partisan Review* and in our later correspondence. I was rather surprised, since I felt this had been cleared up in our letters, but Orwell obviously felt some direct and personal reference was necessary. "There's no reason to let that kind of argument on paper breed personal ill feeling," he remarked. Obviously I had passed whatever test Orwell regarded as necessary before he could accord his esteem, and he wanted to be friendly. From that time we never again mentioned our original disagreement, and whenever our opinions differed, as they often did, I found Orwell blunt and genial in argument.

Now that our relationship was established, I saw Orwell quite often, for at the *Tribune* he was opening the review pages more widely than ever to writers of almost every shade of political opinion, and for young writers then as now reviewing was one of the ways of making one's entry into the literary world. Orwell was not in fact a particularly good editor, though he was an excellent journalist; too often his generosity clouded his discernment about writers and their work. He persuaded many good writers to work for him; I remember articles by E. M. Forster, Herbert Read, Cyril Connolly, Stephen Spender. But he also published a great deal of shoddy trash by young writers who had no promise to fulfil, and he did this mainly, I think, from good nature rather than from lack of judgment. He found it extremely difficult to return an article with a coldly-worded rejection slip, and he said to me more than once that no writer who had earned a hard living by reviewing should ever be trusted with the task of editing.

Sometimes I would call on Orwell in his small, crowded office in the Strand, and talk to him pent behind a desk piled with books and manuscripts, with no room for his long legs. The typewriters would clatter in our ears from the neighbouring desks and the V-2's would go off in the distance like the rockets falling in *Nineteen Eighty-Four*. We would go out to lunch in the upstairs room of a decayed wine tavern on the Strand, sometimes with Herbert Read or Julian Symons. On one such occasion towards the end of the war, London restaurant food was at its worst, the only dish offered was boiled-out cod with bitter turnip tops. I found the combination of flavours appalling, but Orwell, who extracted a boyish enjoyment out of the hardships of the time, ate his fish and greens with relish. "I'd never have thought they'd have gone so well together!" he remarked reproachfully when I sent my plate back almost untasted.

It was in 1944 that my acquaintance with Orwell expanded into friendship, through a series of events that began earlier, in 1943.

XIII

DEFENDING FREEDOM

I N 1943 AT A PARTY in Great Russell Street, I met the very private person who became my wife, and so began the relationship that has sustained my life since then. Her exemplary desire for anonymity I have to respect, even though I do not share it.

By the time we met, my life had shifted in another way. Early in 1943 the National Service authorities decided that my labour on the market garden was not adequately serving the war effort, and I was ordered to report to the Middlesex War Agricultural Committee. I objected to this interference with my freedom to choose how I might be of service, and, since I felt I had acquired enough experience of ditch-digging, I decided to melt into the vast anonymity of London. For a few pounds I turned back my share of the market garden to Jack Humphrey. I left Richmond, gave up my room in the Hampstead Crescent, and joined two young anarchists, Ken Hawkes and Norman Adeane, in an apartment on Parliament Hill. I ceased to attend public anarchist lectures and to visit the Bohemian pubs where I was well known.

Even so, if there had been any real co-ordination between the various security forces I could easily have been picked up, for I continued to wander freely around London at all times of the day and night, to write for *War Commentary*, to publish *NOW*, to contribute to various literary periodicals, and I used Freedom Press, which I visited often at random hours, as a mailing address. These activities of mine were certainly known to the Special Branch of Scotland Yard, Britain's political police, but there can have been no communication between them and the local police forces which acted on behalf of the Department of National Service in picking up people on the run.

There was nothing really thrilling about this clandestine way of life. Perhaps what most impressed me about it was the kind of sympathy for dissidents that had come into being in Britain by 1943, so that I got help not only from pacifists and anarchists, which I had expected, but also from many people actually involved in the war, like soldiers and especially soldiers' wives. Though dozens of people at that time had a good idea where I could be found, nobody ever informed, and I never, at that time, had any feeling of being pursued, though I was careful not to take unnecessary risks of being caught.

My wife and I stayed a little while in the Parliament Hill apartment, and then moved across Hampstead Heath to a house on Highgate West Hill belonging to an architect's widow who was herself a pacifist and already harboured a fugitive furniture designer. We had an enormous attic room whose dormer window looked out on the Heath, and we enjoyed a semi-rural life on the edge of London, for in those days wild duck haunted the heath ponds and, walking out one evening we found the little lane leading from Highgate West Hill to one of the ponds invaded by thousands of tiny frogs.

When the bombardment of London by flying bombs, which we all called doodlebugs, was at its height, we would often take a ground sheet and blankets and sleep out in the hollows of the heath, calculating that there we would be immune from both blast and falling masonry. Sometimes we would climb up to the crest of Parliament Hill to watch the inveterate English gamblers, sitting in deck chairs with stop watches, looking over the great expanse of London and betting on the distance of the explosions, measured by the time lapse between the flash and the sound.

Right at the end of the war we were to be marvellously saved from one of these pestilential machines. Walking home after dinner in Hampstead Village, we were crossing the heath near one of the ponds when we heard the sound of the doodlebug's engine, and saw its redhot cigar shape almost overhead; the engine shut off, and we knew this was the danger point when it would descend. We threw ourselves down beside a fence under some trees and heard the whistling of the falling bomb, and then the explosion which was followed immediately by a drenching shower of water and mud. We stood up, laughing and ludicrously bespattered, and danced around, wildly embracing each other. The bomb had fallen in the mud; if there had been flat dry land as near to us we would certainly have been killed by the blast. It was the last doodlebug of which I ever heard, for the next day the British overran the launching pads at Peenemunde.

WE NOW WANDERED A GREAT DEAL over Britain, bus riding and hitch-hiking. Many of our friends had by now scattered over the country in an exodus rather like that of the devotees of alternative life styles in the 1960s, and their homes often provided the foci of journeys into parts of the country I had never seen before. Albert McCarthy, who had introduced me to jazz and the world out of which it emerged, had gone to live in the New Forest, and there we stayed with him and spent long hours talking to the old satyr Augustus John, as faithful as ever to the anarchist beliefs of his youth. Fredrick Lohr and Laurie Hislam, the leading pacifist anarchists of the time, had migrated to the sheepbitten uplands of South Wales, and we found our way — the last miles on foot over foggy moors — to the damp old slate farmhouse where they lived on a bleak ridge somewhere between Pontypool and Abergavenny. Not far over the hills, but in a completely different terrain, Derek Savage, having abandoned the hope of founding a community in Cambridgeshire, was living in the lush valley of the Wye, in a great brick farmhouse near Symonds Yat, burning out his talent on a series of brilliant and original critical books, *The Personal Principle*, *The Withered Branch*, *Caesar's Laurel Crown*, that represented the peak and, as it now seems, the virtual end of his career, for after the early 1950s Derek was to write nothing more of any importance.

Derek remains in my memory as perhaps the best of those brilliant young men, splendid talkers and writers of youthful precocity, whose sparkling conversation and easy prose dazzled and almost bewildered me when I was their contemporary and yet whose promise in the end was not sustained, and who lapsed into silence while I in my Taurian obstinancy continued. The memory of such friends has taught me the profound truth of the fable of the Tortoise and the Hare. For I have always been, as Coleridge said of William Godwin, "A slow man but a sure," and in the end rather more sure than slow, for over the decades my work has built up the momentum so many of my early friends lost so soon. This leads me to the conclusion that there are different kinds of creativity, some of which flower only in youth and wither never to return, however long the artist may live, and others that mature slowly and reach their finest blossoming when the artist is on the verge of old age.

Looking at my fellow writers in the 1980s, and the painters I know well, I am sure that in recent decades there has been a shift to the latter type, and I often speculate on what that may mean for the future of the human species. Are we losing the spontaneous forces of our youth? Are we beginning to garner only the harvest of ripeness? Either suggests a generic mortality, a falling of the fruit, not far in the future.

Having visited these outlying friends, we would go farther, into unknown terrain, wandering northward from the Wye valley through the old towns of the Welsh Marshes — Monmouth and Hereford and Ludlow. We went on foot through the Wyre Forest, and over the heather-purple hills above Church Stretton and became so enamoured of this Housman land of southern Shropshire that we lingered around Ludlow seeking in vain for the country cottage to which we too could make our retreat. Then we travelled into central Wales, through the wilds of Montgomery and Merioneth, through villages where half the women had goitres and half the children were Mongolian idiots and an unhealthy peace reigned that made one forget the history that was proceeding in the world outside.

We broke out to the sea at Cardigan Bay, staying at Dolgelly in an old stone-built hotel that served marvellous fish and treacle tart. From there we went north through the knot of Snowdonia and round into Lancashire. For the only time in my life, a filthy room in an Oldham public house so turned our gorges that we left it and slept in the Manchester station waiting room until the next train left in the early morning for Keswick in the Lake district. We spent days tramping around Buttermere and Ullswater. It was the edge of winter. One sharp moonlit night we wandered beside Derwentwater, and the white peaks to the west stood out in such miraculous luminosity that in my memory those small and graceful mountains rank for grace of form with the tallest peaks I have since seen, save only for the glittering immensity of Kanchenjunga.

Pressing north, we reached graceful Edinburgh, my favourite among the capitals of Britain, and then Glasgow, which has no grace at all, but which offered us the noble hospitality of a group of anarchist disciples of Max Stirner who spoke a Lallans dialect so broad that it was three days before I began to understand them. North of Glasgow we went into the wooded hills of the Trossachs, with their clear and sparkling cataracts, and then, beyond, into bare hills, and finally up a bleak valley where suddenly, and together, we were taken with a foreboding panic, and turned and hurried back the way we had come. Only that evening, in a little inn in Callendar, did we learn, over our dinner of fried mutton, that the place where we had experienced this strange psychic shock was the Pass of Glencoe of evil memory. For in this part of Scotland, whose uninhabited hills were regarded as tempting to enemy spies dropped in by parachute, all the signposts had been removed.

Glencoe was the farthest point of our wanderings in Britain, but these travels had left us discontented with a life confined to London. Early in 1944 we bought a shepherd's caravan and went through the Chilterns in search of a place to keep it. Finally, in the village of Skirmett in the hills between High Wycombe and Henley-on-Thames, we found a farm with a grove of old elms and an orchard of overgrown apple trees and a yard full of cats and a sympathetic dairy farmer who let us park our van under his trees for a few shillings a month. From that time on, every clement weekend we could spare, and sometimes when I was writing hard for a week or two at a time, we would go down to our home on wheels, which I fitted with bunks and benches and a folding table and a little cast iron stove where we could burn fuel we gathered in the beechwoods. Certainly we were well established by D-day, for our field lay under the great air path for the invasion, and that June night of 1944 we lay awake from nightfall until dawn as flight after flight of bombers seemed to shake the earth as they thundered southward through the darkness and we knew that history was taking another turn.

Otherwise, though it was less than forty miles from London, Skirmett seemed singularly apart from the horrors that were then being perpetrated on the battlefields of Italy and France and in the death camps of Germany and Poland. Provided there are no armies to interfere with it, the agrarian life continues anywhere in its traditional rhythms, war or no war, and the grazing meadows and parched chalkhill oat fields of Skirmett were no exception. Staying there tended to reunite me with the pleasanter aspects of my boyhood, as we walked in the beechwoods, which in spring were bright with bluebells and primroses, and along the lanes embowered with mezereon. In the evening over the roads of crushed flint to the Chiltern village we went to pubs where we would drink and play darts with the mixture of broad-spoken farmhands and well-off commuters who formed the wartime population of the area. The alternation of London and country life helped me with the transition I was going through at the time, from writing mostly poetry and anarchist propaganda, to writing the less committed criticism and biography on which I spent most of my time in the later 1940s. At Skirmett I composed some of the long literary essays that were eventually collected in *The Writer and Politics* (1948), and I began, in 1944, to work on my first important prose work, *William Godwin*.

FROM THE EARLY MONTHS of 1944, I became less closely involved in the affairs of Freedom Press. But I was nevertheless influenced by events within the anarchist movement. Because of their opposition to monolithic party structures, and their emphasis on affinity groups as the desirable basis for action, anarchist groupings have always tended to be fissiparous, and the British movement was no exception. When I entered it, it was very loosely organized in a secret Anarchist Federation of Great Britain. The main groups were in London, Glasgow, and two or three of the provincial industrial cities, and the total membership at that time was certainly less than two hundred. The Federation included a strong syndicalist element, consisting largely of factory workers attempting to radicalize their unions. This faction tended to stand in opposition to the intellectuals of Freedom Press — and also to the stray anarchist-pacifists like me and Alex Comfort — and to demand that the emphasis should be placed on industrial action.

What the syndicalists really wanted was to gain control of Freedom Press and the printing house associated with it, and for this reason its proponents began to accuse Marie Louise, Richards and Hewetson of autocratic methods; any affinity group that resists domination by a wider movement is liable to such accusations. When the crisis came and the Freedom Press group walked out of a Federation meeting, I knew where my own loyalties lay and went with them, for I recognized the dangers of mass dictatorship in the syndicalist concept of industries operated by massive unions. Nevertheless, the split shook my faith in the possibility of moving towards anarchism by the conventional methods of direct action we had all been advocating. I ceased to be one of the active editors of *War Commentary*, though I continued to write occasional articles for it, and to help with small clerical tasks. My former comrades tried to lure me back into closer involvement but I did not respond until outside circumstances changed my mind.

One of the clerical tasks Marie Louise had asked me to do was typing the stencils of a manifesto to the armed forces, in the classic anti-militarist manner, which the group planned to circulate in army camps where they had contacts. It advocated mass disobedience as soon as peacetime came, if not before, and to me it seemed a risky document; I felt that Marie Louise and the others had not considered the very sweeping definitions given to sedition under the special wartime regulations. But I typed the stencils and felt I had done all I could when I had expressed my misgivings, which were ignored.

The matter slipped out of my mind. Then one evening I had a call from Marie Louise asking me to meet her at Camden Town tube station. A thick November fog was beginning to form as I made my way there. Marie Louise and Richards were waiting. They told me the Freedom Press premises near Finchley Road had been raided by a squad of the Special Branch, and that they and the other two editors then active (Hewetson and Philip Sansom) expected to be arrested and tried under the notorious wartime Regulation 39A which gave the authorities a virtually free hand in suppressing anti-war publications and punishing their editors. The police, they said, had shown a special interest in the typewriter on which the appeal to the soldiers had been prepared. I should get it and anything else that might compromise me out of harm's way immediately. And then I should do my best to keep clear, since if they went to prison there would be nobody else left who could run *War Commentary*. At the end of the meeting Marie Louise asked me directly if I would do this.

It was an appeal I could not resist, partly because of our friendship, but even more because I was angry at the way in which the authorities were obviously trying to destroy an opposition paper by removing its staff. I agreed. When I set off home the fog was getting thicker, and I regarded this as providential, since it would make me harder to follow as I skipped from bus to bus and went through a couple of pubs that had rear entrances in back streets to make sure I was not being followed. By the time I had got to our flat and was leaving with the typewriter and a case of papers, it had developed into one of the last of London's classic peasoupers; I was literally unable to see the pavement at my feet when I stood under a street lamp. I made my way to Euston Station; no one could possibly have kept up with me in that monstrous opacity. I caught a night train to Carnarvon, and then went to Beddgelert where I met some friends in an old mountain hotel. We left the compromising papers and the typewriter for the time being in a pacifist farmhouse in a Snowdonian valley, and in two days I returned to London.

If I were to emerge as editor of *War Commentary*, I realized I had to regularize my own position, to come in from the cold of my fugitive status. I registered a change of address, and in a few weeks the National Service bureaucrats had realized that I was again in the open and tried to harry me back to farmwork. I pleaded ill health and sent in a certificate from a friendly doctor. My affairs then took an ironic turn, for the Ministry's own doctor surprised me by discovering a heart weakness of which I had been unaware, so that I need not have gone on the run at all. But the experience had been interesting and I did not regret it.

Meanwhile I turned my attention to the situation that had been created by the actions of the police. I made immediate contact with Herbert Read who had just hidden in his attic at Sear Green some parcels of literature the police had overlooked in their search of Freedom Press. We decided to attack on the civil liberties issue before the police had a chance to do anything further, and within a few days we had persuaded T. S. Eliot, E. M. Forster, Stephen Spender, George Orwell, Dylan Thomas, and a clutch of other well-known writers to sign letters protesting against the raid on Freedom Press.

Some odd confrontations emerged from this exercise. Forster insisted on toning down a phrase in our letter as too radically outspoken; Eliot, in theory by far the more conservative of the two, insisted on the original phrase being restored, not because he agreed with it, but because he regarded Forster as an insufferable fusspot, which he was. Spender, then working at the Foreign Office, was summoned before the Minister and reprimanded for signing the letter; characteristically, he did not resign, but decided to keep away for the duration from civil liberties issues.

Our letters, which appeared in the *New Statesman* and *Tribune*, did not prevent the police from arresting and charging the four editors, who were then let out on bail to await their trial. But I am sure they prevented the persecution being extended, for no further raids or arrests were made. And they gave us a basis on which to form a Defence Committee to which many leading figures in British political and intellectual life adhered. Aneurin Bevan was one of the joint chairmen, and Harold Laski a member of the committee. So were Bertrand Russell and writers like Cyril Connolly and Osbert Sitwell and George Orwell, artists like Augustus John and Henry Moore, and musicians like Michael Tippett and Benjamin Britten. And so, perhaps inevitably, was the popularizing philosopher, C. E. M. Joad. Joad, celebrated for his parsimony, characteristically said to me, "I'll be glad to join as long as I don't have to shell out." The war was nearly won, and everybody felt that for the government to attack a dissident group right at the end boded ill for our freedoms in the days of peace.

We set up a committee room in Hanover Square, the heart of Mayfair. Through its doors passed an extraordinary mixture of volunteers: workmen and writers, old anarchist veterans and young conscientious objectors, gay society photographers and debutantes in rebellion. Even if Joad did not shell out, plenty of other people did. We raised enough money for the defence and we raised public doubts about the prosecution. We got no help at all from the Civil Liberties Association, which had been infiltrated by the Stalinists who in 1945 were still fervently patriotic, so we continued as a permanent Freedom Defence Committee that monitored infringements on freedoms of speech and writing and action for many years after the war.

In the tense days of the trial in the oak-panelled solemnity of the Old Bailey, I would sit in the press gallery, representing *Peace News*, the pacifist paper which Middleton Murry was then editing, and watch with wonder and satisfaction the public benches filling with a peacock array of the people I knew ordinarily in the Bohemian pubs and clubs of Soho and Bloomsbury. I would lunch each day with Herbert Read and Julian Symons, now out of the army, to discuss the way the case was going. In one way it was a great triumph for the anarchists. All the so-called seditious writings — prose and poetry — on which the prosecution based its case were read in court, and the daily papers reported them almost verbatim, so that ideas that had previously reached only a few thousand people through *War Commentary* now reached several millions, courtesy Lord Beaverbrook and Lord Rothermere.

There were moments of pure comedy when the Special Branch detectives got entangled in the complexities of left-wing factional politics, at one point actually inventing a non-existent Surrealist Party that the defence counsel quickly blew to dust. One day I spotted Alex Comfort in the audience. Alex had blown himself up in a chemical experiment as a small boy and one of his hands had no fingers left and only a thumb that seemed to have elongated with use. That day, listening intently to an obscure passage in the evidence, he began to pick his nose meditatively with that long talon of a thumb. I looked across the court and saw

Mr. Justice Birkett in his scarlet robes, equally absorbed in the evidence; he glanced in Comfort's direction and then, equally abstractedly, began to pick his nose with a long and bony forefinger.

We won only partial victory. In court each day Marie Louise looked so much the part of a tragedy queen that the all-male jury sought and found a technicality on which to release her. But the three male editors were found guilty, as indeed they were according to the letter of the wartime regulations, and the judge, praising their idealism and regretting his duty, sentenced them to nine months in Wormwood Scrubbs.

FOR ME IT WAS A BETTER OUTCOME than I had feared. I would not have to edit *War Commentary* alone. An agreeable and experienced fellow editor had been released from the jaws of the law in the person of Marie Louise, and we settled down to the exacting tightrope task of publishing a dissenting paper known for its outspoken criticism in a situation where we knew every word we wrote would be followed with the closest attention by the police on the lookout for slips in legality, and by our fellow dissidents on the lookout for compromises with authority. I think we walked that tightrope well. In Hazlitt's phrase, we "never wrote a line that licked the dust," and while we mocked the police constantly, we never gave them a case they could follow up without the risk of another public outcry.

We edited the paper. We read the piles of radical rhetoric that were submitted in the form of articles, and because little of it was up to our standards, we wrote much of the paper ourselves in joint day-long sessions fuelled by strong Italian coffee. We took the copy to the typesetter who operated at the top of an old warehouse in Covent Garden; we read the proofs; we did the layout of each issue; and then we looked after its production in the antiquated printing house in the East End that the Freedom Group had bought for a song in a bankruptcy sale. And, in mid-career, the week the war in Europe ended in May 1945, we changed the paper's name from *War Commentary* to *Freedom* (which still continues thirty-seven years afterwards) and lost no readers.

They were crowded, urgent days, with all the satisfaction of working to the edge of one's strength in common cause with a woman whose mind and mine seemed in almost perfect timing and who into the bargain was the best of companions, her fine Tuscan gaiety mitigating a fierce political dedication. I have not, in all the forty years since then, written better journalism than I did then for that obscure paper with its four or five thousand readers. In every way it was one of those times of heightened living when one's perceptions and one's mental responses are tuned to their highest level and one has a strange sense of being outside and above oneself.

Apart from editing *War Commentary*, we had to supervise the bookshop which the Freedom group had set up in Red Lion Street after the fearful landlord had expelled them from the premises near Finchley Road as a consequence of the police raid. Red Lion Street had been changed utterly by the war since the days I first went there to visit Charlie Lahr. Houses had been knocked out by bombs, and those that stood between the gaps, like teeth left in an old man's mouth, were shored up with timbers that were already blackened by the weather and beginning to decay. Some of the spaces had been made into fire-fighting reservoirs which on a clear day brightly reflected the sky and the clouds; others had been left for the fireweed to fill all summer long with its magenta flowering. Destruction had brought its own beauty.

Here Vernon Richards had found a decrepit, bomb-wracked shop that was vacant, and during the months they were waiting for their trial he and the others put it into repair. The front part was a shop where we sold our own books and all sorts of political and literary avant garde material. It became a haunt of young writers and radicals and of the nostalgic old mossbacked comrades from the days of Kropotkin and William Morris whom the trial had drawn out of obscurity. The back part served as the office for Freedom Press and as a spartan apartment for Kropotkin's old friend Lilian Wolfe, a tough and tenacious vegetarian who had come out of retirement when she heard of the trial to act as our office manager.

Since Lilian was so efficient, we had to divert little attention to the bookshop, but the running of the printing press was another matter, and this task, which fell increasingly on my shoulders, introduced me to a world and its denizens that even now seems more exotic than many foreign countries in which I have since travelled.

One reached the printing house through an alley off Whitechapel High Street; almost next door was the Whitechapel Art Gallery. The alley opened on to a polygonal court, paved with flagstones and surrounded by buildings four or five storeys high, whose Industrial Revolution brickwork had been sooted and eroded by London smoke and fog into a dingy rottenness that made their collapse seem long overdue. Rubbish was always drifting into the corners of the court, and even when the sun shone there, the dark, dank walls seemed to absorb and smother its brightness, so that the place never looked anything other than drab and slightly sinister, which befitted its notoriety, for this was Angel Court, where Jack the Ripper had committed one of his more atrocious murders.

Express Printers (we kept the old name even if it belied the slowness of our operations) occupied two floors and a basement of one of the buildings on Angel Court. On the upper two floors were the offices of the Jewish Chronicle, the organ of a small Chassidic sub-sect in a state of almost perpetual hostility towards the rest of British Jewry. An odd kind of symbiosis developed between the Chassidim and the anarchists, for they would set up their copy in Yiddish type on their own linotype machine and bring down the formes to be printed on our ancient Wharfdale flatbed press in the basement. Every week there would be a crisis, for the formes were invariably brought down late, and hardly had we put them on the machine when Rabbi Twersky, the *Jewish Chronicle*'s editor, earlocked and bearded and runcible-hatted, would come racing in, urging us on and screaming that if we did not hurry he would never get his paper into the mail before the Sabbath. Our press-man, a taciturn Polish Jew of another sect, stolidly ignored him and let the machine run at its slowest pace.

Apart from me, three people worked at Express Printers. An old Scot named Anderson made up *War Commentary* and *Freedom* and the pamphlets and books we published, working alone in a great composing room filled with disused cases of type where many men must have worked in the days before linotype machines were introduced. The pressman stayed like a troglodyte in his basement, monosyllabically answering the instructions we gave him, and we rarely saw him above ground; once a week a well-worn little prostitute would visit him and they would retire to make love on the reams of newsprint stacked in a dark and mouldy cellar beside the pressroom. The middle floor was my domain. The office was there, and also the stapling machine, the great mechanical guillotine, and the treadle-operated platen press for small printing jobs, all of which I eventually learnt to operate so as to increase our income from whatever minute contracts I might rustle up. And there also worked the third and by far the most interesting member of our staff. He was Ben Lampman, the man of all tasks.

Whitechapel was then largely a Jewish neighbourhood, a network of little markets and streets of dilapidated houses to which the descendants of those who fled the Russian pogroms of the 1800s gave a noisy liveliness I never encountered in the other slums of London. Wandering among the stalls and shops, I heard more Yiddish and Polish than English, and the foods I bought and tasted were quite different in their richness and smoky pungency from the stolid banger-and-tripe fare of the real Cockney districts farther east.

But Ben belonged to the old East End that had existed before the influx of Jewish refugees. He was tall for a Cockney, and very strong, so that he carried with ease the big iron formes filled with lead type when they had to be taken from the composing room down to the pressroom in the basement. He dressed like a barrow boy of the period, in a long tight spiv overcoat, wide-bottomed trousers and sharp-toed shoes, and walked with a swagger; but by inheritance and tradition he was a Thames waterman. The watermen operated barges and lighters on the London reaches of the Thames; in earlier centuries they had also operated passenger boats that were quicker than going by coach or sedan chair through the narrow streets of old London. Even in the twentieth century, unlike other London workers who had their trade unions, they were organized in a guild that began in the Middle Ages. One was a Thames waterman by descent and joined the guild because one's father belonged. Very rarely, in recent generations, had any outsider been allowed into this ancient, exclusive, and very proud body of men.

Ben's father and his brothers still worked on the river and they did so, like most of the watermen, as a family group under contract rather than as wage earners. But Ben had quarreled with them and left the barges, and this was because, having been a great fighter in his youth, he was suddenly converted to pacifism.

Pacifism did not really change the Stepney scrapper. Ben appointed himself bodyguard of the Hammersmith pacifist group; he carried their speaker's stand when they went to preach on Shepherd's Bush and stood beside it to intimidate the hecklers. When the police tried to stop the pacifists from speaking at all, Ben was so enraged that he beat up two policemen at once and spent three months in gaol. The experience made him a dedicated enemy of the state and when he heard by a left-wing grapevine that anarchists were printing a paper in Whitechapel, he came to ask for work. To us he seemed that mythical being, the natural anarchist working man who believed by instinct what we believed by reason. He had never read Kropotkin. He did not even read him when he helped to print his pamphlets for Freedom Press. But he had come by experience to the same conclusions and we welcomed him for it.

And with Ben, because he belonged to a plebeian tradition that preceded the industrial era, I never felt the kind of gap that so often seemed to divide me as an intellectual from a factory worker. It was not that we were interested in the same things, except for our shared hatred of authority and our shared amusement at human follies. It was not even that we spoke the same language, for it took me several weeks to understand what Ben was talking about. It was, I think, the special circumstances of being part of a very small body of dissenters in a wartime world that removed the inhibitions our different backgrounds would otherwise have created and enabled us to behave and speak quite freely with each other.

I have said that we did not speak the same language, and by that I mean that Ben's habitual way of speech was a kind of Cockney patois that had its roots in the seventeenth century. He was always using the rhyming slang the costermongers spoke. This does not mean that the word used actually rhymes with the word for which it is substituted. A phrase that rhymes is found, and then the rhyming syllable is cut off. For example, a Cockney woman will call her husband "My old man," but she may also call him "My old pot" from "pot and pan." Ben used hundreds of these substitute words made from truncating rhyming phrases and disentangling them was like solving a grand code, though in the end I recognized most of them and knew that when he talked about putting on his rock he meant his overcoat, from "rock the boat," and when he suggested going to have "a bit of the old saint" he meant dinner, from "saint and sinner."

Sometimes Ben and I would go out together on expeditions connected with the business of Express Printers that taught me a great deal about East End life and its strange and often grim survivals from earlier times. We had no facilities for binding books, so when we were producing Herbert Read's *Poetry and Anarchism* we loaded the printed sheets into a costermonger's barrow and trundled it through the streets to a bookbinding establishment off the City Road. It was in a dirty street where some of the old brick houses had been knocked down by bombs.

The street was depressing enough, but when we entered the bindery it seemed as though the bad old London of Thomas Mayhew and Gustave

Doré had never come to an end. Crowded into the two floors of a small brick building, working by dim gas flares, were dozens of women sewing and stapling and binding in a stench of putrid glue; all of them were either old or crippled or young girls pale and peaked from under-nourishment. The woman who ran the place was the only red-cheeked well-fed person in sight, and her name, by a grotesque irony, was Dickens. Ben and I were equally appalled, and we trundled off with our barrow to find a bindery where working conditions at least seemed more endurable. On other days we would wander around the little jobbing printers in the back streets, buying up black-market paper to keep the presses running, and on such forays I learned a great deal about the business practices of the East End and the way bargaining was still regarded as a sport fit for men, as it is in the Levant.

Ben and I also spent a lot of time trying out the eating houses of the East End, which in those days were always simple and always cheap and often very good. They exemplified the ethnic variety of the area. Along Aldgate, where the East End melts into the City of London, there were cheap, ill-lit Italian places where the pasta was often superb. Goyd's, the big kosher restaurant and bakery next to Angel Court, was making rich and succulent cakes in the east European tradition right through the war. Just over the street a Cockney named Ernie never ceased to serve the best pork chops, and some of his devoted customers were English girls married to the Muslims, Arabs and Pakistanis, who lived in the area. "Me old pot 'ud kill me if 'e saw me gollopin' this!" one of them said to me as she ordered a helping of bacon after her pork chops.

Some days we would get on a bus in the Commercial Road and go all the way down the East India Dock Road to Limehouse, once the main Chinese quarter of London. Limehouse had a place in Edwardian fiction as the haunt of white slavers and opium dens and Fu Manchu villains. But in the 1940s most of the Chinese had departed, leaving a few restaurants as a reminder of the past. The most famous and the best was Chong Chu's which served a double public. At mid-day one sat among longshoremen eating the docker's dinner of roast and two veg for one and sixpence. And at evening, for those who cared to venture so far into the London hinterland, there was excellent Shanghai food though, as I once discovered, it was wise not to look in the kitchens.

In these East End haunts one often ate better in wartime than in Soho or the West End, perhaps because they were nearer to the docks, and supplies filtered through unofficial channels, which nobody questioned.

One also felt welcome in a way one never did in the more affluent restaurants farther west. After two or three visits the proprietor would greet one and recommend the best black-market offering of the day. After five or six visits the other customers would include one in their conversation. And this happened no matter whether the restaurant was Jewish or Italian or Chinese or plain Cockney. There was a natural and spontaneous democracy about it all, and the only time I felt I was slumming was when I insisted, against Ben's objection, on our going to a place called Joe Eyre's, which George Orwell had told me about in the Whitechapel High Street.

Joe Eyre's was the cheapest restaurant I ever found in London, but also the most pathetic. It was one of those places where the customers sat on benches in cubicles with rotting wooden partitions, and grimy waitresses constantly shouted "Cup and two" to the kitchen, which meant a cup of strong tea and two slices of bread and margarine, butter being too expensive for Joe's vagrant clients. They were all men (I never saw a woman there except the staff) and they had contracted out of society entirely. Even in the full employment world of wartime they had not been able to find a niche. They were ragged and dirty and lost.

Ben, the Thames waterman, had none of the kind of guilty sympathy for such people that Orwell displayed in *Down and Out in Paris and London*. They offended his own pride as the inheritor of an independent working-class tradition. "You'll never get me into bloody Joe's again," he said when we left after our cheap bad meal. "I just 'ave to look at them old bozos and it gives me the Little. Let's go and 'ave a spot of pig to wash 'em away!" (Little being Little Tich, or itch, and pig being pig's ear, or beer.) Having my spot of pig with Ben, I came near to understanding why Orwell, who tried so hard to get at the soul of the down-and-out, never came to understand the real English working man. For in the extraordinary caste system that in those days divided English society into an infinity of layers separated by pride and snobbery, the gulf between Ben, the member of an ancient guild, and the old bozos he despised was just as great as that which opened on the other side between Ben and a member of the House of Lords.

As we wandered around Whitechapel and Stepney and Wapping and Houndsditch, or worked together at our various machines in Angel Court, Ben talked a great deal about the violence of London waterfront life. For him the watermen were the Homeric aristocrats of the great river. The dockers with their unions and their historic strikes he regarded as mere newcomers to the scene. The watermen represented an older and nobler order of things. They did not work for wages. They sold their skills as free men, job by job. They defended their ancient privileges against all comers. And they fought cleanly, with their hands — not, like the dockers, with cargo hooks. The increasingly obvious fact that the waterman's role would be needed less and less as docking operations were mechanized never occurred to him. He was as unaware of its inevitably obsolescence as the Métis in the 1870s had been of the coming extinction of the bison, and many years later when I studied the history of the Métis I was often reminded of Ben. Like Gabriel Dumont, he was a man of great candour, of unswerving loyalty, and of pride in his independent tradition. And under his naive and joking manner the violence was always lurking.

Not that I ever ran into it. He regarded me as a defenceless kind of being whom he had made his friend and whom he would protect if the need arose. Once, in the verbal feuding of the English left during the 1940s, a Trotskyist threatened me with violence. Ben offered to deal with him on my behalf, a service I hastily refused, thinking what havoc a man who had beaten up two rozzers at once might wreak on a single small Marxist whose bark was worse than his bite.

Sometimes Ben talked of East End murders and disappearances, and once he claimed that the Thames watermen knew the perfect, clueless way of "doing" a man, as he put it. You just dropped him overboard, at one of the many spots on the Thames where there was a deep bed of soft mud, and then you floated your barge in towards the shore so that the keel pressed the body into the ooze; held in that suction, it could never rise to the surface. Did he know of such a killing? I asked, meaning had he been involved in one. He merely laughed his innocent laugh and then went on to say that there were bodies lying in the Thames ooze that had been there since the Romans. Of course, he remarked with probable accuracy, the Thames watermen were already plying the river when the Romans built Londinium.

Eventually the anarchist editors came out of gaol and took over again some of their old tasks of editing and manning Express Printers, and I went less often down to Angel Court. Then, when I left for Canada in 1949, that interlude in the East End seemed closed off. I did not try to keep in touch with Ben for I knew that if I wrote to him he would never reply. Writing of any kind was not his strong point. But three years ago, after more than thirty years, a message did come to me in a letter from a London anarchist. Ben had learnt that I was still alive, as he was. He had gone back to the river but, loyal man that he was, still went occasionally to give a hand in Angel Court. One day, if I ever got to Whitechapel again, we must drink a tickle of pig to living friends and dead. Tickle of course means glass, from tickle your fancy.

XIV

THE ENDING OF WAR

THE WAR IN EUROPE came to an end on my thirty-third birthday, the 8th May, 1945, and though we went walking among the beeches and blossoming wild cherries of a deserted Ken Wood rather than join the triumphant crowds in the centre of London, it was still a joyous day for us. It seemed that the great horror of our age was ended; we did not attach great importance to the Japanese war that seemed to be petering out so far away, and so we were unprepared for the greater horror of the atom bombing of Hiroshima in August.

Our failure to expect this was a measure of our scientific innocence, for in hindsight one can find enough clues in the statements of scientists even before the bomb was dropped to have alerted anyone even modestly read in atomic physics. I have never found it easy to understand physics, so that I felt mentally and morally devastated by the news of Hiroshima, which taught me that in an extremity no politician, however democratic his pretensions, is less inclined to inhuman policies than any other.

For this reason I have never been able to share that retrospective and exclusive hatred which, in recent years, has been directed against the Nazis for the extermination of the Jews. If we are to take the Holocaust as a benchmark in human degradation, it seems to me its territory must be extended beyond Auschwitz and the other Nazi death camps to include Hiroshima and Nagasaki, and all the hellholes of the Gulag Archipelago, and the roster of victims must be extended to include not only Jews gassed by Germans, but also Japanese fried alive by Americans, and Russians starved and shot and beaten to death by their fellow Russians. In the demonology of the modern age I have, since

August 1945, placed Truman and Churchill beside the Nazis and Stalin. In Vietnam the communists and the soldiers of American democracy performed equal atrocities; having witnessed the events of World War II, I expected nothing else. Nor, to look into the murky future, do I imagine a difference in ideologies will determine who may launch a Third World War, if it ever takes place. It will be the ruler, whether he resides in the White House or the Kremlin, who feels that his power demands that ultimate outpouring of destruction and terror.

In May 1945, once the immediate euphoria had died down, my main feeling was that of returning from a strange, perilous and exciting world to a condition of grey actuality. This feeling I shared with many others whom the war had taken out of ordinary routines of work and family and liberated them from their everyday cares, offering instead irresponsibility, adventure, a life less dominated by routine. A lucky few found lives of enduring freedom, but most people felt the shades of the prison houses descending once more upon them as they went back to their old jobs and responsibilities.

Not only the people who had accepted the war felt this sense of deflation and depletion once it had ended. Looking at my pacifist friends, I recognized that, like me, they missed the tension and the unpredictability of the war years. If those who fought were left without a physical enemy, we were left without a war to resist, and much we had done over the past six years suddenly lost its immediate relevance. Yet I think the anarchists whose dissent embraced a total criticism of existing society were better off than the mere war resisters, since we were able to continue our central activity of attacking the state without interruption. The failure of politicians in the months and years after May 1945, to meet the expectations on which the war had been fought gave us plenty to criticize.

So Marie Louise and I continued editing *Freedom* much as we had edited *War Commentary*, except that we turned our attention to peacetime problems, but I found *NOW* increasingly difficult to publish. People now had less leisure time to read and less spare cash, so that the sales of maverick books and literary periodicals declined to something like the prewar level, and though George Orwell and other friends put money into *NOW*, I was unable to keep it going beyond 1947.

Since the three imprisoned editors of *Freedom* had lost their remission through trying to smuggle letters out of prison and were not let out late in the summer, Marie Louise and I continued to edit the paper until we handed it over to our returning colleagues in the autumn. We then refused to continue the old system of a large editorial board, since we had learnt that our collaboration worked best without outside interference, and *Freedom* entered on what was undoubtedly its best period when we worked on a roster system; Richards and Hewetson, and then Sansom and Colin Ward, who had joined the group, succeeded us for stretches of six months each. It was a fine arrangement, so far as Marie Louise and I were concerned, during the other two periods when we shared our editing tasks, since we were so attuned to each other mentally and used to each other's ways of working, but we also had the stimulus of functioning in a group whose other members we knew were perpetually watchful and ready for the kind of criticism that is stimulating yet, because it comes from people who understand the problems yet are outside the actual work relationship, is not destructive.

Only late in 1948, when I was already thinking of leaving England, did I finally withdraw from direct participation in Freedom Press and the anarchist movement. I was spending more time on my non-political writing, both from inclination and from necessity, as I shall shortly tell. But the bitter disunity within the anarchist movement had also made me sceptical as to whether our beliefs could ever be effectively manifest as more than a current of thought sustained by individual thinkers and through them influencing society.

The antagonism between Freedom Press and the syndicalist rump of the Anarchist Federation had continued in spite of the trial and imprisonment of the three editors of *War Commentary*. The syndicalists were so envious of the publicity we gained from the trial that they even remained aloof from the Freedom Defence Committee, and carried on a subterranean campaign of vilification. Shortly afterwards they turned to violence. They had recruited a couple of Spanish anarchist refugees who had been *pistoleros* in Barcelona before the Civil War, and also a pair of Irishmen expelled from the IRA, Reilly and Borland, who had been trained in a merciless school of violence and were ready for any kind of shabby adventure. One night two of the English syndicalists, with the two Irishmen and one of the Spaniards, armed with revolvers, forced their way into the flat of Marie Louise and Richards, and extracted money from them on threats of death. They justified themselves with the argument that Freedom Press belonged to all anarchists and its cash must be distributed to those who favoured other forms of propaganda. We immediately called a meeting of all the known anarchists in London.

It was attended even by the old Jewish East End comrades, survivors from Kropotkin's day, who rarely made a public appearance and it censured the violence. But the syndicalists, fearful that we would publicize the incident, now raided Express Printers and smashed the type for the current issue of *Freedom*.

Three of us then decided that we must perform our own raid, this time a moral one, so we went to the basement where the Irishmen lived and confronted the group. Reilly, a gorilla with a brogue, uttered blood-curdling threats; Borland, thin and pale like a cold-eyed Aubrey Beardsley, menacingly flourished his revolver. By ignoring their threats and keeping talking, we persuaded them to attend a general gathering of anarchists similar to the one we had called before so that they could state their case. The meeting took place; the Spaniards, who by now feared their refugee status might be imperilled, did not attend. The remaining syndicalists and the Irishmen indulged in some blustering rhetoric, but quickly realized that the general feeling of the meeting was against them. Then an extraordinary series of melodramatic events destroyed their movement. Borland died of consumption. Reilly was found dead on a bench in Hyde Park a few days later. And the most vicious of the English syndicalists was translated in a different way out of his present existence by inheriting a fortune and a house in Park Lane from a distant relative of whom he had been hardly aware until the lawyers sought him out as the heir.

Their enemies having been dispersed with such miraculous rapidity, the intellectuals of *Freedom Press* now attempted to set up an organization of "pure anarchists," a Federation of Anarchist Groups, whose title was intended to stress the autonomy of the member segments. The dominant theoretical influence was Kropotkin, though Malatesta's example was revered, and room was given for the notions of such strange prophets as Wilhelm Reich and even the Marquis de Sade. To begin with at least, it was decided to ignore the differences between the violent and the non-violent, the followers of Bakunin and those of Tolstoy.

Even Herbert Read emerged from his aloofness to take an interest in these developments. He attended one of the organizational meetings, and in August he wrote me from a summer villa in Braemar ("A Victorian house with its period equipment — amusing but exhausting, a relic of the slave age"): "I am glad to hear that the London Group is taking shape. I would like to see a copy of the programme." I think he hoped it would be a true guild of anarchist intellectuals, which he could have joined, but the old pseudo-proletarian line prevailed, and he held aloof, as did Alex Comfort.

I joined for a while, but I became increasingly aware of the pressures towards orthodoxy to which, as Orwell shrewdly pointed out to me, even anarchists were prone. The more dedicated a militant, I realized, the more priggish and intolerant he was likely to be. Only a few, like Marie Louise with her clarity of mind, seemed to avoid that tendency, and even she once said to me: "One day, George, you'll have to make a choice. You can't be a detached intellectual and a committed militant at the same time." She was striking at the crucial dilemma of the writers of the Thirties and Forties. And, knowing that the infection of orthodoxy would probably ruin me as a writer, I stepped aside in the end to become a free-wheeling radical of my own kind, or perhaps rather of the same kind as Hazlitt and Orwell and Cobbett and the rest of their tribe.

MEANWHILE, THROUGH THE YEARS from 1945 to 1949, my wife and I continued our involvement in the Freedom Defence Committee, which succeeded the original Freedom Press Defence Committee. In the middle of the summer we reorganized it with Herbert Read as Chairman and Orwell, with whom I was becoming increasingly friendly, as Vice-Chairman. When I invited him, Orwell remarked that he did not really like organizations, and hated committee meetings, but he felt our group was congenial enough to make an exception. It was the only exception he ever made, the only occasion on which he accepted office in any organization.

I became Secretary, and we operated the regular business of the Society with a small working committee which, so far as I remember, included John McNair of the ILP, Stuart Morris of the Peace Pledge Union, Vernon Richards representing the anarchists, and Julian Symons representing himself. We would meet in the back room of the Freedom Bookshop, which served as our mailing address. Nobody was paid a salary, we sought out lawyers who would act for nothing, and we typed our letters and appeals on Eileen Orwell's machine which George gave us after her death.

We followed a completely libertarian policy of helping anyone we believed had been persecuted for the expression of opinions. So we found ourselves defending anarchists, pacifists, communists and even fascists, and we took a certain pride in standing up on the issue of free speech for people who in political terms were our bitter enemies, though we drew the line at black marketeers who would sometimes try to bribe us into taking on their cases. There was a surprising unanimity between the working committee and the less involved people, like Read and Orwell and Cyril Connolly, on such matters, and I think our general attitude was best expressed in a letter that Orwell wrote to me early in 1948 from the hospital in Lanarkshire where he was then being treated.

I hope the FDC is doing something about these constant demands to outlaw Mosley & Co. *Tribune*'s attitude I think has been shameful, & when the other week Zilliacus wrote in demanding what amounts to Fascist legislation & creation of 2nd-class citizens, nobody seems to have replied. The whole thing is simply a thinly-disguised desire to persecute someone who can't hit back, as obviously the Mosley lot don't matter a damn & can't get a real mass following. I think it's a case for a pamphlet, & I only wish I felt well enough to write one. The central thing one has (to) come to terms with is the argument, always advanced by those advocating repressive legislation, that "you cannot allow democracy to be used to overthrow democracy — you cannot allow freedom to those who merely use it in order to destroy freedom." This of course is true, & both Fascists & Communists do aim at making use of democracy in order to destroy it. But if you carry this to its conclusion, there can be no case for allowing any political or intellectual freedom whatever. Evidently it is a matter of distinguishing between a real & a merely theoretical threat to democracy, & no one should be persecuted for expressing his opinions, however antisocial, & no political organization suppressed, unless it can be shown that there is *a substantial threat to the stability of the state.*

We got a few people out of prison, which in itself would have been sufficient justification for our activities, and we managed, largely through Orwell's *Tribune* essay "Freedom of the Park," to curb police attempts to prevent the free selling of minority papers near the speakers' pitch at Marble Arch. Once the Labour Party came into power in 1945 the presence of Harold Laski, the party's chairman, on our list of sponsors gave us a small leverage with the Cabinet, and by this means we were able to make sure that individual cases were properly reviewed by the Home Office; but our campaigns on behalf of large groups of victims were less successful.

I remember one mass meeting in Conway Hall, where we urged a general amnesty for all deserters and for all people still in prison, years after hostilities had ended, under various wartime laws and regulations. Herbert Read and Fenner Brockway spoke, and so, to my surprise, did Orwell. He was obviously not happy as a public speaker, and his voice, weakened by the throat wound he had received during the Spanish Civil War, did not carry well. Yet I do not agree with Julian Symons, who was also present and wrote about this occasion, that he was a bad speaker; there was so much unpretentious conviction in his manner and so much plain common sense in what he said, that his audience listened with complete attention and applauded him, more warmly than the practiced orators of the evening.

Yet my impression is that neither Fenner Brockway's professional polish nor Orwell's hesitant honesty had much effect in hastening the end of wartime injustices on the larger scale. And this was not out of keeping in a country where, under the austerity programmes of Stafford Cripps and his puritanical associates in the Labour Party, wartime restrictions and food rationing were unnecessarily continued until the Fifties.

IT WAS AT THIS TIME that my friendship with Orwell developed, and we began to meet informally, outside the ambiance of civil liberties. By the spring of 1945 we were visiting each other in our respective homes, which in Orwell's case was a clear sign of approval. He tended to compartmentalize and grade his personal relationships almost obsessively. Few of the many he knew were invited to his flat in Islington, perched under the roofs of a tall Georgian house in Canonbury Square, a lower-middle-class outpost on the edge of a great workers' district. He lived there with his sister Avril, then unmarried, and his small adopted son Richard, to whom he was extravagantly devoted. Orwell was highly conscious of the geography of classes, and the whole area around Canonbury Square, with its bombed houses and flooded basements and ruins red in summer with fireweed, had the kind of seediness he liked to portray in books like *Keep the Aspidistra Flying* and *Nineteen Eighty-Four*. Such marginal districts gave him a comforting illusion of nearness to the British workingman — that nearness he sought so often and so vainly.

A street or so from Canonbury Square stood a large working-class tavern, a kind of gin palace with cut-glass screens and a big garden filled with tables, where the proletarians would sit on a summer's evening in whole families, with the fathers and mothers downing pints of old-and-mild while the children shouted on the swings the publican had cannily provided. Orwell liked to go there occasionally, always keeping a weather eye open so that he might avoid the embarrassment of running into the communist poet Randall Swingler, who also lived in Canonbury Square and whom he passionately hated. But George did not appear to know any of the workingmen who frequented the pub, and he certainly seemed out of place among them, a rather frayed sahib wearing shabby clothes with all the insouciance an old Etonian displays on such occasions.

Orwell's apartment reflected his attempt to reconcile his intellectualism with his interest in a working-class culture already moribund among the people. It was a dark, almost dingy place, with a Dickensian atmosphere I suspect Orwell deliberately fostered. In the living room stood a great screen plastered over with shellacked pictures cut from magazines, and a collection of china mugs, celebrating various popular nineteenth-century festivals, crowded on top of the crammed bookshelves. Like many good writers, George neither had nor pretended to any developed taste in the visual arts or, for that matter, in music, and he gathered objects around him for their curiosity rather than their aesthetic charm. By the fireplace stood a high-backed wicker armchair of an austerely angular shape I have seen nowhere else, and here Orwell himself would always sit, like a Gothic saint in his niche. The small room he called his study looked like a workshop, with its carpenter's bench, its rack of chisels and its smell of newly cut wood. Orwell would sometimes do a little joinery as a relaxation from writing, though the simple bookcases and brackets he made showed no evidence of any special dexterity. Most of his writing he did by typewriter, sitting at the large round table in his living room.

Whenever we arrived at Orwell's flat, or he walked into our top room at Highgate, his ailing bronchi wheezing from the long climb up several flights of stairs, there was first a period of silence, for George, though gregarious, was also a shy man. Then, after a while, the conversation would warm up over a meal (usually high tea at Orwell's), or sitting before a coal or peat fire, with Orwell butterfingeredly rolling cigarettes of the strongest black shag he could find and drinking tea as dark and almost as thick as treacle. Sometimes, when he was in a reminiscent mood, the talk would develop into an Orwellian monologue.

His voice, which retained a slight but recognizable vestige of the Etonian accent, was rather low and level in tone, and it had a fascinating kind of monotony that seemed to throw into relief the vividness of his descriptions. His monologues mainly concerned those parts of his life dealt with in his autobiographical works and in the semiautobiographical parts of his novels: the writings on Burma; on Paris and Spain; and on those lower depths of English life which then still seemed to any member of the middle class more distant and only slightly less exotic than life in a foreign country. It was a leisurely, rather didactic but nonetheless highly interesting gloss on his various books.

At other times we would be guided by Orwell's passion for odd facts, and would converse on the strangest variety of subjects, hopping erratically from point to point. However banal our topic might appear when we first lit upon it, Orwell would usually discuss it with a thoroughness and humour that lifted it completely out of its intrinsic dullness. He might talk about tea, for example, and the ways of making it, or about various kinds of fuel and their respective merits, and would bring in such a wealth of illustration and reminiscence and so many odd tags of information that one was stimulated to enter the subject as zestfully as he. And then, a week or two later, one would find that the conversation had become embedded in his writing as one of his highly readable essays in the *Tribune*. This close relationship between talk and writing enabled Orwell to be at once such a prolific and such a generally successful journalist. Once an idea had taken shape and even polish in conversation, it was a fairly simple matter to write it down. Some of Orwell's articles, as he admitted rather shamefacedly, were actually typed out immediately and published in their first draft, without any substantial revision, though on his books and on the more monumental essays like those he did for *Horizon* or *Partisan Review* or *NOW* he took much greater pains.

At other times the conversation would range more portentously over political themes, and Orwell would expound his fears about the future of society, and dilate on the weakening of the concern for freedom and truth in the popular consciousness, as well as among writers and politicians. In this way he outlined to me all the themes that emerged in *Nineteen Eighty-Four*, though, with characteristic secretiveness, he talked little about the details of the novel, and until I saw it in print I had only the sketchiest idea of the plot.

One day, I think it was early in 1947, Orwell took out of his bookshelves a paperbound book. "I've been looking for this for a long time," he said, "but I still can't find a copy of the English version." It was *Nous Autres*, the French translation of Zamiatin's *We*, and a few weeks later Orwell wrote for the *Tribune* a descriptive essay on this fascinating anti-Utopia. But he gave no indication of the extent to which the chance acquisition of this volume would help to determine the shape of *Nineteen Eighty-Four*, which bears the unmistakable marks of Zamyatin's influence.

When Orwell talked in the apocalyptic vein he would paint a horrifying Gothic picture of the fate that might befall us, and in this, as some of the more pessimistic parts of *Coming Up for Air* suggest, he was motivated by long-held fears which the reading of *We* merely helped to crystallize in a fictionally viable form. "My God, Orwell *is* a gloomy bird," said Herbert Read, himself no lighthearted conversationalist, after one such session. And often, indeed, it seemed as though one had been listening to the voice of Jeremiah.

Orwell was one of those rare men whom success did not harm. Indeed, there was a noticeable mellowing of his character during the lamentably brief period between the successful publication of *Animal Farm* and the onset, at the end of 1947, of the illness that continued until his death at the beginning of 1950. He became less inclined to imagine himself the victim of literary conspiracies, and he found a great deal of pleasure in sharing his good fortune with others.

When he heard of the acceptance of *Animal Farm* by the American Book-of-the-Month Club, Orwell rang me up and invited me to lunch with him in celebration. By now he had abandoned the dreary taverns of the Strand that one associated with his *Tribune* days, and was patronizing the Greek and Italian restaurants in Percy Street. We met in a Tottenham Court Road pub and as we walked to Percy Street Orwell explained to me at length that we were going to a place he had begun to visit only the previous week because the head waiter in the restaurant where he formerly lunched had objected to his taking off his jacket to eat.

I have forgotten the name of the restaurant to which we did go, but I do remember Orwell standing up, conspicuous because of his height, and hanging his jacket over the back of his chair. With a look he challenged me to follow his example; I did. At that time, wartime restrictions on restaurant meals were beginning to relax, and the lunch was excellent and lavish, with aperatifs, wine and brandy; it was a far cry from the boiled cod and turnip tops in the Strand a few years before, and Orwell seemed to enjoy the change.

Over lunch, Orwell discussed the effect the success of *Animal Farm* would have on his future. I thought at the time his ideas were quite realistic. He planned to put most of the money from the Book-of-the-Month Club into a trust fund for his son Richard. There was nothing in the way he spoke to suggest a premonition that he would be dead within four years; he was merely acting with a sense of caution bred of many illnesses.

He also wanted to buy a house in the Hebrides and told me that he had been thinking about this all through the war; rather sardonically, he said that now his intention was reinforced by a desire to get as far away as possible from the threat of destruction by the atom bomb. From what I know of Orwell's almost perversely obstinate courage, I doubt if this was ever a really important reason; the nostalgia for a simpler and cleaner way of life that emerges so poignantly in *Coming Up for Air* and even gives pathos to parts of *Nineteen Eighty-Four* was, I am sure, a much more pressing motive. Apart from his own feelings, he wanted to bring up his son in the country rather than the city, and later on he was delighted when Richard, still only four, seemed to take enthusiastically to farm life. For the rest, he hoped to abandon journalism and to spend his time writing novels and major critical essays.

By the austere standards of 1946 England, the bill Orwell paid for that lunch was a stiff one — round about six guineas — and I felt obliged to contribute in some way to the celebration of his good fortune. I decided it had to be some unusual treat, and I remembered that one of the Soho pubs, the Dog and Duck, had mysteriously acquired a small cache of real absinthe. So we crossed Oxford Street and stood in the tiny bar, crowded with beer-boozers drinking against closing time, while the barmaid slowly dripped water through a cube of sugar into the milky liquid. Some of our fellow customers were curious, and the barmaid explained at embarrassing length, with dark references to people who wasted good money on frivolities. There was still a lot of puritanical feeling about extravagant spending in London at that time, and we began to realize that the regulars of the Dog and Duck regarded us with suspicious disfavour, so that as soon as the absinthe was ready we drank it quickly and hurried out.

Unwittingly, I had made Orwell unhappy, since the incident underlined the gap between the modest bourgeois luxuries he could now afford to give himself and his friends, and the standards of the working class for which he still felt an obscure though slowly receding admiration. However, that was not what he talked about as we walked away down Frith Street, both feeling a little sheepish. "Didn't it cost rather a lot, George?" he asked solicitously. It cost in fact only a fraction of the bill he had settled half an hour before, but he knew enough of the life of young professional writers — this was the year of my first real book — to realize that the pound I had paid out was one of the very few in my possession. Naturally, like Gordon Comstock in *Keep the Aspidistra Flying*, I dissembled.

It must have been almost immediately after this meeting that Orwell went up to the Hebrides and found the deserted farmhouse, Barnhill, which he bought on the Isle of Jura. From that time we naturally saw much less of him, but letters arrived quite frequently in which he gave vivid little pictures of his life there and kept us posted on his activities. Returning from Switzerland in August 1946, for example, I found a letter waiting for me in which he said he had just started a novel which he hoped to finish in 1947. This was the book that emerged from the gloomy speculations about the world's future to which we had listened during the preceding year. It became *Nineteen Eighty-Four*, and was destined, though none of us then imagined it, to be his last book.

Knowing Orwell's passion for tea, we would save up our rations — since we were coffee drinkers — and every now and again send him a packet of Ty-phoo Tips, which produced the dark, strong brew he liked. One such packet, in September 1946, evoked a letter in which Orwell described existence on Jura; it reflected the intense interest he always took in the concrete aspects of life — particularly rural life — and also in its social overtones.

> Thanks ever so for the tea — it came just at the right moment because this week the whole of the nearest village is being brought here in lorries to get in the field of corn in front of our house, and of course tea will have to flow like water while the job is on. We have been helping the crofter who is our only neighbour with his hay and corn, at least when rain hasn't made it impossible to work. Everything is done here in an incredibly primitive way. Even when the field is ploughed with a tractor, the corn is still sown broadcast, then scythed and bound into sheaves by hand. They seem to broadcast corn, i.e. oats, all over Scotland, and I must say they seem to get it almost as

even as can be done by a machine. Owing to the wet they don't get the hay in until the end of September or even later, sometimes as late as November, and they can't leave it in the open but have to store it all in lofts. A lot of corn doesn't quite ripen and is fed to the cattle in sheaves like hay. The crofters have to work very hard, but in many ways they are better off and more independent than a town labourer, and they would be quite comfortable if they could get a bit of help in the way of machinery, electrical power and roads and could get the landlords off their backs and get rid of the deer. These animals are so common on this particular island that they are an absolute curse. They eat up the pastures where there should be sheep, and they make fencing immensely more expensive than it need be. The crofters aren't allowed to shoot them, and are constantly having to waste their time dragging carcasses of deer down from the hills during the stalking season. Everything is sacrificed to the brutes because they are an easy source of meat and therefore profitable to the people who own them. I suppose sooner or later these islands will be taken in hand, and then they could either be turned into a first-rate area for dairy produce and meat, or else they would support a large population of small peasants living off cattle and fishing. In the eighteenth century the population here was 10,000 — now less than 300.

In letters like these (and there were more of them) one felt that Orwell was not merely displaying his recently-acquired knowledge of the remote Scottish countryside and its way of life. He also expressed a conviction that the so-called progress which had been going on for the past three or four generations, and which had accelerated since his childhood, was disrupting a naturally balanced society in which a frugal but satisfying agrarian existence had been viable. But Orwell allowed for the possibility of that trend eventually being diverted, and I found it an interesting indication of the open and undoctrinaire kind of socialism which he professed that he should consider the re-creation of a peasant class a possible solution to the social ills of rural Scotland. My own feeling is that his close involvement at that time in the life and problems of a group of survivors from the premechanical age such as the Jura crofters was directly related to the passion with which, at the same period, he was sketching out the themes in *Nineteen Eighty-Four*. The predominant one is the possible outcome of an uncritical faith in progress and an unimaginative willingness to accept a managerial society, whether on the American capitalist, the English socialist or the Russian communist model.

The essay I had written on Orwell for Dwight Macdonald appeared in *Politics* in the winter of 1946, after Orwell had returned to London. It was the first serious essay on Orwell's work that had yet appeared, and in places it was very critical, particularly of those inconsistencies of thought which it is easy to pick out in anything Orwell wrote about politics. The day after the issue arrived in England, I went into the Freedom Bookshop, and there I found Orwell. He had just bought *Politics* and was obviously intent on reading the article as soon as he could. I felt rather apprehensive; I had got into trouble with London literary friends over much less critical comments on their work. That evening Orwell rang me up; he liked the essay and thought it was as good a first study as any writer could expect.

Orwell stayed in London from October 1946 to April 1947. It was the hardest winter we had endured for many years, and he suffered from severe attacks of bronchitis which kept him in bed for weeks on end. I remember more than once going round to his flat in the middle of the day and finding him in pyjamas and a shaggy dressing gown, looking exceptionally gaunt and pale, but working at his typewriter on a review or article for some editor to whom he had made a promise he did not wish to break. Money was no longer important to him as it had been in the past, but the years of journalism had established the deadline habit, and he was too workmanlike in his attitude towards writing to feel happy about letting down anyone who was relying on him.

After Orwell left for Jura in April 1947, we did not see him again; for him it was the last of the good summers. He invited us to join him in the Hebrides whenever we felt inclined, and sent an elaborate timetable of trains, boats, buses and hired cars. But that year we could not afford the fares for the two-day journey from London. In 1948 Orwell was perpetually in and out of Scottish hospitals. And in the spring of 1949 we were deeply involved in preparations for our departure to Canada. But we kept up a correspondence, and Orwell's letters not only chronicle the course of his last illness, but also reveal the strength of his passion for writing and the durability of his interest in the political concerns we shared.

I heard from Orwell for the last time in January, 1949. He had left Scotland and was being treated in a sanatorium in the Cotswolds. He seemed relatively content there, and some of the grim old Orwellian humour came back when he discussed his treatment. "They are giving me something called PAS which I suspect of being a high-sounding name for aspirins, but they say it is the latest thing and gives good results. If necessary I can have another go at streptomycin, which certainly seemed to improve me last time, but the secondary effects are so unpleasant that it's a bit like sinking the ship to drown the rats." He was still interested in the affairs of the Freedom Defence Committee, which was now waning fast. Characteristically he expressed regret at not being able to contribute to the funds as generously as in the past. He had found sickness expensive and until *Nineteen Eighty-Four* came off the press he felt he must continue to be economical. With the caution of a professional writer with a long experience of low incomes, he thought that he would be lucky if he made five hundred pounds out of the novel. In spite of the success of *Animal Farm*, he did not realize, or was unwilling to acknowledge, that at forty-five he had become a successful and even a fashionable writer.

XV

IN THE WORLD OF LETTERS

THE ENDING OF THE WAR meant both a narrowing and a broadening of our lives. At last, Europe began to open again, and we could travel to other countries from the island on which we had been cooped for almost seven years. The experience created in us the desire to escape from England that would lead to our departure to Canada in 1949. But we probably would not have made that final journey away from England if our life had not become in some ways more difficult there in peacetime than in war.

I am not suggesting that the years from 1945 to 1949 were uniformly dull or dreary. We had the journeys abroad and old relationships were re-established as friends returned from the wars. We saw a great deal again of Roy and Kate Fuller and of Julian Symons and his wife Kathleen, whom he had married during the war. Roy had returned to his solicitor's work for the Woolwich Equitable and was beginning to build his reputation as one of the leading British poets of the post-1945 era, while Julian, after a couple of years in an advertising agency, took to freelance writing in 1947. He had already published his first detective novel, *The Immaterial Murder Case*, but he was able to take the plunge into independence when he took over Orwell's assignment as regular book reviewer for the *Manchester Evening News*. Orwell had turned up at our flat one evening, and had said he was giving it up. It was just the time when I needed a regular reviewing task and I think George mentioned it because he hoped I would suggest myself. But I valued his good opinion too much to want to appear self-seeking, so I mentioned Julian, who needed the job as much as I did.

Our financial situation had become critical by the simple erosion of the legacy I had received seven years before. In my disinclination to keep my grandfather's money, I had got rid of it quietly and systematically. I gave some of it away to people I liked; I made loans which I knew would never be repaid to cads and cadgers and to some people who were in genuine need. I began to earn a pittance in 1945 writing reviews for small periodicals at half-a-guinea a time, but I was still mainly occupied with *William Godwin* which, after rejection by two major publishers, was finally brought out by a new house, the Porcupine Press, in 1946. We were all rather surprised when the book became an immediate *succès d'estime* which established me as a young writer worthy of serious consideration and Porcupine Press as a promising publishing concern. In major reviews, critics like Harold Nicholson, Charles Morgan, H. N. Brailsford and the anonymous reviewer in the *Times Literary Supplement*, all wrote of it generously. I was delighted by the praise; for the first time in my career I felt I was really accepted into the literary world. I was glad also that my vindication of Godwin as a writer and thinker had been so widely accepted. I had chosen Godwin as the first libertarian philosopher on whom I would write because it seemed to me that he had established the essential doctrines of anarchism on the plane of intellect, and had elaborated what I still think a logically unassailable argument. *Political Justice* I saw as, par excellence, *the* case for the abandonment of government as a way of organizing human societies. I also regarded it as important that anarchists in England should be aware of their own libertarian tradition, exemplified in Godwin and earlier in Gerrard Winstanley, since anarchism had so often been dismissed as a doctrine imported from the continent and associated with intemperate Russians and Latins.

Looking again at *William Godwin* three and a half decades later, I am surprised at the difference in maturity between this book, which did re-establish Godwin as a serious figure in the eyes of English critics and literary historians, and *Anarchy or Chaos*, with its hasty derivative judgments and jejune prose. While I had come to maturity as a poet at the age of about twenty-eight, I reached the same stage of assurance as a prose writer five years later, at about thirty-three. That was the turning point at which my style and my literary persona were established, and though it would be another fifteen years or so before I reached my prime as a writer, I see from this point a consistency of development and a unity of outlook. By the time I published *William Godwin* my world view was established, and my perceptions of existence have not changed greatly since then, so that even now, at the age of seventy, I feel inwardly, as a person, the young man I was in 1946.

I learnt with that first book the salutary lesson, which has been repeated more than once in my career, that there is no reliable correlation between the reviews a book receives and the sales it achieves. Books hardly noticed by the critics have earned me generous royalties, while others that have added greatly to my prestige as a writer have brought me very little in monetary returns. It is largely a matter of mundane considerations like a publisher's advertising budget and his distribution service. The Porcupine Press was too new and too amateurish to be very effective in either of these directions. Only one member of its board had any experience in publishing, and the elegant small houses of the Twenties and Thirties with which he had been associated had not been financially very successful. The other members of the group were small businessmen and professionals with a little money to invest and a great love for books, but no experience of the trade. There was no one among them who had the special flair that makes an inspired publisher, and Porcupine Press was therefore doomed to the failure which — after a few prestige successes — was its eventual fate.

Nevertheless, for the time being my interests and Porcupine's coincided. I had given them the book that put their name as well as mine on the prime pages of the literary papers, and I might have other books as good to offer. They needed an editor with literary expertise and ideas, and I needed a small steady income, which they offered. So I read books for them, sought out likely authors, and started a series of classic pamphlets which got no farther than the first three, Wilde's *The Soul of Man Under Socialism*, Tolstoy's *The Slavery of Our Times*, and Shelley's *A Defence of Poetry*. The centenary of the revolutions of 1848 came up, and I prepared for Porcupine a large celebratory volume, half of which consisted of documents of the times and the other half of contemporary essays by people like Max Beloff, Christopher Hollis, Raymond Postgate and my Cambridge friend, Hugh Ross Williamson. For some reason it aroused Harold Laski's ire, and he reviewed it angrily, which increased sales and taught me another lesson: a hostile review may do a book's sales a great deal of good, certainly far more good than silence. In 1948 Porcupine Press also published my first book of essays, *The Writer and Politics*.

Among the writers I introduced to Porcupine Press were Roy Fuller, Marie Louise Berneri, and Louis Adeane. Roy prepared a little volume of selections called *Byron for Today*, and Marie Louise wrote for them her only major book, *Journey through Utopia*, a critical study of Utopian schemes from Plato down to the modern age. The author was dead and the publishing house on its last legs by the time the book finally appeared in 1950, published not by Porcupine Press, but by Routledge; it has since become one of the standard works on Utopias.

Louis Adeane was a young poet, brother of the furniture designer Norman Adeane with whom I had shared for a while the flat in Parliament Hill Fields. The brothers' real name was Potter and they changed it because they detested their father; Louis did a double shift, for his real Christian name was Donald. He was small and dark, with black hair always tumbling low over his forehead, and a look, during the day at least, of having just arisen from slumber, which was understandable since he used to spend the morning hours until three or four sitting in the all-night underground restaurant in the Leicester Square Corner House, writing in a large leather-bound ledger which he always carried with him.

I rarely joined him there, but the place was the haunt of a number of literary nighthawks, of whom Colin Wilson became eventually the best known. Louis was a much more brilliant and erudite talker than Colin, and at that time I felt he had the brighter future ahead of him. But he became another of the dazzling unfulfilled promises among the friends of my youth. He was a good lyric poet, but published only one small volume, forgotten by all except his friends. He was a shrewd and well-read critic; he had studied Jung intensively and could relate his insights brilliantly to both literary and political topics. Yet he wrote only one prose book of which I am aware and that was never published. It was the book on Herbert Read which, at my urging, Porcupine Press commissioned from him and which, against my recommendation, they eventually rejected because they felt it was too scholarly for their list. I do not know whether this setback or a general dwindling of the will to write was the reason, but from the end of the 1940s Louis ceased to write seriously, and spent the rest of his days until his death two or three years ago (by which time he had again changed his name to Rowan) working as an editor for a series of publishers. He remained attached to literature, but was no longer in the creative sense a part of it. Yet he was very good and very helpful to me in the role of editor he finally chose, and in the years between 1945 and 1949 when we saw each other often, he commented sanely and usefully on the books I was writing.

With *William Godwin* I felt that surge of energy which has continued, with a few intermissions, since the mid-1940s. I began to find a sureness that allowed me to write prose rapidly, with comparatively little time spent on revisions, and I had ideas for books which I wanted urgently to write. I knew Porcupine would not have the funds to produce all of them or even to finance them with respectable advances. They were still operating on pre-war scales with advances of twenty-five or at best fifty pounds.

Louis had become linked with a firm called T. V. Boardman. Boardman was one of those big, phlegmatic, pink Americans who look like white-haired and overgrown babies. He made his money mainly out of thrillers, but he was anxious to add prestige to his publishing house by bringing out what he called "stoodious books." He was encouraged in this by the two stringy English spinsters who presided formidably over his office, his partner Miss Weir, and his secretary, Miss Tweedy. None of them knew much about literature, and they relied greatly on Louis as their editorial adviser. They were willing to pay generously, in terms of London publishing at that time; the advance they offered on each book was £125, which in those days was lavish for a barely-established writer.

For me it was an opportunity to move out of the largely political area in which *William Godwin* had been conceived. The first two books I wrote for Boardman were much more literary but there was a libertarian touch to both of them.

The first, which appeared in 1948, was on *The Incomparable Aphra*. The original impulses that lead one towards writing books are often slight and even laughable. My father had been fascinated by the strange names that ornament the history of literature, and for a period he constantly joked about Mrs. Aphra Behn. Later on, finding references to her, my curiosity was stirred by memory, and I discovered the strange life she had led, her importance in the development of the novel, her special place as the first English professional woman writer, and the intrinsic charm of a great deal of her writing. No real biography had yet been written of her, for Victoria Sackville-West's *Aphra Behn*, which appeared in 1927, had been hardly more than a long essay and paid little attention to the literary qualities of Aphra's writings. My book was, in fact, both the first full-scale biography and the first extensive critical study of Aphra Behn, and as such, though it has long been out of print, it has enjoyed a lasting reputation among feminists.

And justly so. Although Aphra Behn may have attached herself to the Royalist faction in the 1660s (after all the faction more tolerant of the kind of erotic drama she wrote) she was a marvelous fighter for the professional equality of women. She held her own in the male-dominated London theatrical world of the Restoration. Her most notable novel, *Oroonoko*, with its slave hero and its planter villains, can be interpreted as a precursor of abolitionist literature. This libertarian element in her work and her career attracted me to Aphra Behn, as it did to the subject of my second book for Boardman.

In *The Paradox of Oscar Wilde* I balanced the serious and the frivolous sides of Wilde's character and of his literary achievement. My conclusion, that he was a more profound thinker and especially a more acute critic than had generally been recognized, has, I think, been borne out by the seriousness with which modern critics now consider his insights into the nature of artistic creation. Rereading my book thirty years later, I recognize a ponderousness not always appropriate to the subject; Julian Symons accused me justly of attempting to break a butterfly on the wheel when I pursued my search for philosophic profundities into the brilliantly frivolous dialogue of *The Importance of Being Earnest*. And there is a justificatory aspect to the book, as there was to most early books about Wilde, which dates *The Paradox* as belonging to the period when persecution of people for their unorthodox sexual inclinations was even more an issue than it is today.

Certain things had to be said in 1948 by anyone concerned for personal freedom that are no longer necessary today. The bitterness has gone out of the great debate over Wilde that lasted for more than fifty years, and the cause of permissiveness for which in his own way he must be regarded as a martyr has triumphed beyond one's expectations. It will need a new Savonarola, a massive revival of puritanism, to see Wilde again as he appeared to his detractors as well as his supporters in the first half of this century.

Aphra Behn and *The Paradox of Oscar Wilde* were both as well reviewed as *William Godwin*, and *The Paradox of Oscar Wilde* was the first of my books to be published in the United States, by Macmillan of New York. Yet although my standing as a recognized younger writer was certainly well-established, we could not live, in a time of rising prices, on the money I was earning from books alone, and in those years, from 1946 to 1949, I established the pattern of living as a many-sided writer that I have followed ever since. I felt — as I still do — the pride of the man of letters who can turn his hand to any literary task and do it well, whether it is a serious book, a play, a poem, an article or a review.

Boardman, wishing to expand into continental European writing, had accepted Marc Bernard's novel, *Anny*, and Marie Louise and I translated it under the joint *nom-de-plume*, M. L. George. We did a great deal of the work during the fine summer of 1947 in one of the sunny open-air restaurants of Hyde Park. It was a silly book, sentimental under its facile modernity, but it gave us a hundred pounds to share, and I think we made it better in English than it was in French. Later I edited an edition of Charles Lamb's letters for Wrey Gardiner to publish at Grey Walls Press. I wrote literary articles for the *World Review*, which Stefan Schimanski was now editing, and began my long broadcasting career by doing a few talks for the BBC.

But most of all I supplemented my income by book reviewing: anonymously for the *Times Literary Supplement* and openly for Tosco Fyvel who succeeded Orwell at the *Tribune*; for one of the Farjeon girls at *Time and Tide*; and above all for V. S. Pritchett at the *New Statesman*, for whom I wrote on fiction and literary biography. Victor Pritchett paid the best fees and he was generous in another way. To supplement their income, most critics sold the books they reviewed at two-thirds the shop price to a bookseller near the *Times* office who supplied American libraries. Pritchett, with a grin twisted to fit the stubby Latakia-fragrant pipe that always projected from his pugdog face, would invite writers he liked to take their pick of the titles he did not intend to have reviewed, and a visit to his office could often mean a fair bonus in floggable books.

In those years I established a life pattern I have followed ever since. We would get up late and, except on the weekend, the day would be largely taken up with wandering over London, to Freedom Bookshop and Express Printers, to editorial offices and publishers' offices, lunching sometimes with Read at the Reform Club but more often at some cheap place on Soho or Bloomsbury where I might run into one of my friends or enemies, and frequently, on my way, stopping at Elizabeth's flat in Bloomsbury Square, or Jankel Adler's studio, or Charlie Lahr's shop. On these wanderings I encountered most of the personalities of literary London, from Cyril Connolly to Paul Potts the "Canadian Hick Poet" who distributed broadsheets of his execrable poems in Hyde Park, and I felt very much part of a living literary world. I had elder writers to ask for advice and help, writers of my own age with whom I could discuss the work I was doing, and younger writers who already saw me as halfway up the ladder of success they aspired to climb.

I think in the earlier part of a career this fairly intimate mingling with the members of the tribe, with its sense of belonging to a literary community, and its awareness of a city as a vast cultural zoomorph, is good for a writer — perhaps even essential for the proper development of all but the most temperamentally reclusive. One tries the various options of life and of style, and then slowly discards most of them as a literary persona emerges. Finally, physical proximity is no longer necessary to maintain the sense of belonging to the literary community or the consciousness of destination that allows one to work alone. It is many years now since I have found it necessary to live closely among writers.

Finding a place congenial enough for writing became an increasingly tedious problem. The great attic room at Highgate, above the noise of the house and looking out over the peaceful heath, was an excellent workroom, but in the summer of 1947 our landlady asked us to leave. During the war flats had been easy to find, for few people lived in London then if they could avoid it, but with peacetime the city had rapidly filled, and the kind of places we could afford were hard to find.

We moved at the end of autumn to the house of a commercial artist, an anarchist sympathizer, in Kensal Green. But our host, a small pale man with the impossible ambition to become a great landscapist, suffered from phenomenal constipation, and on the fourth or fifth day of one of his costive periods he would become unendurably irascible, so that the peace would be broken at least once and sometimes twice a week by a nagging row over some small household problem.

In the summer of 1948, after more than six months of domestic skirmishing, we moved again, this time to a tiny one-room studio in Church Street, Kensington. Our neighbours were photographers and commercial artists, except for a gentle New Zealand painter, Pat Hayman, who occupied the studio next to ours; he was the only one with whom we became friendly. The studios were noisy during the day, with people all the time walking backwards and forwards before our window, but in the evenings they were deserted and quiet, and the location was good; a few minutes on the bus took us into the centre of London, there were plenty of local eating houses, and every morning I could go down into Kensington High Street and get excellent hot croissants for breakfast. Each weekend we would take the Greenline coach down to High Wycombe and the local bus to Skirmett, and I would write in the quiet of Farmer Smith's orchard.

The last book I wrote in England was *The Anarchist Prince*. Nowadays, when there are many books — biographical and otherwise — on the great anarchists, it is surprising to remember that by the end of the 1940s there existed no book on Kropotkin in English and only sketchy, inadequate attempts at biography in other languages. Quite apart from my admiration for his teachings, Kropotkin had lived an extra-ordinarily interesting and eventful life. The only reason for my hesita-tion about writing on him was that I knew no Russian, and without reading the available sources in that language anything approaching a complete biography would be impossible.

My problem was solved early in 1948 when a dark young man with a strong Balkan accent came one day into Freedom Bookshop. Ivan Avakumović was a Serbian refugee from Tito's Jugoslavia. His father had worked in the Serbian Embassy under the former king, and had remained in London; Ivan, who had studied at Oxford, was then teaching in a private school and hoping for the academic career he would eventually attain. His knowledge of Russian was excellent, and I immediately realized this was the opportunity for which I had been waiting. At our second meeting I suggested we might collaborate on the life of Kropotkin, and he immediately agreed. I then went to Boardman. I think he was at first somewhat perturbed at the idea of a biography of an anarchist, for books about radicals were not yet regarded as the good publishing ventures they became in the 1960s. But he was impressed by Kropotkin's impeccably aristocratic antecedents, and when we offered the title *The Anarchist Prince* (which offended some of Kropotkin's more fundamentalist disciples) he was delighted and immediately commis-sioned the book.

One of my letters, inviting Ivan to tea in Kensal Green, suggests we were already working together by early April 1948. We divided the work so that Ivan traced and translated the available Russian material, and researched in the Public Record Office and the manuscripts collection at the British Museum. I researched literary sources in English and French and visited Paris to search in the National Archives; I found that the Kropotkin files had been carefully culled to remove anything relating to his long term of imprisonment in France.

In those cold war days, the only institution in Russia that replied to our requests for help was the Tolstoy Museum, where some sense of the international obligations of scholarship still lingered. On the other hand, I discovered a number of Kropotkin's old acquaintances still alive in England, and visited people like H. N. Brailsford, G. D. H. Cole and old Edward Pease, the first secretary of the Fabian Society. What they had to tell me about Kropotkin was mainly anecdotal, but my views of the early days of socialism in Britain were widened by visiting these sur- viving pioneers. They had the integrity of men who never expected to see their beliefs become realities; compared with them I found in the later socialists I knew who did achieve office, even in men as radical as Aneurin Bevan and Michael Foot, the insidious corruption of power. I did not see Bernard Shaw, but in the postcard he sent to me about Kropotkin there was also a flavour of that pristine era:

> Personally Kropotkin was amiable to the point of saintliness, and with his red full beard and lovable expression might have been a shepherd from the Delectable Mountains.
>
> His only weakness was a habit of prophesying war within the next fortnight. And it came true in the end.

Not until the early autumn were we really prepared for the writing of *The Anarchist Prince*, but then the work on what turned out to be a massive book of four hundred and sixty pages went surprisingly quickly and very harmoniously. We spent as much time over that winter as we could at Skirmett working in peace, and, to our own surprise and everyone else's, the book was completed, except for the bibliography, before the end of March 1949. It appeared in 1950, and was the first of my books to be translated into French. It represented also the beginning of a hiatus in my writing life, for, after producing an average of one book a year from *William Godwin* to *The Anarchist Prince*, I would bring out only one work, my travel book, *Ravens and Prophets*, between 1950 and 1956, when I published my third biography of a major anarchist thinker, *Pierre-Joseph Proudhon*.

XVI

GOING HOME

O NLY THREE OF OUR FRIENDS understood why, at the beginning of 1948, we decided to leave England for Canada. George Orwell, who had already withdrawn to the Hebrides, was one of them. In April 1948, he wrote me from Hairmyres, the Scottish hospital where he was then being treated: "I wonder how your plan for Canada is working out. I think it's the sort of country that could be quite fun for a bit, especially if you like fishing!" Derek Savage, with his longstanding hatred of the city and his desire to create some alternative way of existence, was predictably approving. And Dwight Macdonald, looking across the Atlantic from New York at a war-ruined Europe, had no doubt at all that we were right in our desire to leave it.

But the rest of our friends looked on our decision with a mixture of incredulity and sadness. The anarchists felt that I was betraying our past association, and perhaps they were right, since I would never have decided to go away from London if I had not concluded that my involvement in anarchism must now be only philosophic. I had in fact come to conclusions very similar to Orwell's when, in that very year of 1948, disillusioned by his own efforts to work with socialist politicians, he discussed in "Writers and Leviathan" the necessary independence of the writer from political organizations of any kind:

But does all this mean that a writer should not only refuse to be dictated to by political bosses, but also that he should refrain from writing *about* politics? Once again, certainly not! There is no reason why he should not write in the most crudely political way, if he wishes to. Only he should do so as an individual, an outsider, at the most an unwelcome guerrilla on the flank of a regular army . . . . Sometimes, if a writer is honest, his writings and his political activities may actually contradict one another. There are occasions when that is plainly undesirable; but then the remedy is not to falsify one's impulses, but to remain silent.

The more doctrinaire anarchists did not understand this, and they have never forgiven me for my withdrawal from activism. Others, who experienced similar perplexities, understood me, and one of my fellow editors of *Freedom*, Colin Ward, has remained my friend to this day. Marie Louise also understood me, because by now she knew me so well, and her understanding made her perhaps sadder than the rest; she had to reconcile her friendship for me, which continued, with the dedication to militancy by which she was held by her loyalty to her father, the anarchist martyr.

My literary friends mostly found it incomprehensible that I should want to abandon, as it seemed to them, a career that looked so promising, with three successful books in succession, for the chances of an unknown country where, so far as any English writer knew in 1948, there was no literary life worth the mention. They all urged me to stay. My income from writing could only increase and sooner or later we would find once again a congenial place to live.

Why did we leave? There were two real reasons, and nobody who did not share them could be expected to understand them. One was the personal myth which told me that Canada was the real home to which I must one day return, the place where I could perhaps live out some of my father's unlived life. The other was the feeling akin to claustrophobia that by the end of the war had made even Britain seem an island too small to be endured.

This was why we sought, between 1943 and 1945, even token departures from England by wandering into Wales and returning, more than once, to Glasgow and Edinburgh. Then, early in 1946, the first visitors began to arrive from Europe. One of them was Marie Louise's younger sister Giliane, who had survived the war in occupied Paris, training as a doctor and successfully concealing her revolutionary antecedents from the Nazis. Giliane was blonde where Marie Louise was dark, and had little of her sister's beauty, but she had a clown's wit and charm and we took to each other immediately. She was living with a young French poet, Serge Senninger, whom I had known already, when he was in London among de Gaulle's entourage.

At Giliane's invitation we made our first escape from England in May 1946. We planned to combine our rediscoveries of the past by going not only to Paris, but also to the Alps. They were still difficult days for travel since currency restrictions persisted until long after the end of the war, and we were allowed only £75 each, but we calculated that, with care, we could spin it over two months, and we succeeded.

Late in May we left on the channel boat from Dover. Our first impression of France revisited was bleak and depressing. There was a mist over the channel, which lifted only slightly as we put in to Calais harbour, to reveal a seafront of broken buildings, of timeless clock towers haggard among the twisted steel wreckage of warehouses and transport sheds. Our hearts fell, and as we settled into the ruin of a train that awaited us we had a terrifying feeling of being on the edge of a continent of death and irremediable decay. The old feeling of anticipatory pleasure that one had always felt on visits before the war was replaced by a half-desire to return to the close little prison of England rather than go on to what we feared we might encounter. Yet as the train drove slowly into the heart of the land, away from the coastal battlegrounds, we entered a landscape where the natural resilience of a peasant culture was already taking over. Farming was still primitive in comparison with the mechanization the war had brought to English farmlands, but the land was green with crops, and the market gardens around Paris were as neatly cultivated and as appealing in their bright geometric patterns as ever.

And then we reached the Gare St. Lazare, and on an impulse, since we had taken the night boat and it was still only noon, we put our bags in the *consigne*, and walked out in those Paris streets I had not seen for almost six years. It was a strange experience, like coming from a world that had vastly changed to a world that, to our immediate eyes, looked hardly changed at all. London had been beaten and bashed by war, with whole areas flattened and the surviving streets gap-toothed and scarred by bombs; Paris was almost untouched, its grandiose buildings a little dirtier, its narrow streets a little danker and shabbier, but essentially the same city one had always known. The plane trees were in leaf along the boulevards, and though the flower beds were not yet back in their prime, the grass was green and the air, in that year when there were still few cars on the streets, was fresh and sweet.

Even more striking was the spirit of the people. They were shabby, shabbier than I had ever seen Parisians before the war, and they did not look particularly well-fed, but there was a spirit and a liveliness to them, a brightness of expression and behaviour that contrasted dramatically with the greyness which seemed to have penetrated every aspect of the Londoner's appearance and mien by 1946. Paris, indeed, had always seemed a more alive and sunny city than London, but the difference in those first years after the war was more striking than it had ever been in the past. For the Londoners there had been no dramatic experience like the Liberation, which released so much vitality in France, but instead a peace that in its drabness and austerity seemed little better than a continuation of the war. Most Londoners wondered what good victory had done them.

We stayed the first night in a shabby student hotel, and next day Serge and Giliane found room for us in their apartment block on top of the hill in the Rue St. Jacques. This part of St. Jacques was a marginal street with the middle class Luxembourg quarter just over the Boulevard St. Michel to the west and the proletarian streets sloping away to the slum of the Rue Mouffetard to the east. The apartment house reflected this juxtaposition of classes. The lower floors consisted of large flats whose tenants lived in that gloom of heavy dark draperies and dropsical furniture which in France was still taken to connote bourgeois respectability. But the upper floors were divided into tiny one-room homes inhabited by students, office workers and skilled craftsmen.

Giliane and Serge each had one of the flatlets, and for the week we stayed in Paris they moved in together and turned over Giliane's top floor room to us. It was Spartan by any standards. No refrigerator, no vacuum cleaner, no bath; just a wash basin, and a plumbing system that glucked and gurgled all the night. There was only one toilet for each floor, between five or six apartments, and neither the genial, drunken concierge nor any of the residents considered it his or her duty to keep it clean. But the kitchen was well-equipped, in the French manner, and there was a balcony from which one could look out over that fantastic Parisian skyscape of gilded domes and Gothic pinnacles, of high-pitched roofs and forests of chimneys like metal cacti, and down into the chasm of the street below. Each morning, we would hear a fluting trill, and, looking down, would see a man in a Basque beret leading his little herd of five or six nanny goats which he would milk for the women who had come down to their doors with jugs or cans.

In spite of the bounding vitality of the people, and especially of the young, life in Paris was still materially very difficult. Bread was rationed, meat was hard to get, wine was expensive, and the black market flourished. Restaurant meals were still expensive even in the humblest eating houses, and this meant that the upper-class establishments around the Etoile and the Opera, were full of well-fed and richly-dressed men and women, while the middle-class cafés were enjoying a quiet business with frugal drinkers, and the little working-class bistros, formerly so full of life and noise, were silent and almost empty. The fashion shops and the jewellers' in the Rue de la Paix were well-stocked, while the flea market on the Rue Mouffetard was crowded with working people buying well-worn clothes for a few francs, and neatly-dressed men picked up cigarette butts in the street. By ten o'clock the Paris which in my memory had never gone to sleep was as quiet as a city of the dead.

Yet, unlike the Londoners, the Parisians were not resigned. Our neighbours in the tiny upstairs flats of the Rue St. Jacques, whether they were socialist, communist, anarchist, or radical Catholic in the manner of Péguy, looked forward to a new France where all the old injustices and inequalities would be swept away. Bread might be scarce and adulterated, but ideas were not, and there was a continual discussion of political and social issues, and a steady flow of new books and magazines from the presses, which seemed to have no shortage of paper.

Le Libertaire, the classic French anarchist magazine, was now selling between 60,000 and 80,000 copies a week (as against *Freedom*'s 5,000). Under the editorship of Albert Camus, *Combat*, the resistance newspaper, had shed its communist affiliations and was leaning towards the libertarian left. There had been a revival of revolutionary syndicalism in the trade unions, André Breton had issued another pro-anarchist manifesto, and a libertarian group of artists, *Art Libre*, linked with the surrealists as well as the anarchists, held an exhibition in which four hundred painters took part.

France was in a ferment in which no orthodoxy of the Right or of the Left seemed secure, and nobody in that week in May seemed to care about putting up with a little inconvenience for the sake of the magnificent future that was coming next year, or at the most in a few years' time. Even the discomforts of the Occupation became a matter of hilarity. Giliane roared with laughter as she described the days of fuel shortage when she tied a saucepan to a pole and cooked her beans by the heat of a street lamp, and her friend and fellow doctor Malou had a great story of the time when an elephant died in the Jardin des Plantes and for a week all the students of zoology feasted on its flesh.

Early in June we went on to Switzerland, travelling by night in a train that had no restaurant car so that we were hungry and thirsty by dawn when we ran through the devastated south-eastern corner of France, where Belfort and Mulhouse were as ruined as Calais, and gangs of dejected grey-clad German prisoners were clearing up the debris. Over the border, Switzerland presented an extraordinary physical contrast; the Basel station neat and orderly, and a little group of anarchists awaiting us, composed, in the old Helvetian tradition of natives, Heini Koechlin and Hans Ehrenzeller, and expatriates, the Warsaw Jew Isy Aufseer and a miner from German Silesia whom everyone called Schlusselbein (Collarbone; I never knew his real name).

With good Swiss efficiency they had found the best cheap place for us to stay, and it did not worry them a great deal that it was a Christliches Hospiz where we sat down for our first meal in a country little affected by the war — a Swiss breakfast with abundant milchcafe and good rolls and fresh mountain butter and cherry jam. We spent a delirious first three days with our anarchist friends in that city of abundance, where there were neat, well-designed new buildings, and unscarred mediaeval streets and squares (their shutters freshly painted and window boxes bright with flowers); and gasthaüse where the bratwurst and roesti melted in one's mouth; and ice cream parlours where unbelievable three-tiered and four-tiered concoctions were being served and shop windows where we gaped at the choice of chocolates and cakes and sausages and watches and clothes, and stood literally paralysed by the abundance so that we did not know what to buy with our scanty pounds; the great Grünewald altar that alone in this city of abundance seemed to relate to what had gone on outside Swiss borders in the last six years, and the detached private nightmares of the Paul Klees in the museum.

Our feelings towards the Swiss were divided. We responded to Ehren-zeller and to Koechlin and his father and brother, who were both doctors, since they had clearly suffered from the self-protective way the Swiss had kept their borders closed, not against the Germans who had no intention of destroying this precious breathing hole in the centre of Europe, but against the fugitives from Nazi tyranny. They, and Aufseer and Schlusselbein, told pitiful stories of the people whom the good free burghers of the Swiss Confederation had sent back to frightful deaths.

In a letter at that time to the American magazine *Report*, I compared the Swiss with the French in a paragraph which I still find an accurate expression of my feelings at that time.

But, spiritually, Switzerland is a dead country in comparison with France. There is a complacency about the people which seems to cover a kind of guilt that they have not shared the war experiences of the rest of the world. And, indeed, in some ways the Swiss *have* suffered mentally from failing to participate in the war. They were neutral for the wrong reasons; instead of adopting a revolutionary defiance of militarism, they accepted the political principles that caused war, and merely evaded the consequences. Far from being a pacifist nation, they can be compared more justly with the jingoist who supports war, but evades fighting to save his own skin. Consequently, they are afflicted with a half-conscious guilt which makes them shut their minds to the experiences out of which European thought and art are beginning to spring forth. Mentally, they are of the age before two wars — the Edwardians of modern Europe. A few are alert and aware, but most — even among the workers — live in an obsolete middle-class culture, a culture of liberal values, Manchester economics and centrist politics. Their minds are as unresponsive to contemporary problems as damp cardboard to writing.

After three days, we left Basel for the Alps, heading for Switzerland's most magnetic mountain, the Matterhorn and travelling on the little cogwheel railway into the peaceful valley of Zermatt where no motor traffic was allowed. We settled in a cheap pension at the end of the village nearest the mountain, with a fine view from the balcony of its gigantic rhinoceros tusk. We stayed more than three weeks, until the end of June. In spite of the hotels and the bright little shops that had come in the wake of the mountain climbers, Zermatt had not yet shed its earlier image as a mountain village devoted to the rearing of cattle and the production of cheese, and many of the weather-blackened old wooden houses of squared logs still remained in the village itself and on the alps to which the peasants were beginning to drive their bell-clanging cattle when we arrived.

Vertigo, and a tendency to hysterical paralysis when I find myself perched on a precipice, have prevented me from undertaking the heroic types of mountaineering, but ever since I climbed Snowden I have loved to walk among mountains, and that visit to Zermatt left me with the enduring desire to live where I can always see snow peaks, as I can from the city where I write these pages.

June was the best month of all for a botanically inclined mountain walker to visit Zermatt. When we arrived the meadows outside old Frau Julen's pension were yellow with tall globeflowers, with the little schusternagel gentians forming a carpet underneath of dark blue and green. We climbed up to the alp of Findelen above the village, and there the spring-lush meadows, watered by primitive channels scooped from half-logs, were roseate with mauve-pink primulas. Each day we would clamber in a different direction out of the valley, following snow frontiers that steadily receded as the hot mountain sun burnt down. We would find slopes red with the little azaleas which the Swiss call mountain roses, and beds of anemones — purple and white and yellow — and meadows of crocuses varying from ivory white to clear amethyst, and big trumpet-flowered gentians on the higher slopes, and always, highest of all, at the very edge of the snow, the miracle of the soldanella, its fringed purple bell actually melting its own way up through the snow to the light.

After a week, Schlusselbein and his girl arrived, and in the evenings we would sit drinking with them in one of the weinstuben in the village, talking about labour struggles in Weimer Germany and the way the communists betrayed the workers to the Nazis. But every day we went off into those mountain solitudes, which were almost deserted since the foreign tourists had not yet returned in large numbers. We would lunch off cheese and fresh mountain butter and bauernbrot and beer or milk straight from the alp in the little huts beside the mountain paths, and for the first time we had a true sense of liberation from the insular imprisonment of wartime England.

At the end of June we went down from the mountains to Bern, where we had a rendezvous with our anarchist friends from Basel. They were celebrating the seventieth anniversary of Michael Bakunin's death in the Swiss capital. It was a strange occasion, at times boring and at other times moving. In Bakunin's day the Swiss Jura and Geneva had been great centres of anarchism, but the movement had declined by the end of the nineteenth century. Nevertheless at the conference which began the celebration there was a notable gathering of old and young comrades from France and Italy as well as Geneva and the Jura. Some of them had links with historic figures, like the aged Luigi Bertoni from Geneva who, in his youth, had known Le Grand Michel and had worked closely with Kropotkin in the early years after his flight from Russia.

The conference was as inconclusive as anarchist conferences usually are, and perhaps its only importance was that it showed anarchism was not a dead doctrine. As a way of thought, if not as an organized movement, it had survived the defeat of the anarchists in Spain and their long suppression in Mussolini's Italy. After it was over, we made our way to the city cemetery, clogging the sidewalks because the police would not allow us to march in procession down the street.

We gathered on the windy hillside at Bakunin's grave. Two or three hundred of us unfurled the black flags among the cypress trees, the remnants of an old movement that miraculously would revive in the 1960s. The old men spoke in German and French and Italian; I nervously made my maiden public speech in English. The only other speaker under seventy was a gaunt Frenchman, André Prudhummeaux. When the speeches finished, the Koechlin brothers produced a flute and a violin, a music stand and sheets of music, and began to play a Mozart sonata in old Michael's memory. The wind blew at the sheets, and more than once we had to run down the paths between the tombs to retrieve them before the music could continue. This gave the occasion an informal warmth which the speeches had not, and which Bakunin would have approved. Back in town, drinking the dry white wine of Neuchâtel that Bakunin liked, Prudhummeaux and I talked the rest of the day away and realized we suffered the same strains between our consciences as writers and our loyalties as anarchists. We became good friends.

We spent the rest of our Swiss holiday in Thun. We knew nothing of the place, but the train had stopped there on our way to Zermatt from Basel, and we had been attracted by the red-roofed castle and the quiet clean glitter of the town and the green lake curving away between wooded hills. Returning, we strolled to the bridge over the river Aar, a swift aquamarine current running out of the lake towards the Rhine. Overlooking its clear waters was a massive eighteenth-century hotel with a facade supported by a series of great arches like the collonade of an antique theatre. We went in through the immense ironbound doors, and the owner showed us a chamber as big as a small house, with deep windows opening through a wall almost three feet thick. The furniture was of massive carved oak, and an enormous tiled stove dominated the room. Next morning we woke to a bright, unclouded day, silent except for the swish of the river against the wall under our window. Then we heard strange music that for a moment, in those antique surroundings, put me in mind of Roland blowing his horn for the last stand at Ronces-valles. But immediately I realized it was an alpenhorn, from one of the nearby hills, and that the tune was the theme that opens the Brahms Fourth Symphony. Only later in the day did we find the plaque record-ing that Brahms had stayed in Thun ninety years before.

Our stay in Thun was punctuated by incidents which leave clear vignettes in my memory still. One early morning, for example, I was walking beside the Aar when I saw a dead mallard floating in the rapid current. Suddenly another mallard dropped rapidly out of the sky, settled on the water near the dead bird, swam for a moment beside it, took the neck in its beak to raise the limp head, then dropped it and, a moment afterwards, flew away.

Some days we would pay a few francs to go on the paddle steamer that chugged past the waterside meadows and the brilliant gardens of the lakeside villages, past the precipitous cliffs of Beatenberg and the little castle of Spiez toylike and gay with geraniums and roses. The white ghost of the Jungfrau loomed in the distance over the green billows of the foothills as we sailed up the channel to Interlaken, that small night-mare of fretwork and cuckoo clocks.

We would also go walking to the south of Thun in the knot of moun-tains surrounding the Stockhorn, miniature replica of the Matterhorn. We walked through flowery meadows and pine forests, and a series of silent and sinister rocky valleys. Overhead eagles circled and the shadows, through some trick of the haze at this time of year, shone with an amethyst luminosity that contrasted strikingly with the grey of the rocks exposed to the sun. The tourists were all away at the Jungfrau and the Matterhorn, leaving us alone, except for the occasional cowherd in whose summer hut we might stop for a snack of black bread and air-dried beef. On one of these walks we descended into a secluded but fer-tile valley on the far side of the Stockhorn, where we talked to an old peasant digging his garden. He asked us, in all innocence, why there were no more German visitors coming to the area; they used to come in parties to climb the mountain. He had indeed heard of the war, as a dis-tant rumour, but he was unaware that Germany had been defeated and had no idea what that meant in the years immediately after peace.

We returned through France, staying another ten days in Paris with Giliane and Serge, going more than once to visit Prudhummeaux in his house at Versailles and to talk about the Spanish Civil War as he had experienced it as a foreign anarchist volunteer. In a few weeks there had been an extraordinary improvement; fruit, vegetables and cheese had become quite abundant and relatively cheap, a sign of the natural resilience of a peasant agriculture. Only meat was still short except for some dubious Canadian canned pork loaf. I was one of the people who suffered poisoning from it, coming down on my second day in Paris with agonizing pain and such a rapid ebbing of vitality that for the first time in my life I thought I was dying. I felt, despite my weakness, a baffled fury. Giliane performed the mediaeval rites that French doctors then still practised, cupping my belly and giving me opium. I recovered, my convalescence greatly assisted by good doses of cognac, so that I was able to go out into the streets on Bastille Day and watch the people dancing far into the night.

That 1946 journey, whose incidents I still remember with such clarity, was not only a first escape from the island prison of England. It also gave us the feeling that, for a few years at least, we would like to take up our lives in a different country. But for the time being we continued our short trips to the continent, and in the dreadful early winter weather of 1947 we spent a short time in Holland, with an anarchist named Jerry Lavies, who had a farmhouse outside Gouda.

The house stood on a tree-screened island of land at the centre of three large, shallow artificial lakes divided from each other by long dikes. At night the great stretches of ice would crack with noises like cannon shots. As soon as I saw the place, I had a strange sense of recognition, for except that the lakes were frozen and the dykes crusted with snow, it was the exact replica of a waterscape with a house in the middle that I had seen in a dream which recurred many times at one period in my early teens. The only difference was that in my dream it was always summer, the water bright blue and the dikes a vivid green.

Denise Levertov, with whom I had recently become friendly, was also staying with Jerry and his wife. Denise was only twenty-three, but had already published her first book of poems, still in the Romantic English style, although she was even then interested in American writing. I remember how fascinated she always was by the volumes of American poetry that James Laughlin and Kenneth Rexroth used to send me. After we all returned to England, she married the young American novelist, hooded-eyed Mitch Goodman. On a rainy autumn night of 1948 I met her in a Red Lion Street pub to say goodbye before she left for New York. There she went through a long period of adjustment until, in the late 1950s, she began to write with a distinctively American tone, emerging as an almost strident social militant. This was the opposite of the rather pre-Raphaelite vagueness that in her English years emanated so naturally from her mixed ancestry, a Welsh mother and a father who was a Russian Jew who became an Anglican priest. I have known few writers with such double careers.

The trip to Holland helped to intensify our discontent with England. Jerry was the most generous of men, a great prow-nosed extrovert who made sure there was always plenty of good Gouda cheese in the house and plenty of Hollands gin to wash it down, and who took us to Indonesian restaurants in Amsterdam where reistafels of twenty dishes were served. But Jerry's generosity could hardly have been so lavishly expressed if, in two years, Holland had not recovered astonishingly from the wartime years when, as some people we met assured us, tulip bulbs had become a much-sought item of food. By 1947, there were few real shortages for the Dutch, and their era of postwar prosperity was in sight.

By the beginning of 1948 we were starting to plan our departure to Canada. We thought, at first, of an experimental period of two to three years, to see how we fitted into the life and how things might develop in England. Nothing in letters from that period, or in my memory, suggests that we thought of a lasting move, though our attitudes did change somewhat as the year went on, largely through our meeting with a young Canadian who had reached England in the crew of a freighter and, being interested in progressive education, had attached himself to Burgess Hill School in Hampstead.

Doug came from Vancouver Island, and he had been long enough away from home to talk lyrically of the climate, the scenery, and the agricultural potential. He was a pacifist anarchist, as we were, and still had visions of a rural community. We rejected such theories but the idea that it might be possible to combine mental and manual work in ways adumbrated by Tolstoy and Thoreau and Kropotkin, began to revive as we talked with Doug through the spring of 1948. The possibility of trying it in a temperate region like the British Columbia coast attracted us; British Columbia further attracted us because it contained rich vestiges of the Coast Indian culture, and also because of the proximity of the Doukhobors, whom I imagined to be far nearer to natural anarchists than I later found to be true. I had been carrying on for some years a correspondence with Pete Maloff, one of the few Doukhobor intellectuals, and I was enthusiastic about the idea of meeting these religious communitarians.

In the middle of 1948 Doug went back to Canada. Almost immediately he wrote to say that he had bought a patch of land on the south-western end of Vancouver Island. If we wished, we could have an acre or so at the price he had paid. He himself was now living by carpentry. He intended to build his own house, and if I wanted to do the same, he would instruct and help me. The pattern was falling into place: land on which to grow our food and produce for sale; a new skill, carpentry, to be learnt (Orwell, an enthusiastic amateur joiner, thoroughly approved!); a new society to explore and turn into the raw material of writing. By the end of 1948 we had made up our minds, and, despite the loudly-expressed misgivings of almost all our friends, we went ahead with our plans.

We went, later in the year, on a sentimental journey to Market Drayton. My conscientious objections had alienated my relatives in the town, and I made no effort to see my Uncle Harold or my Aunt Ethel, but I could not avoid risking a meeting with them as I made my last walk past Runnymede. What I saw finally broke the dream of that little realm of childhood, for the great holly hedge of the inner garden, which had been its mistletoe-crowned sanctum, had been burnt as if the arch-angel's fiery sword had cleft it, and it seemed a sign that all the Edens of youth had been breached.

A few days afterwards we went to Paris for the last research on the Kropotkin book. It was cold and wretched, ice on the streets, fog over the Seine, and the hotel an American student had recommended full of fleas and whores. That too, like the violated garden, seemed a sign it was time to leave old places.

I finished *The Anarchist Prince* and we set about gathering money to settle our debts, pay our passage, and start our life in Canada as best we could. We sold the caravan at Skirmett and, with agony, I sold most of my library. Some precious books and some basic ones, necessary to continue writing; a few artifacts; some relics from my father's collections, we packed into a couple of ancient trunks my parents had brought with them from Canada a third of a century before. Our scanty furniture and my stout blackthorn walking stick we gave to Louis Adeane, with whom we stayed the last few days at the end of March before we took the train to Liverpool. We had booked our passage on one of the Furness Line passenger-cargo boats that sailed from Liverpool via Newfoundland to Halifax. By the time we had paid our fares, we had $750 left to take with us. Dwight Macdonald promised to loan us $1,000, which would be waiting when we reached Victoria on the far west shores of Canada, and that would complete the assets to start our new life.

We said goodbye to our friends. Orwell was now in a sanatorium in Gloucestershire, and it is one of my enduring regrets that we did not have time at the end to go down and visit him. Herbert Read and Muriel Spark, Roy Fuller and Julian Symons, Mervyn Peake and Tambimuttu, all shook their heads and declared we would soon be back; Mulk Raj Anand made the jesting prophecy that we would meet next in India, which turned out to be true. A week before we left I met Marie Louise and we talked long and affectionately, largely about her strange Italian childhood and the years of her father's exile. She was sad we were going, but accepted it as she had eventually accepted my withdrawal from anarchist activism. We decided we would write letters to each other telling about our respective childhoods which some day we might publish as a dialogue. It was a way of continuing the collaboration we had both so valued.

So my wife and I took our train journey across the Midlands to Liverpool. The customs officers and the Special Branch men at the dockside searched our luggage to the last corner and the last page of every book. Then we went on our voyage over the stormy North Atlantic sea. As the great seas beat over the forward lounge I read Henry Mayhew's *London Labour and the London Poor*, which the American anthropologist Harold Orlans, a recently-acquired friend, had offered as a parting gift. We put into St. John's and went ashore, and then sailed on to Halifax, and lay in the harbour on the night of the 13th April.

In a dream that night a male voice said to me, as I lay in an empty room, "Marie Louise is dead." I dismissed it laughingly next morning. It took us five days to traverse Canada by train from Halifax to Vancouver and to cross on the ferry to Victoria. A cable awaited us there. Marie Louise was dead, from heart failure. The book I have finished, which is the first volume of my autobiography, is the substance of the letters I promised and at the time seemed to have no reason left to write.

THIS BOOK, I realize as I end it, has been essentially an account of the experience and influences that went to shape me as a writer, and of my entry into the English writer's world. In a somewhat different way it has performed the same kind of task that I carried out in writing my books — essentially accounts of the creative life — on writers like George Orwell and Herbert Read, Aldous Huxley and Thomas Merton. Such an approach, with the narrator accompanying the protagonist on his journey, has involved its own Proustian selection of memories; it explains the emphases and the deliberate ommissions which I am sure are evident. This narrative has brought me to the mid-point of life, when I abandoned the country of my childhood and the literary world in which I came to maturity, and started what became a quite different way of life — quite different, that is, except for the activity of writing that remained at its centre. And I realize that whatever I write from my present standpoint in time about this later period after my return to Canada is bound to be quite other than the present book; perhaps less narrative in form, perhaps less attached to the protagonist and more concerned with his world and time and worlds beyond, and certainly more reflective.

INDEX

Printed in Canada